Social Aspects of Memory

CW00801765

Social Aspects of Memory presents a compelling study of how ordinary people remember war. Whilst the book focuses on the cities of Sarajevo and East Sarajevo during the 1992–1995 war in Bosnia-Herzegovina, Jeftić also presents narratives from other war-torn cities and countries around the world. This book adopts a unique approach, by looking at how perpetrators and victims (as well as new generations who may not remember the war directly) manage in the aftermath of war. Jeftić explores how our memories of war and violence are formed, and how we can learn to reconcile those memories, individually and as a collective.

Drawing on the author's own extensive empirical research, the book explores the connections between memories of significant war events, transgenerational transmission of memories, bias for in-group wrongdoings and readiness for reconciliation between two groups.

Giving a voice to underrepresented narratives and prioritising the importance of expression as a necessary catalyst for reconciliation, this book is essential reading for those interested in collective and transgenerational memory and memory studies, especially in relation to the aftermath of the 1992–1995 war in Bosnia-Herzegovina.

Alma Jeftić is a PhD candidate in psychology at the University of Belgrade, Serbia; President of the Association of Psychologists in the Federation of Bosnia-Herzegovina – Sarajevo Subsidiary; and a Governing Board member of the Research Network on Transnational Memory and Identity in Europe (Council for European Studies at Columbia University).

Social Aspects of Memory

Stories of Victims and Perpetrators
From Bosnia-Herzegovina

Alma Jeftić

Routledge
Taylor & Francis Group

LONDON AND NEW YORK

First published 2019
by Routledge
4 Park Square, Milton Park, Abingdon, Oxon OX14 4RN

and by Routledge
605 Third Avenue, New York, NY 10017

First issued in paperback 2022

Routledge is an imprint of the Taylor & Francis Group, an informa business

Publisher's Note
The publisher has gone to great lengths to ensure the quality of this reprint but
points out that some imperfections in the original copies may be apparent.

British Library Cataloguing-in-Publication Data
A catalogue record for this book is available from the British Library

Library of Congress Cataloging-in-Publication Data
Names: Jeftic, Alma, author.
Title: Social aspects of memory : stories of victims and perpetrators from
    Bosnia-Herzegovina / Alma Jeftic.
Description: 1 Edition. | New York : Routledge, 2020.
Identifiers: LCCN 2019006995 | ISBN 9780415789554 (hardback) |
    ISBN 9781315222677 (ebook)
Subjects: LCSH: Memory—Social aspects.
Classification: LCC BF378.S65 J44 2019 | DDC 153.1/2—dc23
LC record available at https://lccn.loc.gov/2019006995

ISBN 13: 978-1-03-247555-4 (pbk)
ISBN 13: 978-0-415-78955-4 (hbk)
ISBN 13: 978-1-315-22267-7 (ebk)

DOI: 10.4324/9781315222677

Typeset in Times New Roman
by Apex CoVantage, LLC

To all those who have the courage to listen and to take the step towards understanding . . .

Contents

Preface

At the very beginning I would like to emphasise something: this book is not only about Bosnia-Herzegovina. It is not only about Sarajevo and East Sarajevo. It is about all those people from Bosnia-Herzegovina, Sarajevo, East Sarajevo and other war-torn cities and countries around the world. It is written with two goals: to understand how our memories of past wrongdoings are formed, and to teach us how to reconcile those memories. It takes not only two persons to reconcile, but two persons and two different narratives that they produce. When we move this to the group level, we have two (or sometimes even more) collective narratives that clash.

We live in a world that pushes us to take one side or the other, and, while doing so, to accept our side as the best in all aspects, even when it insults the other. Through this book I tried to give a voice to those underrepresented – ordinary people who survived the terrible war, and those a bit younger, who did not survive it in person, but still feel its consequences. Being a psychologist who prefers quantitative over qualitative methods, I was astonished by the fact that in this case narratives tell more when neither quantified nor converted into numbers. I truly appreciate the strength of each voice I heard during a pretty long period of fieldwork, and I am very thankful for the time all those people devoted to me.

Today, more than 20 years after the war, people are still having trouble talking about the difficult past. Our job as psychologists and peace activists is to provide them the opportunity to say what they think – to express their emotions and traumas. I truly believe that listening is a royal road to reconciliation in situations like this. Therefore, this book, which tells a bit more about social aspects of remembering, bias in memories for in-group wrongdoings, and readiness for reconciliation is a sort of manual of listening for beginners, and all those who would like to practise this virtue in their settings, regardless of where they live.

I truly believe that being judgemental won't pave the road to reconciliation. However, developing historical empathy through listening and learning can direct us towards that important road. If some of the lines written in this book can help us move towards that track even slightly, its major aim will be achieved.

Acknowledgements

It would take another book to name all the wonderful human beings who helped me during my fieldwork and, later, the writing process. Perhaps I will remain indebted to most of them, and the only thing I can do is to continue working towards reconciliation while having them on my mind.

First of all, I would like to thank the professors from the Department of Psychology at the University of Belgrade for their endless support, especially my thesis supervisor, Prof. Dr Dragan Popadić. Also, I would like to thank the professors from the Institute of Psychology, University of Graz, where I spent one academic year as a Go Styria scholarship student. A big "thank you" goes to Prof. Dr Rupert Brown and social psychology doctoral students from the School of Psychology, University of Sussex, where I spent a shorter period of time as a Senior Visiting Research Fellow. Thinking of academic institutions that helped me a lot, I would like to express my gratitude towards professors from the Center for Southeast European Studies at the University of Graz, a small but inspiring group of academics with whom I was privileged to work and collaborate for one semester. In that regard, I extend my gratitude to the Open Society Foundation, thanks to whose Civil Society Scholar Award I could concentrate solely on my research.

So many people helped me during the data collection process. However, I would like to express my sincere gratitude to Dr Zilka Spahić Šiljak, Research Fellow at Stanford University and Director of the Transcultural Psychosocial Educational Foundation in Sarajevo, a person who represents pure inspiration and wisdom. My gratitude goes to Dr Tanja Sekulić, Dr Goran Marković, Dr Sabina Alispahić, Mr Dušan Šehovac and many, many more who helped me during data collection. Also, special thanks go to my colleagues and friends, Jelena Joksimović and Emina Zoletić, for supporting me throughout this process and for always being ready to chat with me.

This project would have been impossible without Ms Lucy Kennedy, Routledge Commissioning Editor, who was the first to recognise it and the first to approach me. I am very thankful to Editor Ceri McLardy, and Editorial Assistant Sophie Crowe, for being meticulous, patient and always ready to help.

I would like to thank my parents, Alma and Siniša, and my grandparents for being my endless support. Without them, all of this would have been impossible. Also, I would like to thank them for teaching me respect, tolerance and understanding, all of which helped me during my field research. They are my biggest strength and support. Being raised in such family is nothing other than a privilege.

I am indebted to all those people who shared their time and stories with me. I truly believe that it was for a good cause, and I hope they are and will continue to be aware of it. Without their willingness and trust, this book would not exist in such a format. Dear Sarajevans and East Sarajevans, thank you from the bottom of my heart.

Last (but not least), I would like to thank Nathan for helping me see the world in a different light and for making me a better person from day to day. There are few people out there who are "one of a kind", and I am happy to have found one of them.

1 Introduction

Sarajevo for beginners: history, culture and politics from the Ottoman Empire to post-Dayton Bosnia-Herzegovina

Foreigners struggle to understand the complicated history of Bosnia-Herzegovina. However, talking to the local people, reading local (and foreign) history textbooks and/or reading local newspapers can make it even more confusing because everyone seems to have a slightly different version of events, seasoned with different conspiracy theories. Therefore, the wisest thing to do is to look at different stories and try to understand those elements that distinguish them.

Sarajevo between the Ottomans and the Austro-Hungarians: history, culture and politics

Sarajevo's history has been determined by its geography, the presence of different foreign powers (Ottomans and Austro-Hungarians), different ethnic groups and complicated relationships between them. Also, it has been the site of three important historical events: the beginning of World War I, the XXII Olympic Games and the longest siege in the history of Europe (the 1992–1995 war).

Over the past six centuries, six different regimes have governed the city, as many as five of them in the twentieth century (Donia, 2009). Contemporary Sarajevo was mostly built up during three major periods of expansion: the first 140 years of Ottoman rule (up to 1600), the Austro-Hungarian rule (from 1883 to 1914) and the formative period of the socialist government (from 1945 to the 1984 Olympic Games).

The most interesting fact about Sarajevo is the diversity of the population that was its trademark from its foundation in the fifteenth century. The city has always been described as a mixture of religions, peoples and influences. The relative numbers of the largest groups in the city have changed many times throughout history, as well as their names. In the first centuries, the differences between the groups were primarily religious, but in the twentieth century the differences were largely based on nationality (Donia, 2009).

Modern Sarajevo and Bosnia-Herzegovina are predominantly inhabited by members of the three largest ethnic groups: Bosniaks, Croats and Serbs. The members of each particular group maintain a secular identity that has developed over time, but also refer to a specific religious tradition from earlier times. Today more than ever, Bosnian Croats feel their Catholic heritage; Bosnian Serbs are calling for their Orthodox origins; while Bosniaks consider Islam and Muslim culture as their most significant heritage. Today's Serbs were formerly called Orthodox, Serbian Orthodox and even Greek Orthodox; Croats were called Catholics, or, very rarely, Latin. Until the end of the twentieth century the Bosniaks were known as Bosnian Muslims, or simply Muslims. In addition, the Jews had become a significant group after their arrival in the sixteenth century; however, very few groups inhabit contemporary Sarajevo. Also, there are groups that refuse to consider themselves as either Bosniaks, Serbs or Croats but only Bosnians, and those are usually children from mixed religious marriages or simply people who decided to embrace what is left of the Yugoslav "brotherhood and unity".

The question of identity is always tough; however, it seems especially complicated in Bosnia-Herzegovina. Not all citizens of Sarajevo expressed primary loyalty towards any of the ethnic groups; therefore, some decided to declare themselves Yugoslavs, especially in the socialist period. About 5 percent of Bosniaks identified as Yugoslavs in the 1991 census, but in Sarajevo and several other cities, about ten percent selected this type of identity (Donia, 2009). This group included many children from mixed marriages and others for whom that identity represented a refuge from all national identities, as well as those who considered themselves primarily citizens of Yugoslavia (Donia, 2009). Bosnia-Herzegovina as a country represents a meeting place of different peoples, customs and religions. It is inhabited by three major ethnic and religious groups: the Roman Catholic Croats, the Muslim Bosniaks and the Eastern Orthodox Serbs. However, during its history Bosnia experienced several changes related to the visibility of these different religious practices, customs and symbols due to the different political regimes. For instance, religion was neither publicly expressed nor practised during communism, while the country underwent a period of increased religiosity after the fall of communism in the 1990s, which was also accompanied by the 1992–1995 war. During the war the engaged parties defined themselves mostly in terms of their religious identities.

However, there have been no strong indicators that could explain why people have become more openly religious since the signing of the Dayton agreement, or whether this increase in religiosity is mostly a result of the conflict or the fall of communism (Hacic-Vlahovic, 2008). It is difficult to conclude with certainty how and why the religious revival occurred at the beginning of the 1990s in Bosnia-Herzegovina, and to what extent the complicated jigsaw puzzle has started to shape both the political and everyday life of ordinary Bosnians. It is also unclear whether people have become more openly religious due to nationalist sentiments, opportunism, their economic standard or intrinsic belief. The data collected during the communist period leave some degree of reasonable doubt as to whether society had actually truly secularized in the first place, or whether people simply pretended to be less religious in order to protect themselves (Hacic-Vlahovic, 2008).

In the fifteenth century, the Ottoman army defeated the mediaeval Bosnian Kingdom in a series of battles and gained control over much of Bosnian territory. At the time of the Ottoman conquest around 1430, the area of Sarajevo was inhabited by Catholics loyal to the Roman Pope (Donia, 2009). In this area, before the conquest, there was a considerable rivalry between the various Christian churches, and conversion from one religion to another was not unusual.

The city of Sarajevo was founded by the Ottoman Empire upon conquering the region. According to the literature, 1461 is most often referred to as the founding year. However, even today there are a number of landmarks built by the first Ottoman governor of Bosnia that have endured over the centuries, such as Konak, the Emperor's Mosque, the Emperor's Bridge, Baščaršija, Sahat-Kula, Gazi-Husref Begova Mosque etc. However, even at that time many Slavs were combining their Christian faith with the remains of so-called pagan customs. Due to the absence of structured church monitoring, Slavic Christians lacked support and therefore became more susceptible to Islam after the Ottoman conquest in the fifteenth century. During the Ottoman era Sarajevo's urban landscape changed; however, religious, cultural and legal changes were even more evident. Nevertheless, circumstances, time and unexpected cases led to the fall of the empire and brought the Austro-Hungarian spirit to Bosnia and Sarajevo. The army of Eugen Savoy entered Sarajevo during the night from the 23rd to the 24th of October 1697 while occupying and at the same time burning a large part of the city. After that, Sarajevo lost its political power, as the headquarters of the country were moved to Travnik. This period was characterized by various political and cultural changes; however, it was also characterized by resistance by the local population, which led to the formation of secret organizations and communities. Nevertheless, the most well-known event from that time is the assassination of Franz Ferdinand and his wife, Sophie, which happened at the Latin Bridge in Sarajevo and still remains a mystery that continues to divide history teaching in contemporary Bosnia-Herzegovina.

It is believed that Gavrilo Princip, a Bosnian Serb and the son of a post-man, killed the Archduke Franz Ferdinand and his wife. Princip was born in 1894 in Obljaj in Bosnia-Herzegovina. After he moved to Belgrade, he joined a militant group called Young Bosnia whose major belief was that it could use violence to help free the region from Austro-Hungarian rule and unite the Southern Slavs. At his trial he described himself as a Yugoslav nationalist, who wanted all Yugoslavs to be united, in any political form, and free from the Austrians.

On 28 June 2014 Archduke Franz Ferdinand of Austria came to inspect the Austro-Hungarian armed forces located in Sarajevo. One of Princip's group threw a bomb at their car, but missed. However, later that day, Princip shot both of them dead. Austria declared war on Serbia a month later. Princip was charged with treason and murder, but under Austro-Hungarian law could not be executed because he was not yet 20 when the crime was committed. Instead, he was jailed for 20 years, but died of tuberculosis in prison in Austria in April 1918.

For many Westerners, the Sarajevo assassination merely confirms their stereotypes of Balkan backwardness and barbarism, and thus has provided a convenient means to divert blame for World War I from their own leaders (Miller, 2007). For many South Slavs, however, 28 June 1914 will always be the beginning of their liberation from centuries of foreign control. However, the Sarajevo assassination has always been looked upon more ambivalently by those who must accept it as their own. Even though Franz Ferdinand had been opposed to war during his lifetime, his assassination provided the reason for a declaration of war on Serbia. The chief of the Austrian General Staff, Franz Conrad von Hötzendorf, welcomed an excuse for a war with Serbia. Most historians would today agree that Berlin's decision-makers put substantial pressure on Vienna to demand retribution from Serbia, and that they were happy to take the risk that an Austro-Serbian conflict might esca-late into a European war. When Austria-Hungary declared war on Serbia on 28 July, it was the end for the Belgrade government.

In describing the journey of Princip and his colleagues to Bosnia, and the assassination of the Archduke, Vladimir Dedijer brings out very well the great element of luck involved and also points out that the trial of the assassins was fair even if their subsequent fate was barbarous (Dedijer, 1966). Dedijer (1966) emphasizes that while Princip was suffering through his dying hours in Theresienstadt in April 1918, the Bosnian horizons were lit every night by the burning of feudal landlords' konaks (large houses or official residences that were very common in the former Ottoman Empire).

However, Balkan countries have continued to teach their children a dif-ferent interpretation of the killing of the Archduke and his wife that set the conflict in motion. Princip is portrayed in the history textbooks of the vari-ous former Yugoslav countries either as a terrorist or as a rebel with a cause.

These perceptions reflect contemporary divisions in a region that is still recovering from the 1992–1995 war. While they were part of Yugoslavia, children in all these countries were taught the same history. Now they all have their own versions of the truth.

Nenad Sebek, former executive director of the Centre for Democracy and Reconciliation in Southeast Europe, analyzed school textbooks in the region and concluded that the unified discourse disappeared with ex-Yugoslavia, and now the past is being adjusted to fit whatever discourse the ruling elites in these countries want at the present moment. In the ethnically divided Bosnia-Herzegovina, there is no commonly held view either about Princip or about the origins of World War I, since three different teaching curricula have been applied: two curricula in the two entities (the Federation of Bosnia-Herzegovina and the Republic of Srpska), as well as areas of Bosnia-Herzegovina that currently apply the Croatian teaching curriculum.

For the Bosniaks and Croats, Princip was a Belgrade-backed political assassin, while for Bosnian Serbs, the murder served only as a pretext for Austria-Hungary and German to commit military aggression against Serbia. These divisions are also reflected in different ways of commemorating the same event. A series of events were held in Sarajevo, including exhibitions, concerts and a meeting of young peace activists from around the world. However, Bosnian Serbs held their own events in the eastern town of Visegrad, programmed by the film director Emir Kusturica, while a statue of Princip was due to be installed in East Sarajevo (Džidić et al., 2014).

In mainly Bosniak areas (like Sarajevo, the Bihac region in the northwest and the central Zenica-Doboj area), school textbooks highlight Princip's links to Serbia: the textbook used in Sarajevo says that Princip's group, Young Bosnia, was "supported by secret organizations from Serbia", while the Bihac textbook states more directly that the plotters were "supported by Serbia". The Zenica textbook describes Young Bosnia as a "terrorist organization". The history book used by Bosnian Croat pupils also describes Young Bosnia as a "terrorist" group. But in the Serb-dominated Republic of Srpska, Young Bosnia is simply described as an "organization", and textbooks stress that Austria-Hungary "used" Franz Ferdinand's assassination "to blame Serbia" and declare war on the country. This description of the outbreak of the conflict is similar to the one contained in textbooks used in Serbia itself.

History teachers from different regions of Bosnia-Herzegovina have divided views on the whole event. For instance, Zeljko Vujadinovic, a history professor from Banja Luka in the Republic of Srpska, believes that what we are looking at is the current political mind-set transferred to the past (Džidić et al., 2014). Comparisons of Young Bosnia with the pre-World War I Al-Qaida were just a result of the 1990s conflict. Therefore, the characterization of Young Bosnia and Princip as terrorists is an attempt to place the blame for huge worldwide events on Serbian territorial expansion policies (Džidić et al., 2014). Sarajevo history professor Zijad Sehic agreed that the past had been redrawn in the aftermath of the 1992–1995 conflict in Bosnia-Herzegovina, and it was only after the collapse of Yugoslavia that Princip was described as a Serbian nationalist rather than a fighter for Yugoslav brotherhood and unity (Džidić et al., 2014). Therefore, now, in the absence of Yugoslavia, Princip is glorified as a Serbian hero, and his actions are defended as something that was supposed to contribute to the stabilization of the country and better group relations.

At the entrance of what would later be known as Princip Bridge in Sarajevo, one of the first examples of a monument to a contradictory past was erected. A monument named "Spomenik umorstvu", or "Monument to murder", was taken down almost as soon as the Kingdom of Serbs, Croats and Slovenes took over in late 1918. Then it was broken up, with one of its 10-meter columns going to a stonecutter in Trebinje, the other to a quarry in Sarajevo. In contrast, the massive central medallion engraved with the images of Ferdinand and Sophie has spent the last 60 years collecting dust and a thick layer of patina in the basement of Sarajevo's Art Gallery. Also, a plaque in Sarajevo commemorating the 1914 assassination contains the following words: "From this place on June 28 1914 Gavrilo Princip assassinated the heir to the Austro-Hungarian throne Franz Ferdinand and his wife Sofia". The memorialization process seems more focussed on using history in the name of truth and tourism rather than misusing it politically.

The communist Partisans who liberated Sarajevo claimed that 1945 was the fulfilment of everything that 1914 had stood for: the struggle and courageous self-sacrifice of Bosnia's youth for justice and freedom; the liberation from the Germanic oppressor; the awakening of a revolutionary consciousness; and the spirit of brotherhood and unity embodied in the mixed ethno-religious backgrounds of the Young Bosnians and Partisans alike. Therefore, Gavrilo Princip was someone who had made the dream come true. According to an article published in *Oslobodenje* for Vidovdan 1945, just as the 19-year-old Princip, gun in hand, had lunged towards the Archduke's car, the youthful Partisans had thrown themselves before Nazi tanks (Miller, 2007). On 7 May 1945, in a mass meeting in Car Dušan park that was attended by the president of the parliament of Bosnia-Herzegovina and other local, national and foreign dignitaries, Princip was glorified as a national hero and martyr (Miller, 2007). Following several speeches, the procession crossed "Princip Bridge" to dedicate a new plaque on the assassination site. To cheers of "Glory to the unforgotten national hero and his comrades", Borko Vukobrat, who hailed from Princip's hometown of Bosansko Graho, unveiled a tablet that certainly went further than that of

1930 in terms of glorifying the Sarajevo assassination: "The youth of Bosnia and Herzegovina dedicate this plaque as a symbol of eternal gratitude to Gavrilo Princip and his comrades, to fighters against the Germanic conquerors" (Miller, 2007). The first opportunity for the newly independent Yugoslavia to commemorate the Sarajevo assassination found the site transformed into a World War I memorial.

While in 1930 political leaders were banished from the ceremony to dedicate a small plaque to Princip, in 1953 the president of the National Committee of Sarajevo, Dane Olbina, gave the keynote address at the opening of the Museum (Miller, 2007). Nevertheless, the footprints, the museum, street names and other emblems of the assassination, not to mention the heroic rhetoric surrounding it, would persist through the 1984 Winter Olympic Games and, indeed, right up to the end of communist Yugoslavia (Miller, 2007). Then they swiftly, and quite publicly, became elements of fierce contestation between Yugoslavs. During a televised parliamentary debate over Bosnian independence in February 1991, a delegate from the Serbian Democratic Party (SDS), which opposed an independent Bosnia-Herzegovina, threatened his Muslim and Croat colleagues with the words: "The sovereign of your sovereign state would never make it past the Gavrilo Princip Bridge" (Miller, 2007), to which a Muslim representative responded that in an independent Bosnia, the Princip Bridge would not bear the name of a terrorist. Soon thereafter, someone scrawled the bridge's original name, Latin Bridge, on the wall of the Young Bosnia Museum.

During the war itself, the museum was closed and barely saved from bombs and vandals; the street names were removed; and the footprints were ripped from the sidewalk. As the ideology that held Yugoslavia together and determined how it would remember the Vidovdan conspirators disintegrated in a massive explosion of nationalist energy, the carefully constructed memory of the assassination evaporated with it (Miller, 2007). Western commentators with little or no experience in the region explained it all as more proof of the Balkan peoples' inborn inclination for violence. Nevertheless, something had to be done after the conflict, and in 2004 city officials decided upon a simple granite plaque that states, truthfully enough: "From This Place on June 28, 1914, Gavrilo Princip Assassinated the Heir to the Austro-Hungarian Throne Franz Ferdinand and His Wife Sofia".

The position of Sarajevo in Yugoslavia: the glow of the Olympic city

Sarajevo became part of the Kingdom of Yugoslavia after World War I. It represented the centre of the Bosnian region and Drinska Banovina; however, it did not play any other significant political or economic role.

During World War II Sarajevo experienced various attacks following a German bombing. The Kingdom of Yugoslavia was invaded by the Axis Powers (also known as the Axis and the Rome-Berlin-Tokyo Axis, which fought against the Allied forces), and Bosnia was ceded to the newly established Independent State of Croatia. However, the Axis led to the persecution of those native citizens who were considered "undesirables". It was a time when many nationalist movements were established and tried to murder those who were not advocating their propaganda. A group of 108 Muslim citizens of Sarajevo signed on 12 October 1941 the Resolution of Sarajevo Muslims, which condemned the killings committed by nationalist movements and their sympathizers (Hadžijahić, 1973). They also made a distinction between those Muslims who participated in such persecutions and those who condemned such killings and tried to rescue their neighbours. However, at that time many Serbs, Romani and Jews were killed in the Holocaust, which negatively affected the Jewish community in Sarajevo.

However, Sarajevans were trying to resist, and the most influential actor in that process was a National Liberation Party (NLA) Partisan named Walter Perić. According to an old but well-known legend a new German officer came to Sarajevo in order to find Walter. He asked his subordinate to show him Walter, and the man took him to the top of the hill overlooking the city and said: "*Sehen Sie diese Stadt? Das ist Valter*". Even though Walter was killed while fighting on the day of Sarajevo's liberation (6 April 1945), he has since become the icon of the city, and the legend about him has been retold ever since.

After the liberation Sarajevo became the capital of the Republic of Bosnia within the Socialist Federal Republic of Yugoslavia. During that period huge investments were made, especially in building new residential blocks, developing industry and trying to transform Sarajevo into one of the Yugoslavs' biggest cities. Also, the population increased, which contributed not only to the vividness of the city, but also to the recognition of its power and growth. Such growth led to one of the extremely important moments in the history of Sarajevo: the 1984 Winter Olympics.

Sarajevo got the privilege of hosting the 1984 Winter Olympics in a period that was, according to Nicolas Moll (2014), marked by the deepening of the economic crisis and of the rivalries between the republics in Yugoslavia. Therefore, Sarajevo and the Olympics were glorified as the power which would bring all Yugoslav republics together and contribute to great prestige, *brotherhood and unity* and peace. However, these values were promoted not only by the Yugoslav authorities but also by the Organizing Committee of the Sarajevo Winter Olympics, which also wanted to use this opportunity to strengthen the economic and political role of Bosnia-Herzegovina within Yugoslavia (Moll, 2014).

Although the organization of the Sarajevo Winter Olympics was supposed to bring strong cohesion to the Yugoslav countries, it also faced strong opposition in the years before the Games officially started. Resistance was encountered in several republics, Slovenia particularly. In 1979 the Slovenian leadership asked the President of Yugoslavia, Josip Broz Tito, to either cancel or postpone the Games, emphasizing economic stabilization as the highest priority and the Winter Olympics as a financial disaster (Organizacioni komitet XIV zimskih olimpijskih igara '84, 1984). The leadership of Bosnia-Herzegovina rejected those claims and explained them as Slovenia's jealousy towards Bosnia's winter tourism and promotion of the country in general; therefore, they managed to convince Tito not to postpone or cancel the Sarajevo Winter Olympics (Dizdarević, 2011). However, that did not stop the resistance in other republics. For instance, the Serbian newspaper *Novosti* in November 1980 published this type of text: "Shall we allow the 1984 Olympics to be just Bosnian and wait for TV broadcast, as if Sarajevo were the same as Gothenburg or Sapporo, or will the 14th Winter Olympics be ours, Yugoslav, as well?" (*Novosti 8*, 15 November 1980; according to Moll, 2014). Fights were especially related to the financing of the Sarajevo Winter Olympics because in the original proposal Bosnia was supposed to cover two-thirds of all expenses while the rest of the expenses were supposed to be covered by the other republics. However, further negotiations led to a different agreement according to which Bosnia-Herzegovina had to cover 80 percent of the total expenses, which further led to a tax of 0.2 or 0.3 percent imposed on each worker's income in Bosnia-Herzegovina in 1982 and 1983, which also contributed to great dissatisfaction within the country (Pedrotty, 2010). Although Bosnia-Herzegovina financed the Sarajevo Winter Olympics to the greatest extent, the official narrative of the Organizing Committee continued to highlight that the whole of Yugoslavia had contributed financially, which further emphasized the Yugoslav dimension of the Games (Organizacioni komitet XIV zimskih olimpijskih igara '84, 1984).

Regardless of public rebellions and debates, the Sarajevo Winter Olympics were successfully organized in 1984. It drew a lot of positive attention from both the national and international community, especially after Jure Franko won the first medal ever for Yugoslavia. Therefore, the Sarajevo Winter Olympics became a very important site of memory for Yugoslavia, but, more important, for the citizens of Sarajevo, who accepted it as a symbol of unity and success. Therefore, it is very interesting to see what happened to such a symbol during the following years, which brought war, destabilization and the complete dissolution of Yugoslavia. The 1992–1995 war also directly affected the Olympic sites around the city of Sarajevo, especially the Igman and Bjelasnica mountains, where skiing competitions had been held, as well as the Trebevic Mountain, where the bobsled run was organized. Those areas became direct combat zones, while Mount Jahorina, the former venue of alpine skiing for women, was behind the siege line and under the control of the Army of the Republic of Srpska. Several Olympic sites in the city of Sarajevo were shelled and destroyed, including the Olympic Museum and the Zetra Sports Center building, where the figure skating competitions and the closing ceremony of the Sarajevo Winter Olympics were held.

Images of 1984 and of the same sites during the siege were regularly used to appeal for the solidarity of the international public, for example, the music video "Help Bosnia Now" by the Sarajevo pop group Aid in 1992 was recorded in the destroyed Zetra building, as well as postcards from the Sarajevo Design Group Trio showing the five Olympic rings superimposed with grenade impacts or transformed into barbed wire, together with the inscription "Sarajevo 1984–1994" (Moll, 2014, p. 136). The year 1994 was especially significant because the tenth anniversary of the Sarajevo Winter Olympics was organized within the besieged city of Sarajevo, and it seemed as if people understood it as two different occasions when Sarajevo was the centre of the world. However, while on the first occasion (the Winter Olympics), Sarajevo was a popular and well-known centre, on the second occasion (war and siege), the world turned its head away. The tenth anniversary of the Olympic Games in 1994 was very actively commemorated in Sarajevo, where a special organizing committee for the celebration of the jubilee was established under the presidency of the mayor of Sarajevo and with the participation of the new Olympic Committee of Bosnia-Herzegovina and the support of the government of Bosnia-Herzegovina (Moll, 2014). The organizers chose the motto "The flame is still alive", while a moment of silence was held in Lillehammer during the opening ceremony of the Winter Olympics in 1994. International Olympic Committee President Samaranch also visited the besieged Sarajevo and promised help with the reconstruction of the destroyed Olympic venues. It is interesting to notice that at that time the whole emphasis was moved to Sarajevo as the Olympic city without mentioning the neighbouring states, as if the international community together with the citizens of Sarajevo wanted to emphasize the past glow of the city that was going through a horrible siege in the middle of Europe.

However, on the other side of the siege line, the tenth anniversary of the Sarajevo Winter Olympics was also marked. After its establishment in 1992, the Republic of Srpska created its own Olympic Committee in 1993, which in February 1994 organized an anniversary of the 1984 Games on Jahorina, in the form of a three-day event entitled "Olympic Days", opened by Momčilo Krajišnik, president of the Republic of Srpska Assembly (Moll, 2014). These two anniversaries were organized in two divided, but parallel worlds, and the year 1994 showed that the 1984 Sarajevo Winter Olympics had become a divided site of memory equally presented in both Sarajevo and East Sarajevo.

The total division of the Olympic heritage continued during the war, but also influenced post-war anniversaries that occurred in 1999, 2004 and 2009. After the ratification of the Dayton Peace Agreement, the line between the Federation of Bosnia-Herzegovina and the Republic of Srpska continued to divide this Olympic heritage: Jahorina and parts of Trebević belonged to the Republic of Srpska, while Igman, Bjelašnica and other parts of Trebević were part of the federation. Also, these mountains were in two different municipalities: Sarajevo and East Sarajevo. In 1999 a very modest anniversary was organized in the Federation of Bosnia-Herzegovina, while the Republic of Srpska did not organize any kind of event, as in that period they were all very much focussed on the Kosovo crisis (Daily Oslobođenje, 10 February 1999). However, in 2004 the Republic of Srpska and the Federation of Bosnia-Herzegovina agreed to unite and to organize the first post-war joint anniversary. That was also some sort of beginning of negotiations over the organization of the European Youth Olympic Festival (EYOF). In 2011 the European Olympic Committee granted the organization of the 2017 EYOF to both the municipalities of Sarajevo and East Sarajevo, which also highly influenced the Olympic Games anniversary held in 2014. One of the most important events during the anniversary organized in 2014 was a gala event in Zetra with Jane Torvill and Christopher Dean, who returned to Sarajevo for the first time since they had won the gold medal in ice dancing in 1984. Their visit was co-organized by both municipalities (Sarajevo and East Sarajevo), and it somehow presented their joint effort to raise the Olympic flame again. In 2017 both sides engaged in the joint activities in order to make all necessary preparations for the EYOF. This initiative also shows that people still share positive memories of the Sarajevo Winter Olympics, and such memories can be used (to a certain extent) as a connecting symbol between the two entities.

In order to analyze whether and how memories of the Sarajevo Winter Olympics can influence inter-entity relations, Nicholas Moll conducted a survey on both the associations and memories of 90 people of different generations and from different areas of Bosnia-Herzegovina. The major results of his study led to the following observations: almost all associations were positive or very positive; among the positive attitude towards the Sarajevo Winter Olympics a unifying factor plays a major role (expressions in terms of "Sarajevo", "Bosnia-Herzegovina", and never "East Sarajevo", "Federation", "Republic of Srpska" etc.); the most positive associations were given by people who grew up in Sarajevo before or after 1984, and mostly those people regretted that the Olympic heritage is not glorified and reconstructed enough nowadays (Moll, 2014).

The fall of Yugoslavia and the beginning of the war: the longest siege in the history of Europe

The Dayton agreement and the emergence of two entities

The Dayton Peace Agreement was reached on 21 November 1995 by the presidents of Bosnia-Herzegovina, Croatia and Serbia with the major aim to end the war in Bosnia-Herzegovina. Besides that, it outlined a General Framework Agreement for Peace in Bosnia-Herzegovina, which kept Bosnia as a single state made up of two parts, the Federation of Bosnia-Herzegovina (Bosniak-Croat majority) and the Republic of Srpska (Serb majority). Sarajevo remained the capital city.

The Dayton Peace Agreement was cheered in 1995 because it stopped the shooting; however, very soon it was understood as an official and international formalization of the division of the country and people into three political and territorial entities, based on the different ethno-religious backgrounds of people in Bosnia-Herzegovina (Macek, 2009, p. 40). At the very beginning people felt a sense of relief as they were able to walk freely in the streets knowing that there were no snipers aiming at them (Macek, 2009, p. 202). However, in 1996 new graffiti appeared saying, "kad se saberem-oduzmem se" (when ! pull myself together-! fall apart). It can be understood as a sign of despair that appeared after people faced the real consequences of the war. A deeply divided country, scarce resources, lack of job opportunities and destroyed architecture were some of the triggers of this despair.

There was hope that the international community would help to rebuild the city of Sarajevo and the country in general. Regardless of the lack of resources, the signs of war trauma were present; however, there was no adequate psychological and psychiatric assistance in that period. The post-war period has been characterized by the wish to "bottle things up" and behave as if nothing had happened. Both the lack of a desire to talk and the inability to talk in the first place contributed to even deeper divisions between the ethnic groups because of the constant feeling of fear and instability. Dayton brought an atmosphere of artificial peace that helped people become more obsessed with the divisions and differences than with the possibilities for reconciliation and economic awakening. Unfortunately, such consequences deeply affected people in both entities, and their influence is still present.

Sarajevo and East Sarajevo two decades later

Two decades later Sarajevo and East Sarajevo are two cities very close to each other geographically, but very distant in terms of political cooperation. Even though it is called the "Jerusalem of Europe", Sarajevo still suffers from a lack of resources, low salaries and a serious brain-drain. However, East Sarajevo, which consists of the suburban municipalities of pre-war Sarajevo, is not in a better position in terms of economic progress and job opportunities. It seems that 22 years after the war the new battle has started: the battle for survival and economic prosperity.

The connections between the two cities are pretty bad. While it takes around 25 minutes to get from Sarajevo to East Sarajevo by car, there are few buses operating between the two. Besides that, taxi drivers are not allowed to drive between the two entities; therefore, they usually remove their sign and pretend to drive in a private mode. Also, the animosity between Sarajevo as an urban place and East Sarajevo as being formed of suburban municipalities is present and influences their further willingness to cooperate. In the following chapters this difference will be emphasized especially in terms of the readiness to reconcile between the two sides.

Reconciliation exists mostly in research or political speeches. However, it is hard to talk about reconciliation when we consider that the two sides have been experiencing serious poverty and lack of opportunities for the younger population. Also, so much war trauma has been repressed but transmitted to the next generation, which makes it hard to talk about the war events and to open up the real discussion about it. Inability to talk goes in line with political speeches that in most cases produce more hatred and fear from the other side (and such speeches are happening in both Sarajevo and East Sarajevo). Therefore, the current situation, more than 20 years after the war, can be understood as an atmosphere of fear combined with occasional expressions of misunderstanding and impulsive aggression.

References

Daily Oslobodjenje, 10 February 1999
Dedijer, V. (1966). *The road to Sarajevo*. London: Simon and Schuster.
Dizdarević, R. (2011). *Put u raspad: stenogrami izlaganja Raifa Dizdarevića u raspravama iza zatvorenih vrata državnog i političkog vrha Jugoslavije* [The road to decomposition: The stenographs of Raif Dizdarevic's expositions in debates behind the closed doors of the state and political summit of Yugoslavia]. Sarajevo: Institut za historiju [Institute for History].
Donia, R. J. (2009). *Sarajevo: A biography*. London: Hurst.
Džidić, D., Ristic, M., Domanovic, M., Ivanovic, J., Peci, E., & Marusic, S. J. (2014, May 6). World War I: History divides Balkan schoolchildren. *BIRN*. Retrieved August 20, 2014 from www.balkaninsight.com/en/article/world-war-i-history-divides-balkan-schoolchildren
Hacic-Vlahovic, A. (2008). (De)secularization in Bosnia-Herzegovina: An examination of religiosity trends in a multi-ethnic society. *Amsterdam Social Science*, *1*(1), 72–86.

Hadžijahić, M. (1973). Muslimanske rezolucije iz 1941 godine [Muslim resolutions of 1941]. In 1941. *Istorija Naroda Bosne i Hercegovine* [1941. History of the peoples of Bosnia-Herzegovina] (pp. 275–283). Sarajevo: Institut za istoriju radničkog pokreta.

Macek, I. (2009). *Sarajevo under siege: Anthropology of wartime.* Philadelphia, PA: University of Pennsylvania Press.

Miller, P. (2007, May–June). *Compromising memory: The site of the Sarajevo assassination.* Woodrow Wilson International Center for Scholars, East European Studies. Retrieved from www.wilsoncenter.org/sites/default/files/MR333Miller.doc

Moll, N. (2014). An integrative symbol for a divided country? Commemorating the 1984 Sarajevo Winter Olympics in Bosnia and Herzegovina from the 1992–1995 war until today. *Croatian Political Science Review*, *51*(5), 127–156.

Novosti 8, 15 November 1980.

Organizacioni komitet XIV zimskih olimpijskih igara '84. [Organising Committee of the 14th Winter Olympics]. (1984). *Hvala Sarajevo. Poruke zahvalnosti gradu i zemlji domaćinu XIV zimskih olimpijskih igara* [Thanks messages to the host city and the host country of the 14th Winter Olympics]. Sarajevo: Svjetlost.

Pedrotty, K. M. (2010). Yugoslav unity and Olympic ideology at the 1984 Sarajevo Winter Olympic Games. In H. Grandits & K. Taylor (Eds.), *Yugoslavia's sunny side: A history of tourism in socialism (1950–1980s)* (pp. 335–363). Budapest and New York, NY: CEU Press.

2 The siege of Sarajevo between "Mnene" and "anamnesis"

Listening is the key to reconciliation . . . The more we listen, the more we hear . . . The more we hear, the less we ignore . . . That said, listening is the royal road to understanding.

This chapter provides a theoretical overview of collective memories, social reconstruction of the past, formation of dangerous memories and their transgenerational transmission. However, the integral part of this chapter is empirical research on collective memories of four war events among two generational groups of Sarajevans and East Sarajevans.

Collective memory for traumatic events

Memory is prone to errors and "sins" (Schacter, 2001). However, memory for in-group wrongdoings is not only error-prone, but also includes stereotypes, prejudice and family influences. With the aim of analyzing the possible ways to integrate survivors' memory distortions and further formation of difficult memories, I will provide empirical research on bias in memories for in-group wrongdoings among two generational groups of Sarajevans and East Sarajevans, starting with a brief overview of the position and role of memory and remembrance in conflict, the role of the transgenerational transmission of trauma, and ending with the history-teaching practice in contemporary Bosnia-Herzegovina.

Memory and remembrance in conflict have been commonly studied in line with their contribution to the creation and maintenance of commemoration ceremonies, public events and culture in certain societies (Igartua & Paez, 1997; Ross, 2001; Hewer & Roberts, 2012). Common culture, rituals, ceremonies and commemorations constitute a society's past. The same past is brought into the present by shaping it according to the characteristics of that society. Connerton (1989) says that societies become more connected and unified through collective memory. The past becomes present only through symbolic interactions, narratives and discourses. All groups and societies have their own myths and stories, which are transferred to new generations by tradition, rituals, ceremonies and public events. Igartua and Paez (1997) discovered four factors of generational cycles of remembrance while studying cultural trauma in the Spanish civil war: the existence of the necessary psychological distance, an accumulation of the social resources to cope with commemoration activities, progressive ageing and the selective memories of those involved, and the consequences of ageing on socio-political repression. In this way memory becomes part of culture and is further transferred cyclically through generations, adjusting to the context and needs of each cycle. The importance of culture in this context is of extreme importance as it contributes by losing or gaining some content and by being changed for the next generations.

Apart from the culture having a huge influence on memory, group belonging can also direct the way in which one remembers the past. According to Halbwachs (1992), members of groups differ in the way they remember a common past. It is very common that members remember the past in ways that would put their group in a more favourable position, or at least in a way that provides explanations and justifications for in-group wrongdoings. Depending on the present needs and the *zeitgeist* to which they belong, social groups remember the same past events in different ways. Liu (1999) found that the events in the history of New Zealand were remembered differently and described with different words by the indigenous and Anglo populations in the country, while Gaskell and Wright (1997) found differences between lower- and upper-class British residents in the quality of memory that was measured by clarity, importance and emotional reaction to Margaret Thatcher's resignation. Cairns et al. (1998) discovered significant differences in the memories of British- and Irish-identified people of Northern Ireland about recent social and political events, while Devine-Wright and Lyons (1997) found that different social groups (traditional vs non-traditional) in Ireland associate different values and feelings with historical landmarks because they remember the history of these places differently. As a result, Trinity College, the oldest university in Ireland, which did not open its doors to Roman Catholics until the 1960s, was associated with feelings of shame, confusion and anger by the traditionalists, while the same place meant hope, pride and fascination for the non-traditionalists. Such memories lead to the formation of different stories around the same events which can further be transmitted through generations and therefore enable a group to create its own deeply rooted interpretations and beliefs.

These interpretations are connected to both in-group and out-group interactions which Ross (2001, p. 159) defined as psycho-cultural interpretations:

"shared, deeply held world views that help groups make sense of daily life and provide psychologically meaningful accounts of a group's relationship with other groups, their actions and motives". Such group narratives include information about "the deep fears and threats to identity that drive ethnic conflict" (p. 165), which further influences how the community explains conflict and what kind of motives they attribute to others' behaviours in the conflict.

People are more likely to attribute their own success to internal factors, and their failure to external factors, which is found in intergroup relations as well. Doosje and Branscombe (2003) analyzed the types of attributions the Dutch made for their colonization of Indonesia and for the German invasion of the Netherlands (the Dutch were the aggressors in the former case and the victims in the latter). What they discovered is that when the Dutch were the victims, they were more likely to make internal/character attributions for the negative behaviour of Germans (e.g., Germans are aggressive by nature), while when they were the aggressors in Indonesia, they made more external/contextual attributions (e.g., "it is important to consider the acts of the Dutch in a historical context") (Doosje & Branscombe, 2003). However, this pattern was emphasized by the strength of national identification (i.e., the stronger the Dutch identity, the more internal attributions for the out-group's negative historical behaviour and the more external attributions for the in-group's negative historical behaviour). Furthermore, Branscombe and colleagues have provided strong evidence for the relationship between categorization, identification, understanding history and feelings for one's in- and out-group (Branscombe & Miron, 2005; Branscombe & Doosje, 2004). They have shown that members of high status groups are more likely to feel collective guilt when inequality between groups is framed as in-group privilege (e.g., white privilege), as opposed to out-group disadvantage (e.g., black disadvantage) (Powell, Branscombe, & Schmitt, 2005), and that categorizing oneself at a more inclusive level (e.g., humans vs North American Jews and Native Canadians) resulted in more forgiving attitudes towards the members of groups that had done harm in the past (e.g., Germans and White Canadians) (Wohl & Branscombe, 2005). Besides that, ethnic and national identification with the group plays a role in both forgiving attitudes and readiness to reconcile by itself.

Two approaches in the study of ethnic and national identification exist in contemporary psychology. According to the first one, national identification equals in-group identification. This approach is rooted in social identity theory, and it treats in-group identification as a unidimensional construct. Recent literature on this topic proves that in-group identification can be seen as a multidimensional construct, and this view is even more represented in psychology (e.g., Cameron & Lalonde, 2001; Jackson, 2002; Cameron, 2004; Leach et al., 2008; Bilali, 2012).

Tajfel (1978) conceptualizes social identity as a combination of three components: evaluative, cognitive and affective. However, the approach that treats in-group identification as a multidimensional process puts the emphasis on national identity as a form of attachment to the group. Such attachment can be defined (and expressed) as either patriotism or nationalism.

According to Bar-Tal (1993), patriotism is a healthy national self-concept, which corresponds to the positive love towards one's own country. Contrary to patriotism, nationalism can be described through several dimensions; however, the most common one is the view according to which one believes that one's own group is superior to other groups, and that dimension is called in-group superiority (Kosterman & Feshbach, 1989).

According to Roccas, Klar, and Liviatan (2006) there are two dimensions of in-group identification: glorification and attachment. Glorification corresponds to the elements related to nationalism, such as beliefs in in-group superiority and deference to group norms and symbols. Attachment represents cognitive and emotional attachment to the in-group (for instance, one defines oneself as a group member or declares a commitment to the group). The glorification dimension possesses a strong evaluative component in that it defines in-group as either positive or negative, a process that has driven predictions regarding the effects of the strength of in-group identification. Roccas, Sagiv, Schwartz, Halevy, and Eidelson (2008) further distinguish two dimensions of in-group glorification: deference and superiority. However, only superiority constitutes an evaluative component, because one way in which group members can maintain an in-group's positive image is to view their group as better than other groups (superior to the other groups), which is very relevant in case of intergroup conflict. In-group superiority is what drives favourable in-group interpretations of an in-group's harmdoing. Therefore, if one is motivated to perceive one's group in a positive light, that may drive distortions and legitimizations of past events where the in-group was the perpetrator and committed certain wrongdoings. Roccas and colleagues (2006) used this rationale to suggest that the glorification dimension (i.e., positive evaluation dimension), rather than group attachment, drives denial of in-group responsibility for harmdoing and legitimization of past in-group harms. However, Liu and Hilton (2005) and Bilali (2012) also concluded that social representations of the in-group's history might in turn influence the degree and the way in which individuals identify with their group. That is in line with Billig's (1995) statement that at a collective level, historical memories form the content of group identity.

Sometimes, and in order to enhance their identity, groups distort the past by silencing or reinterpreting the negative events in their history, and by embellishing and glorifying history to portray the in-group favourably (Baumeister & Hastings, 1997). Therefore, the nature of in-group identification might lead to biases in historical memories, but the characteristics and uses of historical memories might also influence how individuals relate to their groups.

Construals of historical events related to group conflict

According to Phinney (1990), identity can be constructed as a life story in an endless number of idiosyncratic ways by different individuals with different personalities, interests and abilities, within the same socio-historical context. Even if we are unaware of cultural stories from our society/ environment, they can affect our autobiographies (Freeman, 2002). Freeman (2002) suggested that psychologists study the "narrative unconscious", which he defined as the culturally rooted aspect of one's history that has not yet been part of one's story (at least, not at the conscious level). In that sense, storytelling, movies, books, media and photographs are completely unconscious factors until they are brought to the forefront by some events and happenings. According to Chase (2002), we learn about not only individual people's stories once we hear them, but also about the cultural, ideological and historical resources that these stories draw on, resist, encompass and transform.

People resist or modify collective narratives because they strive to bring order and meaning into their individual and also collective worlds. However, many people derive meaning from their group memberships, and their lives are usually intertwined with collective structures and processes. Individual experiences are often determined by membership in collectives and shared societal beliefs (Bar-Tal, 2006), defined as enduring beliefs shared by society members on topics and issues that are of special concern for a particular society, and which contribute to a sense of uniqueness for the society's members (Bar-Tal, 2000). Societal beliefs are organized around thematic clusters like societal goals, self-image, conflicts, aspirations, conditions, norms, values, societal structures, images of out-groups, institutions, obstacles and problems.

According to Bruner (1990), people conceive of collective narratives as social constructions that coherently interrelate a sequence of historical and current events; they are accounts of a community's collective experiences, embodied in its belief system, and represent the collective's symbolically constructed shared identity. Therefore, the collective narrative of the society provides a basis for common understanding, good communication, interdependence and the coordination of social activities, all of which widely contribute to the functioning of the social system. However, collective narratives often feature a public agenda, media reports, existing historical narratives and storytelling. Formed in such a way, they also contribute to the formation and maintenance of conflict especially in divided societies such as Bosnia-Herzegovina. Usually the society constructs an appropriate psychological repertoire which consists of shared beliefs, attitudes, emotions and capacities, while narratives are of special importance.

While the narrative of the collective memory focuses on the society's remembered past, the ethos of the conflict focuses on the present situation only. Following Bar-Tal (1998), the collective memory component of the narrative has the following characteristics: it is shared by group members and is treated by many of them as a truthful account of the past and a valid history of the group, and it does not necessarily tell the factual history of the past, but intends to tell the past that is functional for the group's present existence and functioning.

Usually opposing groups in a conflict offer different, contradictory and selective narratives. It is not only the case during storytelling or in the media, but also in regular history classes. By selectively including or excluding certain historical events and processes from the collective memory, a group characterizes itself and its historical experiences that count in unique and exclusive ways (Irwin-Zarecka, 1994). One's history is perceived by group members as unique, distinctive and exclusive because it tells the particular story of the group's past and outlines the boundaries for a group's description and characterization. In Bosnia-Herzegovina three different histories have been taught via the official curricula, while even more various histories/narratives/interpretations exist among residents.

Bias for in-group wrongdoings: victim vs perpetrator

The vast majority of research in social psychology has been devoted to the study of victims and perpetrators and their responses to wrongdoings committed by their own group (e.g., Castano & Giner-Sorolla, 2006; Leidner & Castano, 2012; Leidner, Castano, Zaiser, & Giner-Sorolla, 2010, Leidner, Li, Petrović & Orazni, 2017), as well as wrongdoings suffered by their own group (e.g., Cehajic, Brown, & Castano, 2008; Leidner, Castano, & Ginges, 2013). It is widely known that when confronted with the wrongdoings committed by their own in-group people tend to use various types of defensive mechanisms, such as moral disengagement strategies (Bandura, 1999, 2002) that can include denial, dehumanization of victims, moralization of out-group directed violence (in the form of different excuses for and justifications of the wrongdoings committed). Such strategies contribute not only to the justification of the wrongdoings committed and conflict per se from the perpetrators' side, but also to the lack of a wish to reconcile and lack of interest in pursuing justice (Leidner et al., 2010). Also, such defensive mechanisms lead to the distortion of conflict-related narrative, which becomes further changed, retold and transmitted in line with a particular justification strategy. However, the modification of narratives as well as attitudes towards reconciliation and justice is under the influence of defensive mechanisms in the victims' group. In-group victimization experiences can easily evoke vengeful feelings towards the perpetrator group that can in turn lead to group-based retribution (Lickel, 2012).

It is not unusual that victims and their families want transgressors (and sometimes even their relatives who were not directly involved in the wrongdoing) to be punished. For instance, a desire for retribution as out-group punishment among Jewish Israelis and Palestinians, both of whom commonly self-identify as victims of the Israeli-Palestinian conflict, apparently originated in their dehumanization of their respective antagonistic group (Leidner et al., 2013). Therefore, we can conclude that victims almost always seek retribution, especially in cases of larger offences, war crimes and genocide. Keeping that in mind, one can assume that understanding conflict requires integrating and putting into perspective both perpetrators' and victims' perspective. Also, the process of trauma healing and reconciliation can start only in situations when both groups declare what exactly they think about the conflict and what kind of perspective their group members can take in that regard. However, not much research has been done so far in order to examine both perspectives. The perspective-based model of reconciliation proposed by Shnabel and Nadler (2008) theorizes that victims have the need to be empowered and appreciated, while perpetrators have the need to be socially accepted; therefore, these two needs are considered to be prerequisites for reconciliation. Nevertheless, the authors neither compared the responses of both victims and perpetrators nor tried to examine in-group and out-group bias, as they only analyzed victims' responses to the messages delivered/sent by the perpetrators. Li et al. (2017) in their cross-cultural research determined that Serbs who strongly glorified Serbia were more supportive of future violence against, and less willing to reconcile with, Bosniaks after reading about Serbian victimization by Bosniaks rather than Serbian transgressions against Bosniaks. However, they also did not examine both victims' and perpetrators' perspectives; therefore, the conclusion is drawn based on data obtained from one side (one-sided perspective). Besides that, both different perspectives and also the ways in which they clash have not been examined yet, as well as differences in interpretations of past events. Therefore, this research will try to fill these gaps by providing both victims' and perpetrators' perspectives and analysis of their contribution to the process of reconciliation.

Remembrance, forgetting and reconciliation: Sarajevo and East Sarajevo 23 years after the war

Societies involved in intractable conflicts form a conflict-supporting narrative that provides justification for and explanation of the conflict as a whole as well as narratives about its specific events and relevant people (Oren et al., 2015). Until now a large amount of research has been done in the area of conflicting narratives, memories of the past and its contribution to reconciliation, not only in the area of psychology, but also in sociology, political science and history (White, 1987; Zerubavel, E., 2003; Zerubavel, Y., 1994; Elkins, 2005; Wertsch, 2002). Dominant specific and metanarratives about the past present the collective memory of the society, defined as representations of the past that are collectively adopted by the group members (Kansteiner, 2002). While analyzing the Israel-Palestine conflict, Bar-Tal (2013) came to the conclusion that conflicting narratives include several main themes: the justness of one's own group's goals, security, delegitimization, positive collective self-image, collective self-victimhood, patriotism, unity and peace. One of the aims of this research is to analyze to what extent the mentioned themes are present in conflicting narratives provided by the participants from Sarajevo and East Sarajevo.

Sarajevo and East Sarajevo belong to two different entities: the Federation of Bosnia-Herzegovina and the Republic of Srpska, and inhabitants of the two cities were on opposite sides during the 1992–1995 war in Bosnia-Herzegovina. All participants reported on their memories of four specific war events. A short description of the events as well as their significance and reason for inclusion in the questionnaire are provided here:

- The massacre in "Vase Miskina" street, also known as the Sarajevo massacre in the bread queue, was the first artillery attack during the siege of Sarajevo carried out by Bosnian Serb forces on 27 May 1992. It is considered one of the most horrific crimes, and it has been commemorated ever since.
- The Markale massacres were two bombardments carried out by the Army of the Republic of Srpska targeting civilians at the Markale marketplace, located in the historic core of Sarajevo (the first one occurred in 1994, and the second one in 1995). The latter attack was the stated reason for NATO air strikes against Bosnian Serb forces, which were supposed to lead to the Dayton Peace Agreement and the end of the war in Bosnia-Herzegovina. Commemorations of both massacres have been organized on a yearly basis in Sarajevo.

- Killings of Serbs in Kazani–Trebevic: between 1992 and 1993 Serbs from Sarajevo were taken against their will to Trebevic, the mountain above Sarajevo, by Bosniak members of the Bosnian Army and killed. The exact number of the victims has been under discussion, and "Kazani" is the only documented case of the suffering of Serbs from Sarajevo until now.
- NATO air strikes against Bosnian Serb forces happened after the second Markale massacre (1995) and were intended to lead to the end of the siege of Sarajevo and the war in Bosnia-Herzegovina.

The above-mentioned events were chosen in accordance with the manifestation and influence characteristics of a major event (Nets-Zehngut, 2015), and the number of commemorations organized each year. However, the last two events are the only two documented cases in which Bosnian Serbs were victims; therefore, these two were the only two to be chosen for the purpose of this research.

It is important to mention that participants from Sarajevo (mostly Bosniaks and some Croats and Serbs) were victims in the first two events while participants from East Sarajevo were perpetrators, and vice versa for the other events. Even though the air strikes were conducted by NATO, the main reason for the attack was the Markale massacre; therefore, in the dominant narrative both Bosniaks and NATO were blamed. Also, two generational cohorts of participants were recruited in order to explore transgenerational transmission of traumatic memories. Transgenerational transmission of trauma has been explored previously, especially in children of Holocaust survivors (Fossion, Rejas, Servais, Pelc, & Hirsch, 2003; Kellermann, 2013). However, this research will not explore the direct transgenerational transmission (parent-child), but the slightly indirect transmission (two generational cohorts that represent groups of people of different ages but born in the same area, such that one group survived the war and the other was born after the war). The point is to analyze how the social context and media together influence the memories of the younger generation, as well as to establish the foundations for the "remembrance for peace" project.

The main aims of this research are as follows:

1 to examine bias in memories of the events that took place during the 1992–1995 war in Bosnia-Herzegovina in two generational cohorts from the area of Sarajevo and East Sarajevo;
2 to examine the content and bias of memories of the younger cohort;
3 to examine differences in narratives of war events between Serbs from Sarajevo and Serbs from East Sarajevo in two generational cohorts;

4   to analyze the relation between ethnicity, bias in memories of war events and readiness for reconciliation;
5   to propose the elements of the mediation model of difficult memories based on the process of remembrance and the transmission of the proposed indicators that are integrated in both individual and collective memory.

Hypotheses

The main hypotheses are:

H0: Participants from Sarajevo and East Sarajevo won't express more bias in the memories of the events in which members of their group were victims, regardless of age.

H1: Participants from Sarajevo and East Sarajevo will show more bias in memories of the events in which members of their group were victims, regardless of age.

It is expected that the differences will arise when comparing the responses of the three ethnic groups of the same generation. Each generational group will be analyzed in line with the following indicators: the accuracy of the dating of events (time perspective), willingness to recall the events, number of victims mentioned, the attribution of guilt, the attribution of the role of victim and the readiness to commemorate the events. These characteristics are based on the phenomenological characteristics of memories, theories of memory bias (Schacter, 2001) and Bar-Tal's (2013) theory on the formation of narratives of conflict. Therefore, the main hypothesis will be divided into six sub-hypotheses that relate to each indicator, for each generational group separately.

I generation

$H0_a$: There is no difference between the three ethnic groups in the first generation of participants in their ability to recall the date of the events.

$H1_a$: There is a difference between the three ethnic groups in the first generation of participants in their ability to recall the date of the events.

$H0_b$: There is no difference between the three ethnic groups in the first generation of participants in their willingness to remind themselves of the events.

$H1_b$: There is a difference between the three ethnic groups in the first generation of participants in their willingness to remind themselves of the events.

$H0_c$: There is no difference between the three ethnic groups in the first generation of participants in the number of victims they mention for each event.

$H1_c$: There is a difference between the three ethnic groups in the first generation of participants in the number of victims they mention for each event.

$H0_d$: There is no difference between the three ethnic groups in the first generation of participants in the attribution of guilt they express while describing each event.

$H1_d$: There is a difference between the three ethnic groups in the first generation of participants in the attribution of guilt they express while describing each event.

$H0_e$: There is no difference between the three ethnic groups in the first generation of participants in the attribution of the role of victim they express while describing each event.

$H1_e$: There is a difference between the three ethnic groups in the first generation of participants in the attribution of the role of victim they express while describing each event.

$H0_f$: There is no difference between the three ethnic groups in the first generation of participants in their willingness to mark four events through commemorations and memorials.

$H1_f$: There is a difference between the three ethnic groups in the first generation of participants in their willingness to mark four events through commemorations and memorials.

II generation

$H0_a$: There is no difference between the three ethnic groups in the second generation of participants in their ability to recall the date of the events.

$H1_a$: There is a difference between the three ethnic groups in the second generation of participants in their ability to recall the date of the events.

HO$_b$: There is no difference between the three ethnic groups in the second generation of participants in their willingness to remind themselves of the events.

H1$_b$: There is a difference between the three ethnic groups in the second generation of participants in their willingness to remind themselves of the events.

HO$_c$: There is no difference between the three ethnic groups in the second generation of participants in the number of victims they mention for each event.

H1$_c$: There is a difference between the three ethnic groups in the second generation of participants in the number of victims they mention for each event.

HO$_d$: There is no difference between the three ethnic groups in the second generation of participants in the attribution of guilt they express while describing each event.

H1$_d$: There is a difference between the three ethnic groups in the second generation of participants in the attribution of guilt they express while describing each event.

HO$_e$: There is no difference between the three ethnic groups in the second generation of participants in the attribution of the role of victim they express while describing each event.

H1$_e$: There is a difference between the three ethnic groups in the second generation of participants in the attribution of the role of victim they express while describing each event.

HO$_f$: There is no difference between the three ethnic groups in the second generation of participants in their willingness to mark four events through commemorations and memorials.

H1$_f$: There is a difference between the three ethnic groups in the second generation of participants in their willingness to mark four events through commemorations and memorials.

The following hypothesis corresponds to the difference in responses among two groups of Serbs: differences in readiness for reconciliation in the first and the second generational group.

H2: It is expected that the responses of Serbs from Sarajevo will be more similar to the narratives of Bosniaks from Sarajevo than the responses of Serbs from East Sarajevo according to all the indicators, except when describing the event in Kazani, regardless of age.

It is important to clarify that it is expected that the narratives of Serbs from Sarajevo will be more similar to the narratives of their Bosniak neighbours, since they spent the war in the same area and survived the same war trauma, while the narratives from Serbs from East Sarajevo will be different since they spent the war in the other area and transmitted a different type of memories to their younger generation. Also, before the war, the territory of present East Sarajevo belonged to suburban munici-palities of the city of Sarajevo; therefore, the communication between these groups was hindered due to the urban-rural difference that has been present until now.

H3: It is expected that Bosniaks and Serbs from Sarajevo will be less ready to reconcile with Serbs from East Sarajevo as measured on all four subscales, regardless of age.

The hypothesis H3 follows the logic of hypothesis H2 and expects Bosniaks and Serbs from Sarajevo to have similar attitudes towards Serbs from East Sarajevo due to the cohesion formed over the war (I generation), and closure through school and other networks (II generation).

Method

Participants

The research included a total of 150 participants, divided into two groups:

1 the "old" generation: participants who were between 18 and 70 years old at the beginning of the war in Bosnia-Herzegovina (1992) and who lived in Sarajevo and contemporary East Sarajevo during the war and who still live in the same area (89 participants);
2 the "young" generation: high school students from Sarajevo and East Sarajevo who were between 15 and 19 years old when the research was conducted (2016–2017) (61 participants).

An equal number of female and male participants was ensured in both groups. However, equal numbers of Bosniak and Serb participants from Sarajevo, and Serbs only (Bosniaks do not live in East Sarajevo in a certain number) from East Sarajevo, could not be ensured after coding of narratives was performed. The narratives obtained through structured interviews were later coded by two independent evaluators; therefore, data that were incomplete were not taken into consideration (unan-swered questions or answers that did not correspond to the question).

In order to ensure representativeness of the sample, the first group of participants for both cohorts was recruited through specific organizations/associations/groups to which the majority of them belonged: high schools in both entities (only students born in Sarajevo and East Sarajevo were chosen, and only Serbs from both places and Bosniaks from Sarajevo) and the Orthodox Church and mosque. The first stratum was used to reach more participants who had the basic demographic characteristics (snow-ball sampling method). However, social networks such as Facebook were used in order to recruit participants more easily. It is worth mentioning that only those participants who had never left Sarajevo/East Sarajevo before, during and after the war were chosen (for the first generational group), while for the second generational group only those who were born in Sarajevo/East Sarajevo and who had been living there since then were chosen. That caused a certain reduction in sample size, because most of the people actually left one or the other city either before or during the war (and some of them even after the war or by the time this research was conducted). Therefore, data obtained through this sample have to be understood in line with the mentioned restriction. Also, very few Bosniaks live in the area of East Sarajevo (in most cases they simply own summer houses there but do not live there permanently); therefore, they were omitted from the East Sarajevo group (only Serbs were chosen there). More demographic data is given in the following tables.

Table 2.1 Ethnicity as declared by participants

	Number	Percent
Bosniak	49	32.7
Serb	101	67.3
Total	150	100.0

Table 2.2 Residential ethnicity

	Number	Percent
Bosniak from Sarajevo	49	32.7
Serb from Sarajevo	52	34.7
Serb from East Sarajevo	49	32.7
Total	150	100.0

Table 2.3 Place of residence during the 1992–1995 war

	Number	Percent
Sarajevo	61	40.7
East Sarajevo	29	19.3
Total	90	60.0

Table 2.4 Current place of residence

	Number	Percent
Sarajevo	101	67.3
East Sarajevo	49	32.7
Total	150	100.0

Table 2.5 Age of participants

Age	Number	Percent
40–70	90	60.0
15–19	60	40.0
Total	150	100.0

Table 2.6 Level of education

	Number	Percent
High school student	18	12.0
University student	42	28.0
Primary school degree	7	4.7
Secondary school degree	41	27.3
Two-year university degree	5	3.3
University degree	36	24.0
MA degree	1	0.7
Total	150	100.0

Instruments

All participants filled in the Readiness for Reconciliation Scale (Petrović 2005), while semi-structured interviews were performed in order to analyze their memories of four specific war events and their opinion on the commemoration of those events – the Memories for War Events Interview.

The Readiness for Reconciliation Scale (Petrović 2005) is a 5-point Likert-type scale that consists of 40 items. The scale has a high level of reliability (Cronbach alpha 0.97). It consists of four subscales: distrust and blaming the other side (Cronbach alpha 0.94), willingness to cooperate (Cronbach alpha 0.94), forgiveness (Cronbach alpha 0.89) and rehumanization (Cronbach alpha 0.89).

The semi-structured interview consisted of the same seven questions for each of the four events, and was specially designed for the purpose of this research. It was designed to measure the readiness of the participant to recall the event, his/her first association to the event, the ways through which he/she heard about the event, what happened during the event (in his/her opinion), and his/her opinion on whether or not that event should be commemorated and marked.

Procedure

Interviews were conducted at the very beginning, and the scale upon completion of the interview. The interviews were not time-limited, and participants were allowed time to think and provide the most accurate answer, to their knowledge. All participants were informed that there were no true and false answers and that their privacy was guaranteed.

Answers to the interview questions were later coded and analyzed by two independent evaluators. The coding was performed according to the list of indicators prepared based on the phenomenological characteristics of memories, Schacter's theory on sins of memory and Bar-Tal's theory on the construction of conflict narratives. The following characteristics and their indicators were used for the process of narrative analysis (indicators numbered 3, 4, 5, 6 were analyzed by two independent evaluators, and Cohen Cappa coefficient of agreement was quite satisfactory $\kappa = .86$):

1   the accuracy of dating of the event (does not remember, can recall the year when the event happened, can recall both month and year when the event happened);
2   frequency of recall (never, sometimes, often);
3   estimated number of victims;
4   attribution of guilt (categories: other group is not guilty, other group is guilty but with several justifications, other group's guilt can be questioned, other group is guilty, guilt is not mentioned);
5   attribution of the role of victim (categories: members of my group are victims, both groups are victims, victims were not mentioned);

6   need for marking the memory for the event (categories: it is important
      to mark the events in which one side were victims, it is important to
      mark the events in which both sides were victims, it is not necessary to
      mark this event).

The first two (1, 2) indicators were responses to multiple-choice questions;
therefore, there was no need for further coding. The following theories were
taken into consideration while preparing the coding list (and helped in its
construction): phenomenological characteristics of memories (Sutin and
Robins, 2006), themes around ethos of conflict (Bar-Tal, 2000), Schacter's
seven memory errors (seven sins of memory) (2001).

Ten relevant dimensions of phenomenological characteristics of autobiographical memories proposed by Sutin and Robins (2006) were used
as a theoretical background for narrative analyses: vividness, coherence,
accessibility, time perspective, sensory details, visual perspective, emotional intensity, sharing, distancing and valence. Since the current research
does not deal with autobiographical memories per se, but with the traumatic narratives of a difficult past, this list was modified such that only
time perspective, sensory details, visual perspective, emotional intensity
and valence and distancing were used while analyzing narratives (during
both quantitative (time perspective) and qualitative analyses (the rest of the
characteristics)).

The narrative of the ethos of conflict is supported by society's collective
memory, and it includes the following themes according to Bar-Tal (2000):

1   goals – members of the same group have a tendency to justify their own
      goals, indicate their importance and provide explanations and rationales
      (their major goal is to influence all members to embrace these goals and
      to fight for them);
2   security – both group members and society in general are trying to
      emphasize the importance of security, safety and survival, together
      with the conditions important for their achievement and maintenance
      (if necessary, they can easily recruit more people to perform hostile
      acts and wars, while explaining it as aiming to achieve peace and
      harmony for all);
3   delegitimization – during conflict, members of one group are usu-
      ally trying to delegitimize members of the opponent group in order
      to justify violent acts they are planning to commit (or already
      committed) towards them and in order to suppress or deny their
      humanity;

4   self-image – group members or societies in general are trying to preserve a positive self-image and therefore have the tendency to attribute
positive traits, values and behaviours to their own members, and to promote characteristics related to courage, heroism, humanness, morality
and fairness, while at the same time they tend to attribute completely
opposite traits to their opponents;

5   victimization – group members and societies have a tendency to present
themselves as victims in the context of intractable conflict, as well as to
exaggerate their own victimhood;

6   patriotism – group members and societies have a tendency to build
attachment to the country and its society by imposing and propagating
loyalty, love, care and sacrifice, with the major aim to increase cohesiveness and dedication, and serve an important function for mobilizing
the society members to actively participate in the conflict and endure
hardship and difficulties;

7   unity – group members and societies tend to promote feelings of
belonging and solidarity in order to ignore internal conflicts and to unite
against external threats (such threats are sometimes invented);

8   peace – societal beliefs of peace refer to peace in general as the ultimate
desire of the society, where peace is presented and understood as an
ultimate goal of the society.

Both groups and societies in general actively influence the maintenance of
such societal beliefs to form and strengthen the society's ethos of conflict.
Therefore, these beliefs constitute part of the shared repertoire of the members of the society, contribute to a common understanding and provide a
basis for good communication, interdependence and the coordination of
social activities, all of which are necessary for the effective functioning of
social systems (Bar-Tal, 2000). However, narratives of conflict also consist
of different (and difficult) memories as more or less shared representations
of past events among group members.

Schacter (2001) described seven memory errors which he called *sins of
memory*. The first three are *sins of omission* that involve forgetting, and the
second four are *sins of commission* that involve distorted or unwanted recollections (based on Schacter, 2001):

1   Transience represents the decreasing accessibility of memory over
time.

2   Absent-mindedness includes lapses of attention and forgetting to
do things and therefore operates both when a memory is formed

(the encoding stage) and when a memory is accessed (the retrieval stage).

3   Blocking represents the temporary inaccessibility of stored information.
4   Suggestibility includes the incorporation of misinformation into memory due to leading questions, deception and other causes.
5   Bias corresponds to retrospective distortions produced by current knowledge and beliefs.
6   Persistence includes unwanted recollections that people cannot forget, such as the intrusive memories of post-traumatic stress disorder.
7   Misattribution corresponds to the attribution of memories to incorrect sources or believing that someone has seen or heard something you have not.

According to Schacter (2001), these errors often seem to be sins, but they are actually an integral part of the mind's heritage because they are so closely connected to features of memory that make it work well. These seven sins cannot be easily minimized or avoided, even when it comes to the analysis of narratives of conflict and traumatic memories. They illuminate how memory draws on the past to inform the present, preserves elements of present experience for future reference, and allows people to revisit the past at will (Schacter, 2001). However, in this research (and while preparing the coding list), mostly bias and misattribution were taken into consideration as these two actually were expected to appear in traumatic narratives of a difficult past which is perceived quite differently depending on the position of one's in-group.

Results

The results are presented in two parts: analysis of memories of four events according to the six indicators; relation between ethnicity and readiness for reconciliation.

Part Ia: Analysis of memories according to the Six indicators (I generation)

a   When did the event happen?

The responses to this question are given in the tables and charts below (for each of the four events).

Markale

Table 2.7 Indicator I (Markale event)

Ethnicity	When did the event happen?			
	Exact date	Year only	Do not remember	Total
Bosniak from Sarajevo	12 40.0%	15 50.0%	3 10.0%	30 100.0%
Serb from Sarajevo	3 9.7%	17 54.8%	11 35.5%	31 100.0%
Serb from East Sarajevo	3 10.3%	13 44.8%	13 44.8%	29 100.0%
Total	18 20.0%	45 50.0%	27 30.0%	90 100.0%

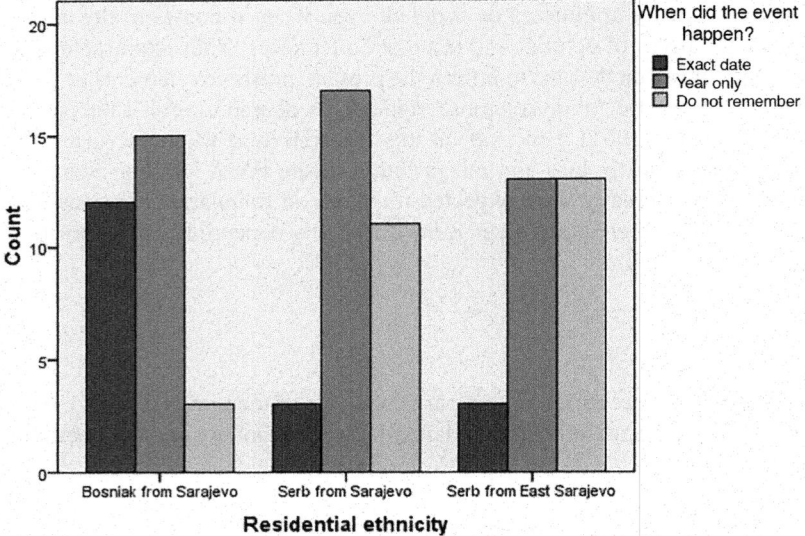

Chart 2.1 Indicator I – Markale

The results of the chi square test (X^2 (4, N = 90) = 15.74 p = .003) showed that there is a moderate association between ethnicity and the ability to recall the date of the event (r(88) = .30 p = .004); therefore, the null hypothesis is rejected.

Kazani

Table 2.8 Indicator I (Kazani event)

Ethnicity	When did the event happen?			
	Exact date	Year only	Do not remember	Total
Bosniak from Sarajevo	1 3.3%	10 33.3%	19 63.3%	30 100.0%
Serb from Sarajevo	2 6.5%	15 48.4%	14 45.2%	31 100.0%
Serb from East Sarajevo	0 0.0%	5 17.2%	24 82.8%	29 100.0%
Total	3 3.3%	30 33.3%	57 63.3%	90 100.0%

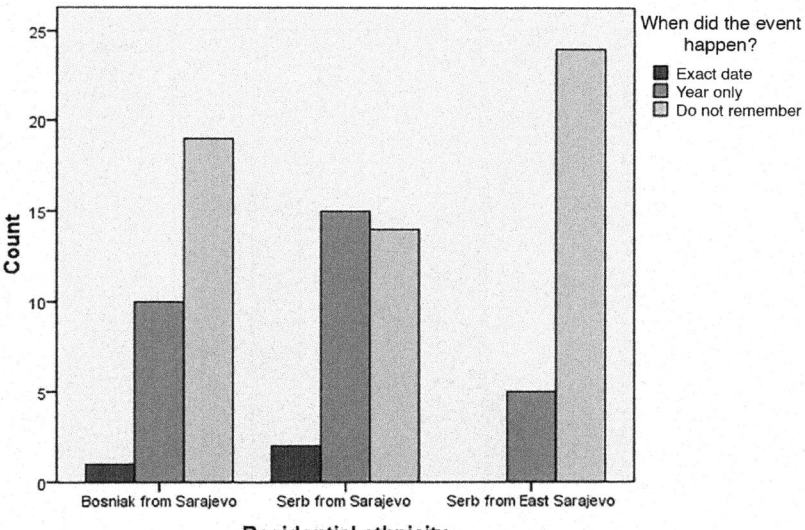

Chart 2.2 Indicator I – Kazani

The results of the chi square test (X^2 (4, N = 90) = 9.58 p = .048) revealed that there is a weak association between ethnicity and the response to this question (r(88) = .0.25 p = .019); therefore, the null hypothesis ($H0_b$) is rejected.

Vase Miskina

Table 2.9 Indicator I (Vase Miskina event)

Ethnicity	When did the event happen?			
	Exact date	*Year only*	*Do not remember*	*Total*
Bosniak from Sarajevo	8 26.7%	19 63.3%	3 10.3%	30 100.0%
Serb from Sarajevo	5 16.1%	14 45.2%	12 38.7%	31 100.0%
Serb from East Sarajevo	2 6.9%	14 48.3%	13 44.8%	29 100.0%
Total	15 16.7%	47 52.2%	28 31.1%	90 100.0%

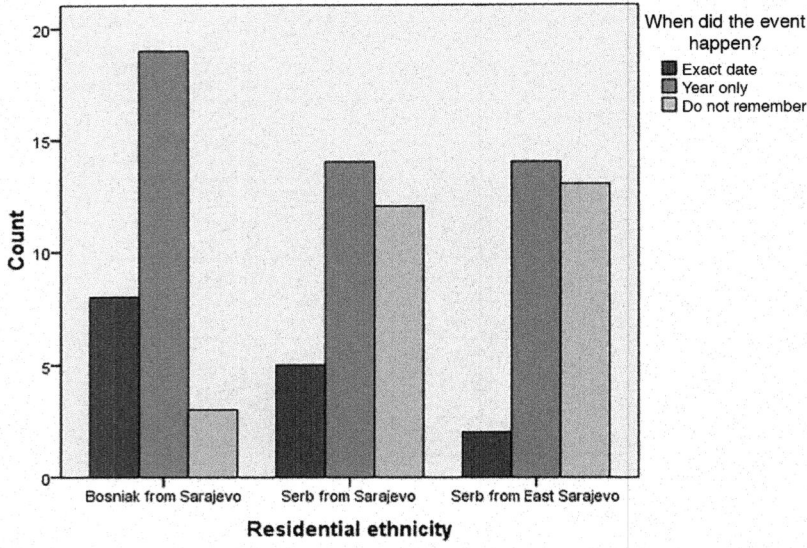

Chart 2.3 Indicator I – Vase Miskina

The results of the chi square test (X^2 (4, N = 90) = 11.18 p = .025) showed that there is a weak association between ethnicity and the ability to recall the date of the event (r(88) = .28 p = .007); therefore, the null hypothesis is rejected.

NATO

Table 2.10 Indicator I (NATO event)

Ethnicity	When did the event happen?			
	Exact date	*Year only*	*Do not remember*	*Total*
Bosniak from Sarajevo	2 6.7%	24 80.0%	4 13.3%	30 100.0%
Serb from Sarajevo	3 9.7%	21 67.7%	7 22.6%	31 100.0%
Serb from East Sarajevo	5 17.2%	20 69.0%	44 13.8%	29 100.0%
Total	10 11.1%	65 72.2%	15 16.7%	90 100.0%

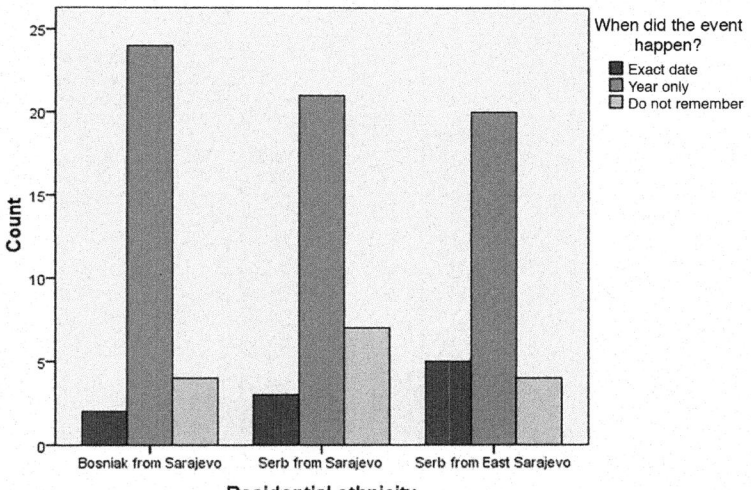

Chart 2.4 Indicator I – NATO

The results of the chi square test (X^2 (4, N = 90) = 2.95 p = .57) showed that there is not enough evidence to suggest an association between ethnicity and participants' ability to recall the date of the event (r(88) = −.107 p = .316); therefore, the null hypothesis is accepted.

b Does the participant ever remind himself/herself of the event?

The responses to this question are given in the tables and charts below (for each of the four events).

Markale

Table 2.11 Indicator II (Markale)

| Ethnicity | Does the participant remind himself/herself of Markale? | | | |
	Often	Sometimes	Never	Total
Bosniak from Sarajevo	11 36.7%	17 56.7%	2 6.7%	30 100.0%
Serb from Sarajevo	3 9.7%	21 67.7%	7 22.6%	31 100.0%
Serb from East Sarajevo	3 10.3%	20 69.0%	6 20.7%	29 100.0%
Total	17 18.9%	58 64.4%	15 16.7%	90 100.0%

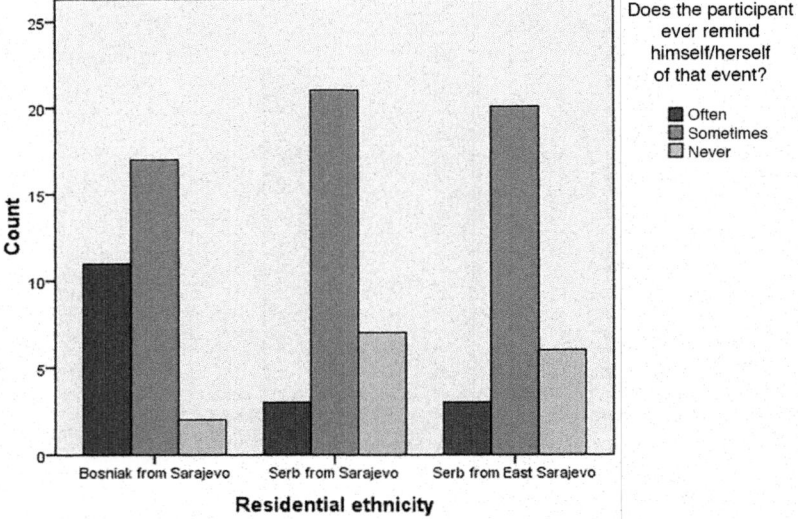

Chart 2.5 Indicator II (Markale)

The results of the chi square test (X^2 (4, N = 90) = 10.69 p = .03) showed that there is a weak association between ethnicity and participants' readiness to remind themselves of this event (r(88) = .2 p = .059); therefore, the null hypothesis is rejected.

Kazani

Table 2.12 Indicator II (Kazani)

Ethnicity	Does the participant remind himself/herself of Kazani?			
	Often	*Sometimes*	*Never*	*Total*
Bosniak from Sarajevo	0 0.0%	18 60.0%	12 40.0%	30 100.0%
Serb from Sarajevo	1 3.2%	22 71.0%	8 25.8%	31 100.0%
Serb from East Sarajevo	0 0.0%	15 51.7%	14 48.3%	29 100.0%
Total	1 1.1%	55 61.1%	34 37.8%	90 100.0%

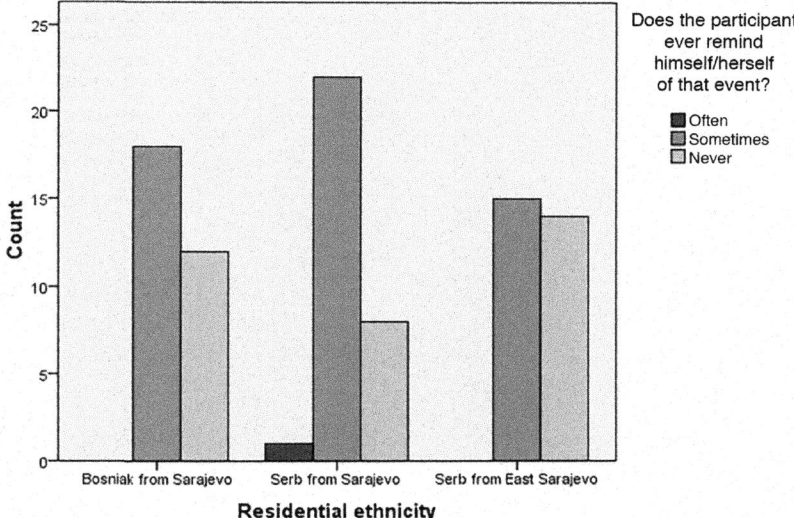

Chart 2.6 Indicator II (Kazani)

The results of the chi square test (X^2 (4, N = 90) = 4.88 p = .3) showed that there is not enough evidence to suggest an association between ethnicity and participants' ability to remind themselves of the event (r(88) = .128 p = .228); therefore, the null hypothesis is accepted.

Vase Miskina

Table 2.13 Indicator II (Vase Miskina)

Ethnicity	Does the participant remind himself/herself of Vase Miskina?			
	Often	*Sometimes*	*Never*	*Total*
Bosniak from Sarajevo	5 16.7%	22 73.3%	3 10.0%	30 100.0%
Serb from Sarajevo	4 12.9%	20 64.5%	7 22.6%	31 100.0%
Serb from East Sarajevo	2 6.9%	17 58.6%	10 34.5%	29 100.0%
Total	11 12.2%	59 65.6%	20 22.2%	90 100.0%

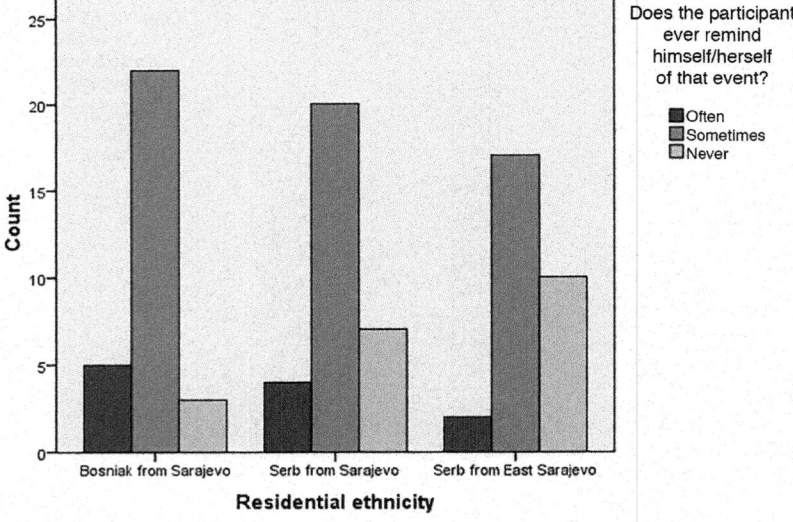

Chart 2.7 Indicator II (Vase Miskina)

The results of the chi square test (X^2 (4, N = 90) = 5.64 p = .23) showed that there is not enough evidence to suggest an association between ethnicity and participants' ability to remind themselves of the event (r(88) = .228 p = .031); therefore, the null hypothesis is accepted.

NATO

Table 2.14 Indicator II (NATO)

Ethnicity	Does the participant remind himself/herself of the NATO bombing?			
	Often	*Sometimes*	*Never*	*Total*
Bosniak from Sarajevo	0 0.0%	21 70.0%	9 30.0%	30 100.0%
Serb from Sarajevo	2 6.5%	20 64.5%	9 29.0%	31 100.0%
Serb from East Sarajevo	12 41.4%	14 48.3%	3 10.3%	29 100.0%
Total	14 15.6%	55 61.1%	21 23.3%	90 100.0%

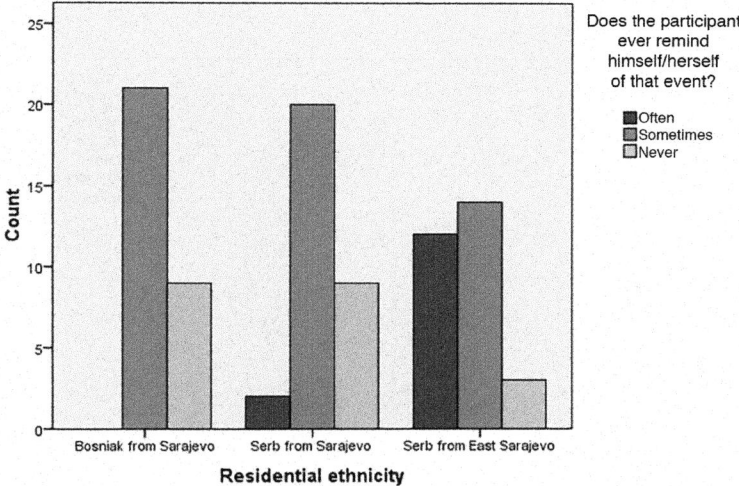

Chart 2.8 Indicator II (NATO)

The results of the chi square test (X^2 (4, N = 90) = 23.08 p = .00) revealed that there is a medium but negative association between ethnicity and the response to this question (r(88) = −.43 p = .00); therefore, the null hypothesis ($H0_b$) is rejected.

c   Number of victims mentioned per event

The responses to this question are given in the tables and charts below (for each of the four events).

Markale

Table 2.15 Indicator III (Markale)

Ethnicity	Number of victims mentioned			
	No victims	*1–100 killed and wounded*	*Over 100 killed and wounded*	*Total*
Bosniak from Sarajevo	2 6.7%	13 43.3%	15 50.0%	30 100.0%
Serb from Sarajevo	2 6.5%	17 54.8%	12 38.7%	31 100.0%
Serb from East Sarajevo	8 27.6%	21 72.4%	0 0.0%	29 100.0%
Total	12 13.3%	51 56.7%	27 30.0%	90 100.0%

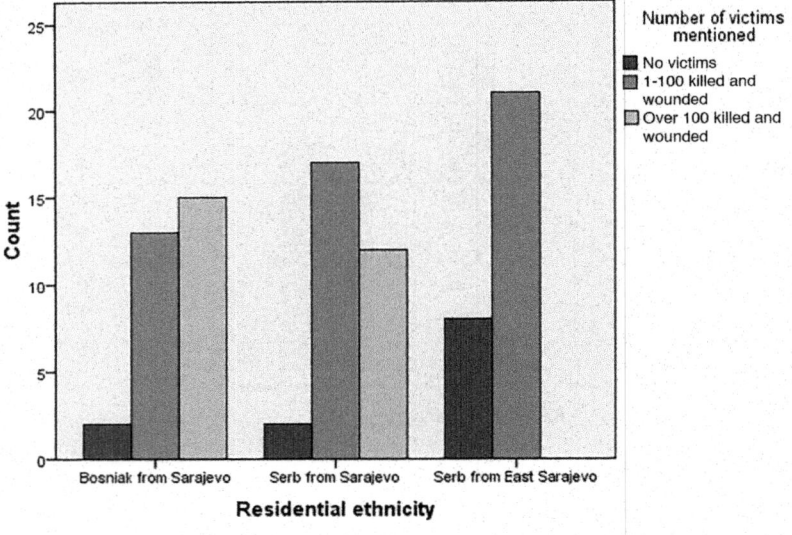

Chart 2.9 Indicator III (Markale)

The results of the chi square test (X^2 (4, N = 90) = 22.23 p = .00) revealed that there is a strong but negative association between ethnicity and the reported number of victims (r(88) = −.484 p = .00); therefore, the null hypothesis ($H0_c$) is rejected.

Kazani

Table 2.16 Indicator III (Kazani)

Ethnicity	Number of victims mentioned			
	No victims	1–100 killed and wounded	Over 100 killed and wounded	Total
Bosniak from Sarajevo	5 16.7%	22 73.3%	3 10.0%	30 100.0%
Serb from Sarajevo	13 41.9%	12 38.7%	6 19.4%	31 100.0%
Serb from East Sarajevo	3 10.3%	23 79.3%	3 10.3%	29 100.0%
Total	21 23.3%	57 63.3%	12 13.3%	90 100.0%

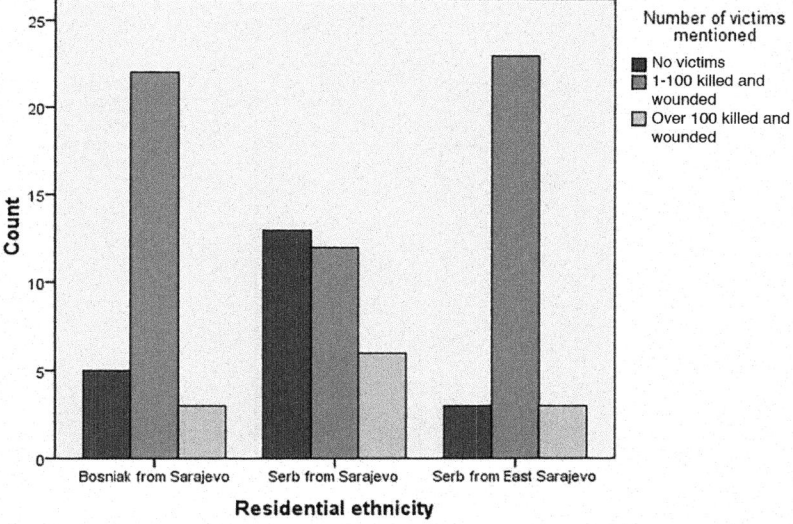

Chart 2.10 Indicator III (Kazani)

The results of the chi square test (X^2 (4, N = 90) = 13.36 p = .011) showed that there is a weak association between ethnicity and the reported number of victims (r(88) = .092 p = .387); therefore, the null hypothesis ($H0_c$) is rejected.

Vase Miskina

Table 2.17 Indicator III (Vase Miskina)

Ethnicity	Number of victims mentioned			
	No victims	*1–100 killed and wounded*	*Over 100 killed and wounded*	*Total*
Bosniak from Sarajevo	2 6.7%	11 36.7%	17 56.7%	30 100.0%
Serb from Sarajevo	2 6.5%	23 74.2%	6 19.4%	31 100.0%
Serb from East Sarajevo	8 27.6%	20 69.0%	1 3.4%	29 100.0%
Total	12 13.3%	54 60.0%	24 26.7%	90 100.0%

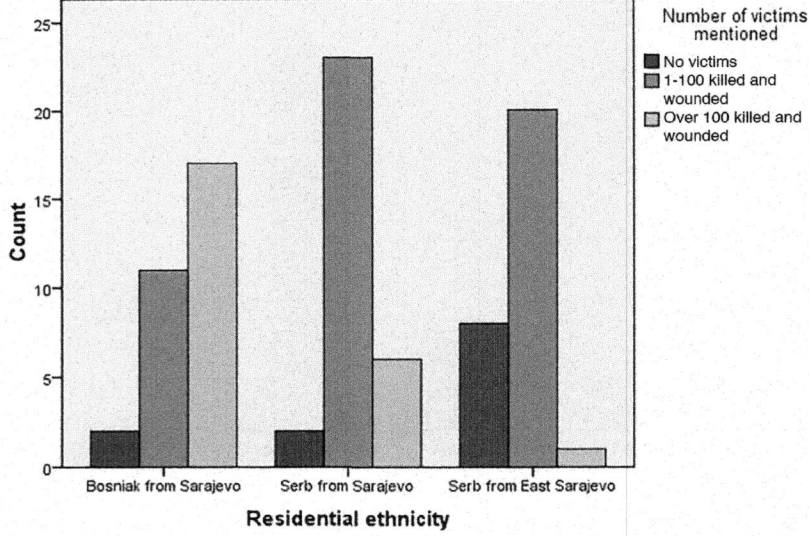

Chart 2.11 Indicator III (Vase Miskina)

The results of the chi square test (X^2 (4, N = 90) = 27.28 p = .00) revealed that there is a moderate negative association between ethnicity and the reported number of victims (r(88) = −.458 p = .00); therefore, the null hypothesis ($H0_c$) is rejected.

NATO

Table 2.18 Indicator III (NATO)

Ethnicity	Number of victims mentioned			
	No victims	*1–100 killed and wounded*	*Over 100 killed and wounded*	*Total*
Bosniak from Sarajevo	26	3	1	30
	86.7%	10.0%	3.3%	100.0%
Serb from Sarajevo	12	15	4	31
	38.7%	48.4%	12.9%	100.0%
Serb from East Sarajevo	0	16	13	29
	0.0%	55.2%	44.8%	100.0%
Total	38	34	18	90
	42.2%	37.8%	20.0%	100.0%

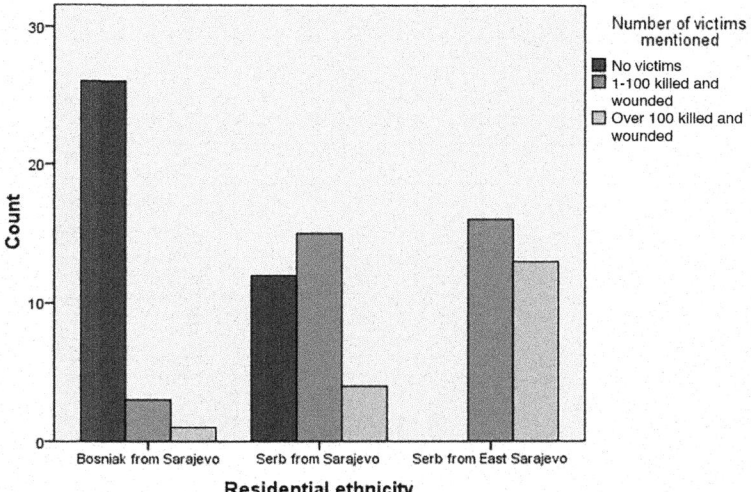

Chart 2.12 Indicator III (NATO)

The results of the chi square test (X^2 (4, N = 90) = 49.36 p = .00) showed that there is a strong association between ethnicity and the reported number of victims for this event (r(88) = .66 p = .00); therefore, the null hypothesis ($H0_c$) is rejected.

d   Attribution of guilt

The responses to this indicator are given in the tables and charts below (for each of the four events).

Markale

Table 2.19 Indicator IV (Markale)

Ethnicity	Attribution of guilt								
	Guilt is not mentioned and other group is not guilty	Other group is guilty	Other group is guilty but with several justifications	Both groups are guilty	Third party is guilty	My group is guilty	My group is guilty but with several justifications	My group is not guilty	Total
Bosniak from Sarajevo	2 6.7%	21 70.0%	4 13.3%	1 3.3%	2 6.7%	0 0.0%	0 0.0%	0 0.0%	30 100.0%
Serb from Sarajevo	1 3.2%	1 3.2%	2 6.5%	0 0.0%	11 35.5%	4 12.9%	11 35.5%	1 3.2%	31 100.0%
Serb from East Sarajevo	1 3.4%	13 44.8%	3 10.3%	3 10.3%	6 20.7%	0 0.0%	1 3.4%	2 6.9%	29 100.0%
Total	4 4.4%	35 38.9%	9 10.0%	4 4.4%	19 21.1%	4 4.4%	12 13.3%	3 3.3%	90 100.0%

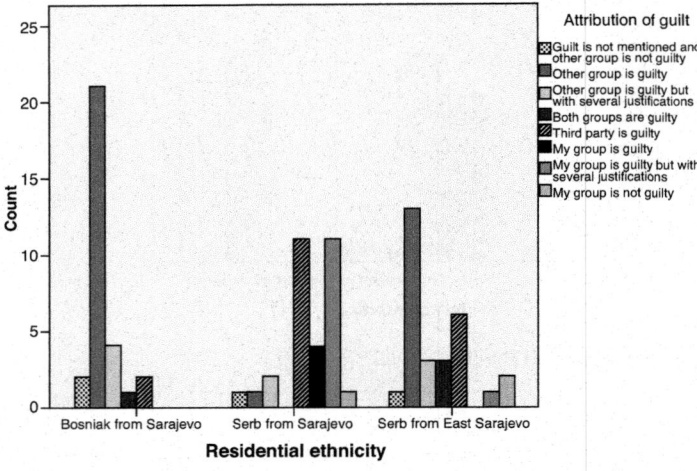

Chart 2.13 Indicator IV (Markale)

The results of the chi square test (X^2 (4, N = 90) = 56.08 p = .00) showed that there is a very weak association between ethnicity and the reported attribution of guilt for this event (r(88) = .013 p = .9) (Spearman correlation equals .24); therefore, the null hypothesis ($H0_d$) is rejected.

Kazani

Table 2.20 Indicator IV (Kazani)

Ethnicity	Attribution of guilt								
	Guilt is not mentioned and other group is not guilty	Other group is guilty	Other group is guilty but with several justifications	Both groups are guilty	Third party is guilty	My group is guilty	My group is guilty but with several justifications	My group is not guilty	Total
Bosniak from Sarajevo	1 3.3%	0 0.0%	0 0.0%	0 0.0%	6 20.0%	9 30.0%	12 40.0%	2 6.7%	30 100.0%
Serb from Sarajevo	2 6.5%	8 25.8%	12 38.7%	0 0.0%	9 29.0%	0 0.0%	0 0.0%	0 0.0%	31 100.0%
Serb from East Sarajevo	3 10.3%	12 41.4%	8 27.6%	1 3.4%	5 17.2%	0 0.0%	0 0.0%	0 0.0%	29 100.0%
Total	6 6.7%	20 22.2%	20 22.2%	1 1.1%	20 22.2%	9 10.0%	12 13.3%	2 2.2%	90 100.0%

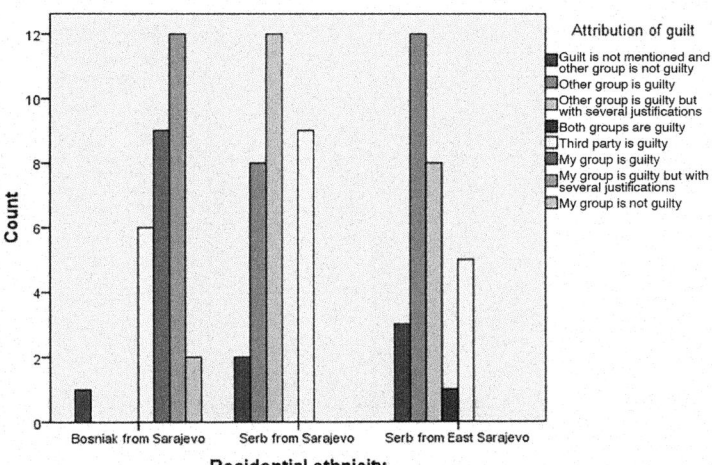

Chart 2.14 Indicator IV (Kazani)

The results of the chi square test (X^2 (4, N = 90) = 72.7 p = .00) showed that there is a strong negative association between ethnicity and the reported attribution of guilt for this event (r(88) = −.56 p = .00); therefore, the null hypothesis ($H0_d$) is rejected.

Vase Miskina

Table 2.21 Indicator IV (Vase Miskina)

Ethnicity	Attribution of guilt								
	Guilt is not mentioned and other group is not guilty	Other group is guilty	Other group is guilty but with several justifications	Both groups are guilty	Third party is guilty	My group is guilty	My group is guilty but with several justifications	My group is not guilty	Total
Bosniak from Sarajevo	2	23	4	0	1	0	0	0	30
	6.7%	76.7%	13.3%	0.0%	3.3%	0.0%	0.0%	0.0%	100.0%
Serb from Sarajevo	1	2	1	1	8	6	11	1	31
	3.2%	6.5%	3.2%	3.2%	25.8%	19.4%	35.5%	3.2%	100.0%
Serb from East Sarajevo	0	8	2	1	9	1	1	7	29
	0.0%	27.6%	6.9%	3.4%	31.0%	3.4%	3.4%	24.1%	100.0%
Total	3	33	7	2	18	7	12	8	90
	3.3%	36.7%	7.8%	2.2%	20.0%	7.8%	13.3%	8.9%	100.0%

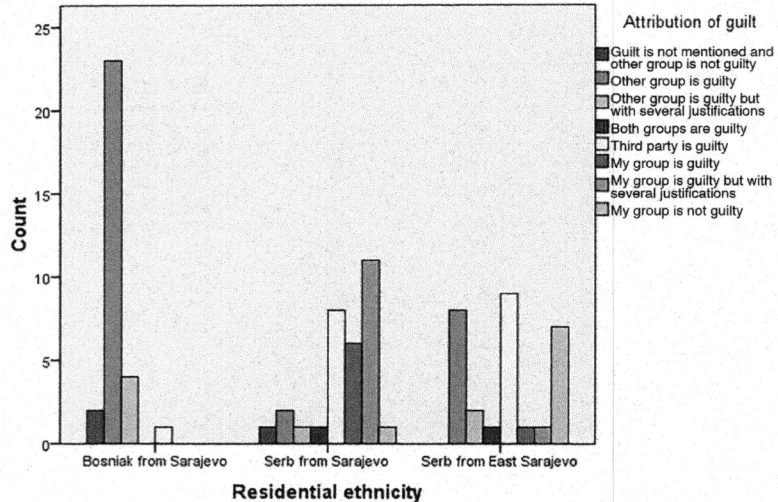

Chart 2.15 Indicator IV (Vase Miskina)

The results of the chi square test (X^2 (4, N = 90) = 70.21 p = .00) showed that there is a moderate association between ethnicity and the reported attribution of guilt for this event (r(88) = −.313 p = .003); therefore, the null hypothesis ($H0_d$) is rejected.

NATO

Table 2.22 Indicator IV (NATO)

Ethnicity	Attribution of guilt								
	Guilt is not mentioned and other group is not guilty	Other group is guilty	Other group is guilty but with several justifications	Both groups are guilty	Third party is guilty	My group is guilty	My group is guilty but with several justifications	My group is not guilty	Total
Bosniak from Sarajevo	7	1	2	0	15	1	0	4	30
	23.3%	3.3%	6.7%	0.0%	50.0%	3.3%	0.0%	13.3%	100.0%
Serb from Sarajevo	1	0	0	0	30	0	0	0	31
	3.2%	0.0%	0.0%	0.0%	96.8%	0.0%	0.0%	0.0%	100.0%
Serb from East Sarajevo	1	6	0	1	20	0	0	1	29
	3.4%	20.7%	0.0%	3.4%	69.0%	0.0%	0.0%	3.4%	100.0%
Total	9	7	2	1	65	1	0	5	90
	10.0%	7.8%	2.2%	1.1%	72.2%	1.1%	0.0%	5.6%	100.0%

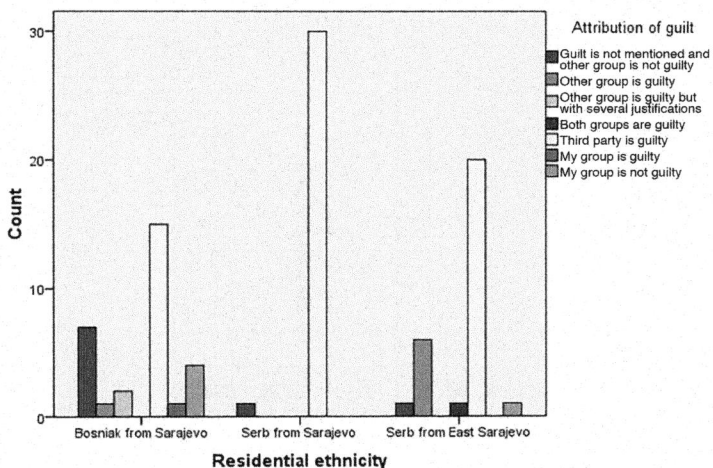

Chart 2.16 Indicator IV (NATO)

The results of the chi square test (X^2 (4, N = 90) = 35.39 p = .00) showed that there is a weak negative association between ethnicity and the reported attribution of guilt for this event (r(88) = −.045 p = .003); therefore, the null hypothesis ($H0_d$) is rejected.

e   Attribution of the role of victim

The responses to this question are given in the tables and charts below (for each of the four events).

Markale

Table 2.23 Indicator V (Markale)

Ethnicity	Members of my group are victims	Members of the other group are victims	Both groups are victims	Neither my nor the other group are victims	Total
Bosniak from Sarajevo	22 73.3%	0 0.0%	8 26.7%	0 0.0%	30 100.0%
Serb from Sarajevo	2 6.5%	1 3.2%	28 90.3%	0 0.0%	31 100.0%
Serb from East Sarajevo	18 62.1%	2 6.9%	8 27.6%	1 3.4%	29 100.0%
Total	42 46.7%	3 3.3%	44 48.9%	1 1.1%	90 100.0%

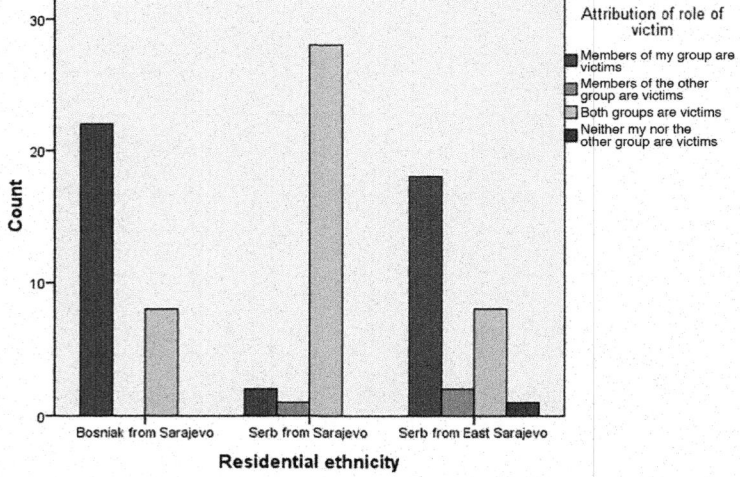

Chart 2.17 Indicator (Markale)

The results of the chi square test (X^2 (4, N = 90) = 37.6 p = .00) showed that there is a weak negative association between ethnicity and the reported attribution of the role of victim for this event (r(88) = −.113 p = .287); therefore, the null hypothesis (H0$_e$) is rejected.

Kazani

Table 2.24 Indicator V (Kazani)

Ethnicity	Members of my group are victims	Members of the other group are victims	Both groups are victims	Neither my nor the other group are victims	Total
Bosniak from Sarajevo	0 0.0%	26 86.7%	2 6.7%	2 6.7%	30 100.0%
Serb from Sarajevo	31 100.0%	0 0.0%	0 0.0%	0 0.0%	31 100.0%
Serb from East Sarajevo	22 75.9%	0 0.0%	4 13.8%	3 10.3%	29 100.0%
Total	53 58.9%	26 28.9%	6 6.7%	5 5.6%	90 100.0%

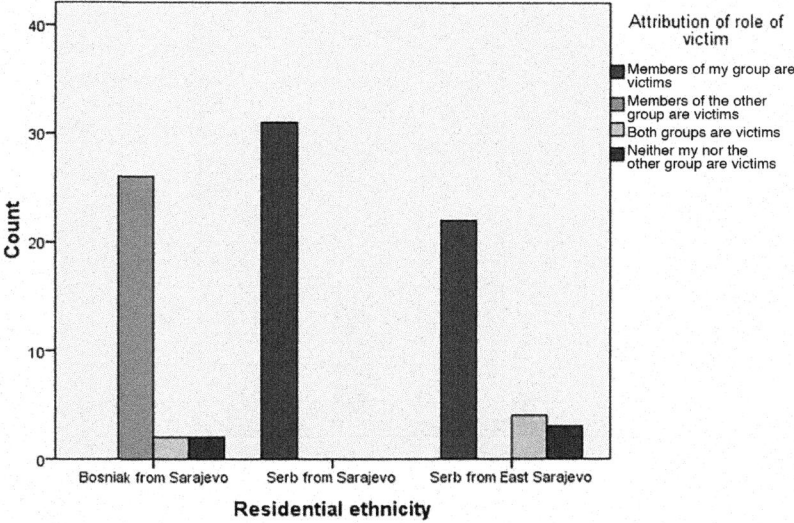

Chart 2.18 Indicator V (Kazani)

The results of the chi square test (X^2 (4, N = 90) = 87.24 p = .00) showed that there is a weak negative association between ethnicity and the reported attribution of the role of victim for this event (r(88) = −.115 p = .280); therefore, the null hypothesis ($H0_e$) is rejected.

Vase Miskina

Table 2.25 Indicator V (Vase Miskina)

Ethnicity	Members of my group are victims	Members of the other group are victims	Both groups are victims	Neither my nor the other group are victims	Total
Bosniak from Sarajevo	20 66.7%	0 0.0%	10 33.3%	0 0.0%	30 100.0%
Serb from Sarajevo	3 9.7%	1 3.2%	26 83.9%	1 3.2%	31 100.0%
Serb from East Sarajevo	10 34.5%	2 6.9%	14 48.3%	3 10.3%	29 100.0%
Total	33 36.7%	3 3.3%	50 55.6%	4 4.4%	90 100.0%

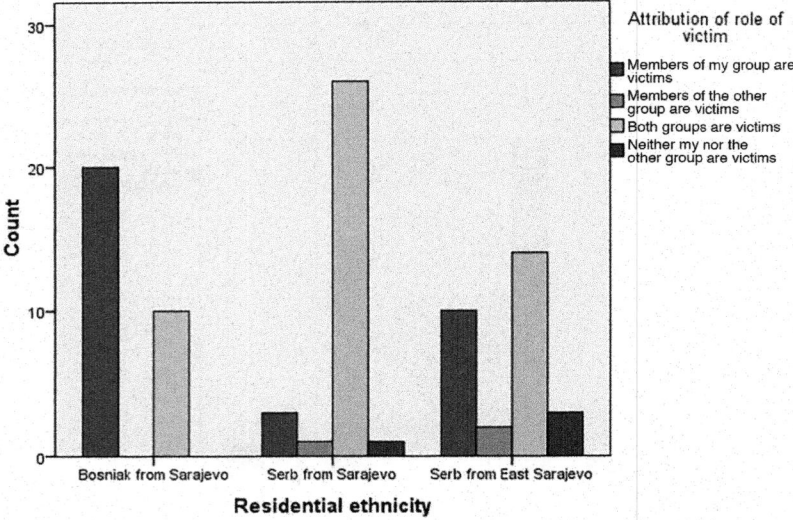

Chart 2.19 Indicator V (Vase Miskina)

The results of the chi square test (X^2 (4, N = 90) = 26.79 p = .00) showed that there is a weak association between ethnicity and the reported attribution of the role of victim for this event (r(88) = .134 p = .280); therefore, the null hypothesis ($H0_e$) is rejected.

NATO

Table 2.26 Indicator V (NATO)

Ethnicity	Members of my group are victims	Members of the other group are victims	Both groups are victims	Neither my nor the other group are victims	Total
Bosniak from Sarajevo	0	4	3	23	30
	0.0%	13.3%	10.0%	76.7%	100.0%
Serb from Sarajevo	13	0	3	15	31
	41.9%	0.0%	9.7%	48.4%	100.0%
Serb from East Sarajevo	27	0	2	0	29
	93.1%	0.0%	6.9%	0.0%	100.0%
Total	40	4	8	38	90
	44.4%	4.4%	8.9%	42.2%	100.0%

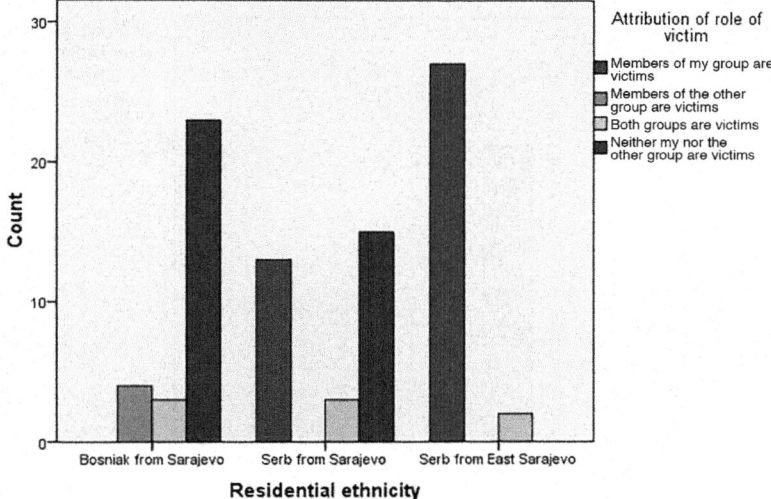

Chart 2.20 Indicator V (NATO)

The results of the chi square test (X^2 (4, N = 90) = 57.97 p = .00) showed that there is a negative association between ethnicity and the reported attribution of the role of victim for this event (r(88) = −.705 p = .00); therefore, the null hypothesis ($H0_e$) is rejected.

f   Should the event be commemorated?

The responses to this question are given in the tables and charts below (for each of the four events).

Markale

Table 2.27 Indicator VI (Markale)

Ethnicity	Yes	No	I do not know	Total
Bosniak from Sarajevo	27	1	2	30
	90.0%	3.3%	6.7%	100.0%
Serb from Sarajevo	23	1	7	31
	74.2%	3.2%	22.6%	100.0%
Serb from East Sarajevo	13	12	4	29
	44.8%	41.4%	13.8%	100.0%
Total	63	14	13	90
	70.0%	15.6%	14.4%	100.0%

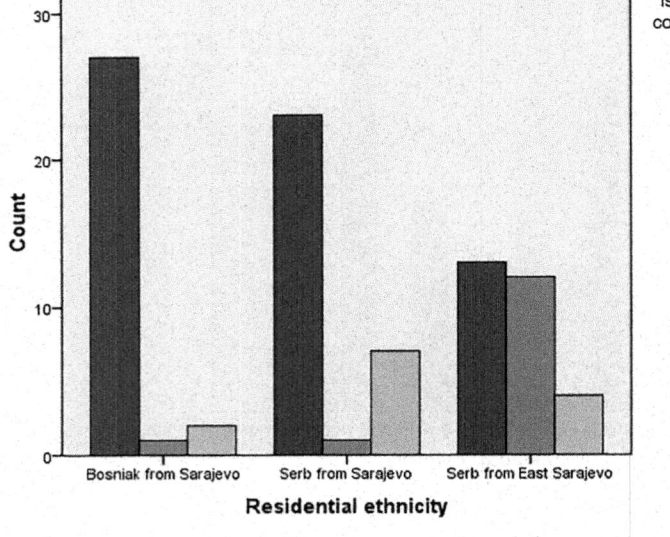

Chart 2.21 Indicator VI (Markale)

The results of the chi square test (X^2 (4, N = 90) = 25.45 p = .00) showed that there is a weak association between ethnicity and the reported necessity to commemorate the victims of this event (r(88) = .261 p = .013); therefore, the null hypothesis ($H0_f$) is rejected.

Kazani

Table 2.28 Indicator VI (Kazani)

Ethnicity	Yes	No	I do not know	Total
Bosniak from Sarajevo	22	4	4	30
	73.3%	13.3%	13.3%	100.0%
Serb from Sarajevo	31	0	0	31
	100.0%	0.0%	0.0%	100.0%
Serb from East Sarajevo	21	4	4	29
	72.4%	13.8%	13.8%	100.0%
Total	74	8	8	90
	82.2%	8.9%	8.9%	100.0%

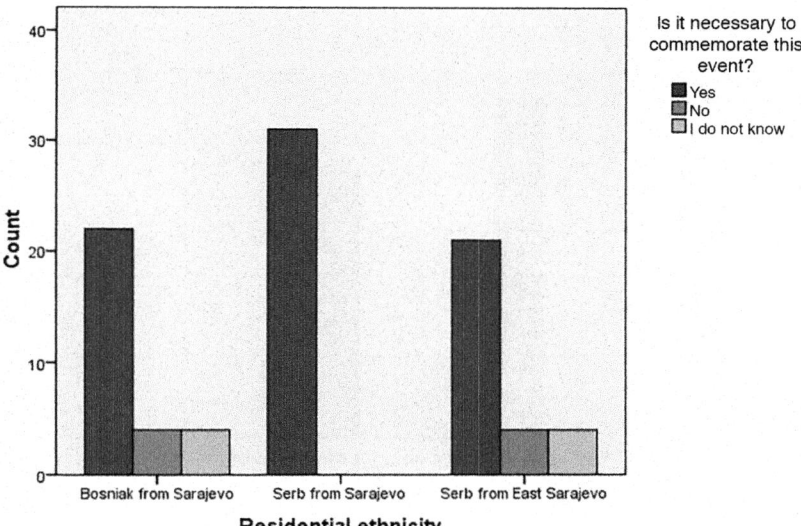

Chart 2.22 Indicator VI (Kazani)

The results of the chi square test (X^2 (4, N = 90) = 10.23 p = .037) showed that there is a weak association between ethnicity and the reported necessity to commemorate the victims of this event (r(88) = .111 p = .297); therefore, the null hypothesis ($H0_f$) is rejected.

Vase Miskina

Table 2.29 Indicator VI (Vase Miskina)

Ethnicity	Yes	No	I do not know	Total
Bosniak from Sarajevo	28 93.3%	1 3.3%	1 3.3%	30 100.0%
Serb from Sarajevo	23 74.2%	4 12.9%	4 12.9%	31 100.0%
Serb from East Sarajevo	18 62.1%	6 20.7%	5 17.2%	29 100.0%
Total	69 76.7%	11 12.2%	10 11.1%	90 100.0%

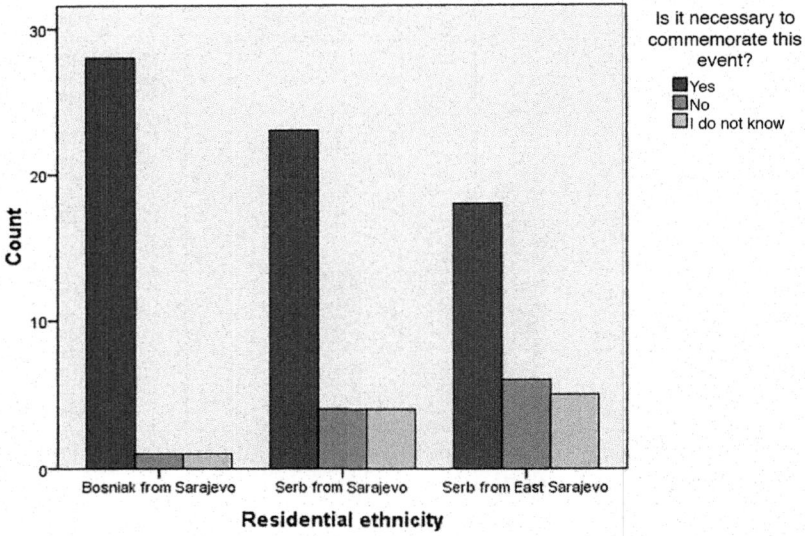

Chart 2.23 Indicator VI (Vase Miskina)

The results of the chi square test (X^2 (4, N = 90) = 8.27 p = .082) showed that there is not enough evidence to suggest an association between ethnicity and the reported necessity to commemorate the victims of this event (r(88) = .243 p = .021); therefore, the null hypothesis ($H0_f$) is accepted.

NATO

Table 2.30 Indicator VI (NATO)

Ethnicity	Yes	No	I do not know	Total
Bosniak from Sarajevo	8 26.7%	13 43.3%	9 30.0%	30 100.0%
Serb from Sarajevo	14 45.2%	10 32.3%	7 22.6%	31 100.0%
Serb from East Sarajevo	22 75.9%	5 17.2%	2 6.9%	29 100.0%
Total	44 48.9%	28 31.1%	18 20.0%	90 100.0%

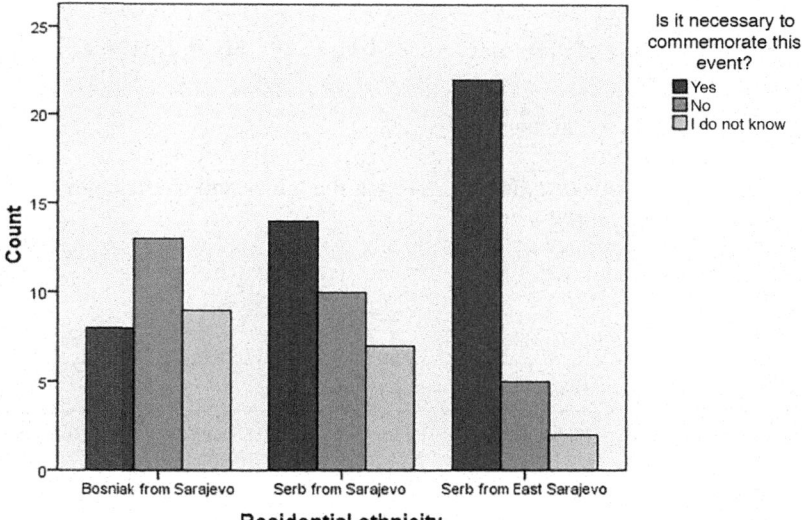

Chart 2.24 Indicator VI (NATO)

The results of the chi square test (X^2 (4, N = 90) = 14.77 p = .005) showed that there is a weak association between ethnicity and the reported necessity to commemorate the victims of this event (r(88) = −.375 p = .000); therefore, the null hypothesis ($H0_f$) is rejected.

Brief discussion

The null hypothesis was rejected 18 times, which proves the influence of ethnicity on responses. However, we may see that the association was not strong in all of these 18 cases but only in association with the Indicator III – the number of victims (Markale and NATO events) – and Indicator IV – the attribution of guilt (Kazani event).

When comparing the responses of Serbs from Sarajevo (I generation) and Serbs from East Sarajevo (I generation), we can see that in almost all cases there is no similarity in response and/or association related to the same ethnicity. On the contrary, Serbs from Sarajevo (I generation) did not show similarities with Bosniaks (I generation), which could have been expected based on the fact that they spent the war together in the same city. However, it seems that Serbs from Sarajevo developed their own narrative that resembles neither Bosniaks' narrative nor other Serbs' narrative, but their own narrative of the war.

Part Ib: Analysis of memories according to the Six indicators (II generation)

a   When did the event happen?

The responses to this question are given in the tables and charts below (for each of the four events).

Markale

Table 2.31 Indicator I (Markale event)

Ethnicity	When did the event happen?			
	Exact date	*Year only*	*Do not remember*	*Total*
Bosniak from Sarajevo	2 10.5%	7 36.8%	10 52.6%	19 100.0%
Serb from Sarajevo	0 0.0%	16 76.2%	5 23.8%	21 100.0%
Serb from East Sarajevo	0 0.0%	1 5.0%	19 95.0%	20 100.0%
Total	2 3.3%	24 40.0%	34 56.7%	60 100.0%

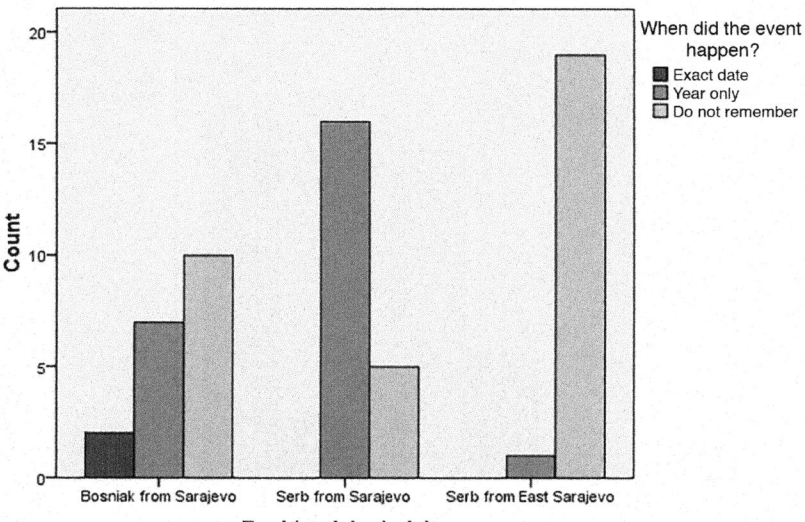

Chart 2.25 Indicator I – Markale

The results of the chi square test (X^2 (4, N = 60) = 26.6 p = .000) showed that there is a moderate association between ethnicity and the ability to recall the date of the event (r(58) = .490 p = .000); therefore, the null hypothesis ($H0_a$) is rejected.

Kazani

Table 2.32 Indicator I (Kazani event)

	When did the event happen?			
	Exact date	*Year only*	*Do not remember*	*Total*
Bosniak from Sarajevo	2 10.5%	17 89.5%	0 0.0%	19 100.0%
Serb from Sarajevo	6 28.6%	15 71.4%	0 0.0%	21 100.0%
Serb from East Sarajevo	3 15.0%	17 85.0%	0 0.0%	20 100.0%
Total	11 18.3%	49 81.7%	0 0.0%	60 100.0%

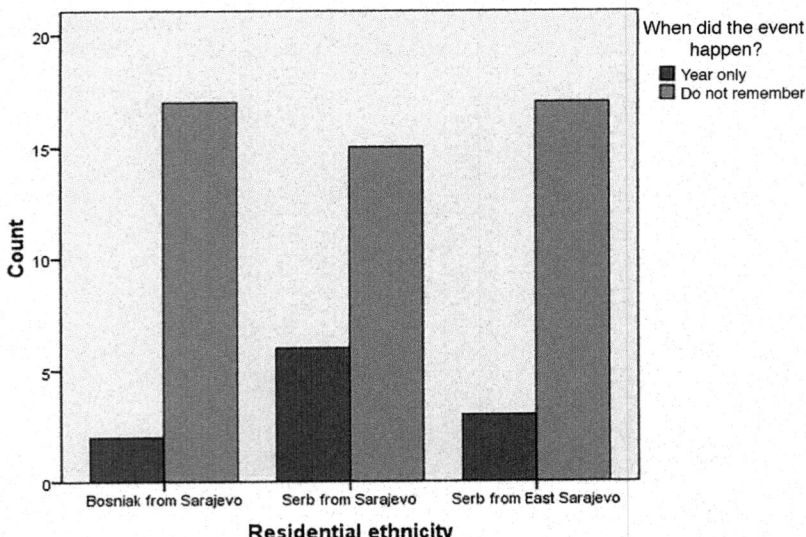

Chart 2.26 Indicator I – Kazani

The results of the chi square test (X^2 (4, N = 60) = 2.39 p = .302) revealed that there is a weak association between ethnicity and the response to this question (r(58) = .024 p = .857); therefore, the null hypothesis (H0$_b$) is rejected.

Vase Miskina

Table 2.33 Indicator I (Vase Miskina event)

Ethnicity	When did the event happen?			
	Exact date	*Year only*	*Do not remember*	*Total*
Bosniak from Sarajevo	1 5.3%	1 5.3%	17 89.5%	19 100.0%
Serb from Sarajevo	1 4.8%	13 61.9%	7 33.3%	21 100.0%
Serb from East Sarajevo	0 0.0%	1 5.0%	19 95.0%	20 100.0%
Total	2 3.3%	15 25.0%	43 71.7%	60 100.0%

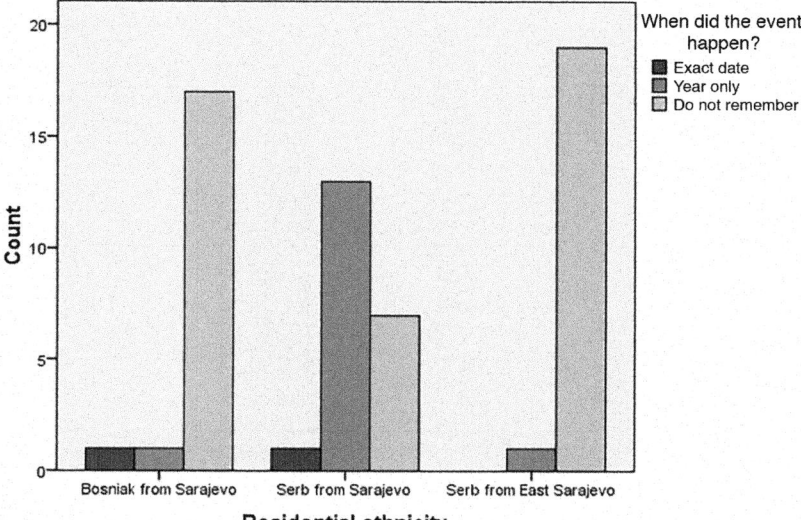

Chart 2.27 Indicator I – Vase Miskina

The results of the chi square test (X^2 (4, N = 60) = 15.82 p = .003) showed that there is a moderate association between ethnicity and the ability to recall the date of the event (r(58) = .409 p = .001); therefore, the null hypothesis is rejected.

NATO

Table 2.34 Indicator I (NATO event)

Ethnicity	When did the event happen?			
	Exact date	*Year only*	*Do not remember*	*Total*
Bosniak from Sarajevo	1	4	14	19
	5.3%	21.1%	73.7%	100.0%
Serb from Sarajevo	0	14	7	21
	0.0%	66.7%	33.3%	100.0%
Serb from East Sarajevo	1	12	7	20
	5.0%	60.0%	35.0%	100.0%
Total	2	30	28	60
	3.3%	50.0%	46.7%	100.0%

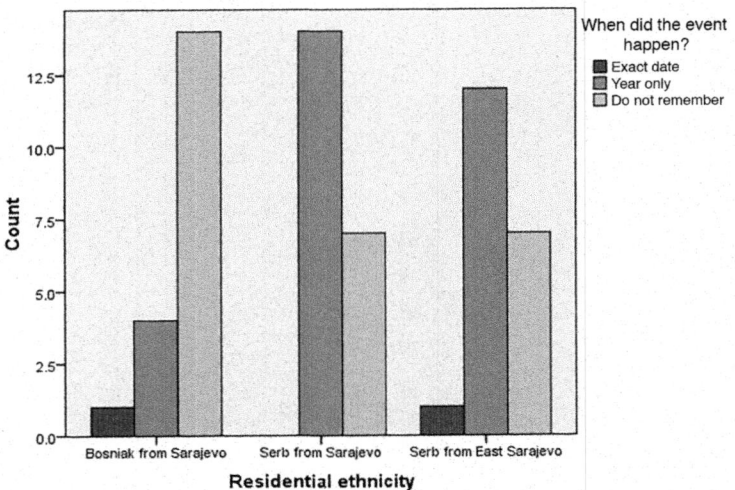

Chart 2.28 Indicator I – NATO

The results of the chi square test (X^2 (4, N = 60) = 10.18 p = .037) showed that there is a weak association between ethnicity and the ability to recall the date of the event (r(58) = −.214 p = .1); therefore, the null hypothesis is rejected.

b   Does the participant ever remind himself/herself of the event?

The responses to this question are given in the tables and charts below (for each of the four events).

Markale

Table 2.35 Indicator II (Markale)

Ethnicity	Does the participant remind himself/herself of Markale?			
	Often	*Sometimes*	*Never*	*Total*
Bosniak from Sarajevo	5 26.3%	11 57.9%	3 15.8%	19 100.0%
Serb from Sarajevo	4 19.0%	10 47.6%	7 33.3%	21 100.0%
Serb from East Sarajevo	1 5.0%	6 30.0%	13 65.0%	20 100.0%
Total	10 16.7%	27 45.0%	23 38.3%	60 100.0%

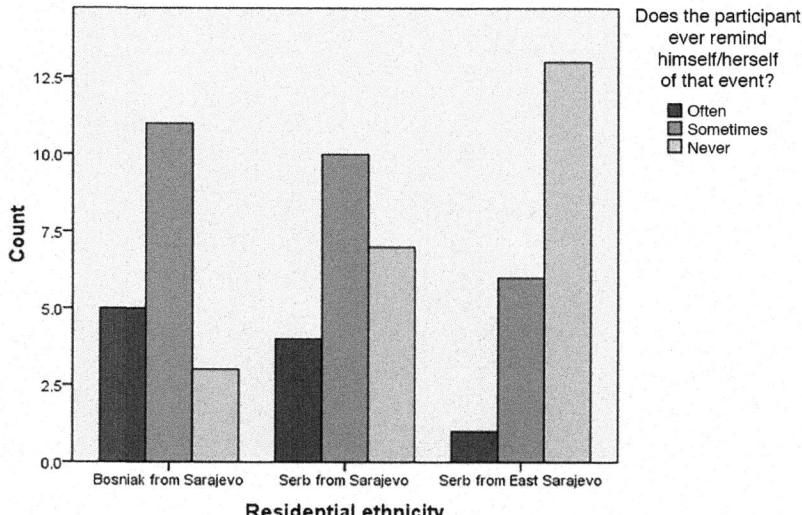

Chart 2.29 Indicator II (Markale)

The results of the chi square test (X^2 (4, N = 60) = 10.87 p = .028) showed that there is a moderate association between ethnicity and participant readiness to remind himself/herself of this event (r(58) = .402 p = .001); therefore, the null hypothesis is rejected.

Kazani

Table 2.36 Indicator II (Kazani)

Ethnicity	Does the participant remind himself/herself of Kazani?			
	Often	Sometimes	Never	Total
Bosniak from Sarajevo	0 0.0%	5 26.3%	14 73.7%	19 100.0%
Serb from Sarajevo	0 0.0%	6 28.6%	15 71.4%	21 100.0%
Serb from East Sarajevo	0 0.0%	4 20.0%	16 80.0%	20 100.0%
Total	0 0.0%	15 25.0%	45 75.0%	60 100.0%

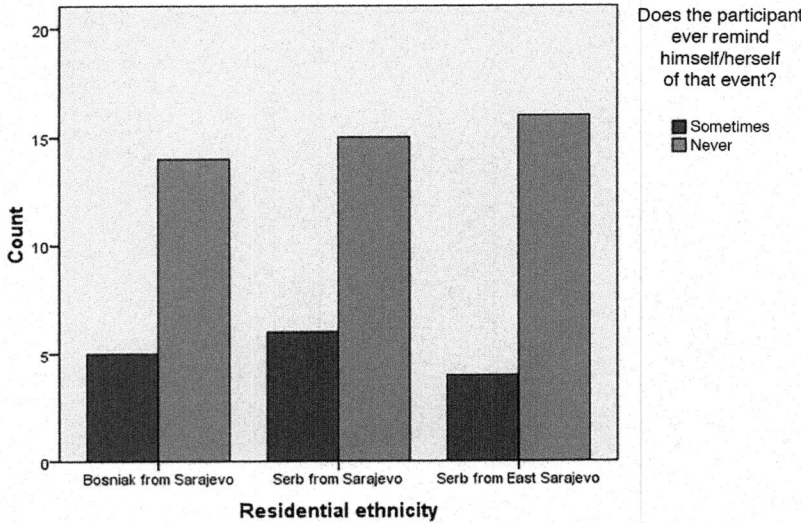

Chart 2.30 Indicator II (Kazani)

The results of the chi square test (X^2 (4, N = 60) = .427 p = .808) showed that there is not enough evidence to suggest an association between ethnicity and participants' ability to remind themselves of the event (r(58) = .128 p = .228); therefore, the null hypothesis is accepted.

Vase Miskina

Table 2.37 Indicator II (Vase Miskina)

Ethnicity	Does the participant remind himself/herself of Vase Miskina?			
	Often	Sometimes	Never	Total
Bosniak from Sarajevo	1	6	12	19
	5.3%	31.6%	63.2%	100.0%
Serb from Sarajevo	2	10	9	21
	9.5%	47.6%	42.9%	100.0%
Serb from East Sarajevo	0	0	20	20
	0.0%	0.0%	100.0%	100.0%
Total	3	16	41	60
	5.0%	26.7%	68.3%	100.0%

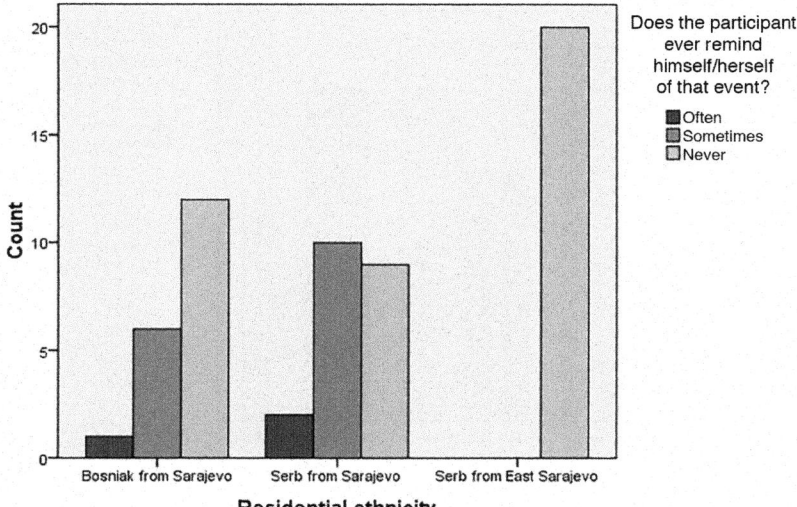

Chart 2.31 Indicator II (Vase Miskina)

The results of the chi square test (X^2 (4, N = 60) = 15.82 p = .003) showed that there is a moderate association between ethnicity and the ability to recall the date of the event (r(58) = .409 p = .001); therefore, the null hypothesis is rejected.

NATO

Table 2.38 Indicator II (NATO)

Ethnicity	Does the participant remind himself/herself of the NATO bombing?			
	Often	*Sometimes*	*Never*	*Total*
Bosniak from Sarajevo	0 0.0%	5 26.3%	14 73.7%	19 100.0%
Serb from Sarajevo	0 0.0%	9 42.9%	12 57.1%	21 100.0%
Serb from East Sarajevo	0 0.0%	12 60.0%	8 40.0%	20 100.0%
Total	0 0.0%	26 43.3%	34 56.7%	60 100.0%

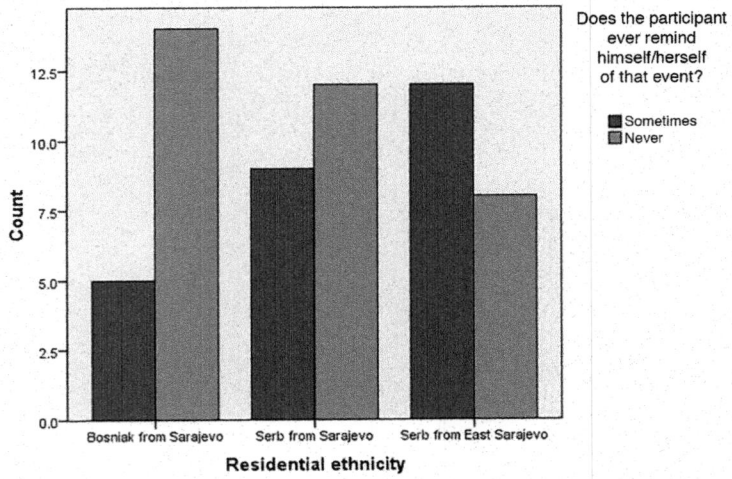

Chart 2.32 Indicator II (NATO)

The results of the chi square test (X^2 (4, N = 60) = 4.51 p = .105) revealed that there is a moderate but negative association between ethnicity and the response to this question (r(58) = −.259 p = .045); therefore, the null hypothesis ($H0_b$) is rejected.

c   Number of victims mentioned per event

The responses to this question are given in the tables and charts below (for each of the four events).

Markale

Table 2.39 Indicator III (Markale)

Ethnicity	Number of victims mentioned			
	No victims	*1–100 killed and wounded*	*Over 100 killed and wounded*	*Total*
Bosniak from Sarajevo	0 0.0%	6 31.6%	13 68.4%	19 100.0%
Serb from Sarajevo	0 0.0%	12 57.1%	9 42.9%	21 100.0%
Serb from East Sarajevo	6 30.0%	14 70.0%	0 0.0%	20 100.0%
Total	6 10.0%	32 53.3%	22 36.7%	60 100.0%

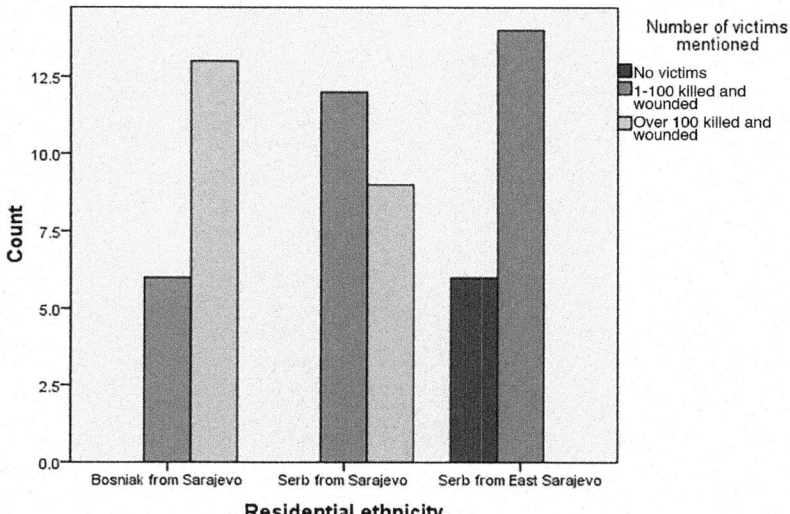

Chart 2.33 Indicator III (Markale)

The results of the chi square test (X^2 (4, N = 60) = 27.56 p = .00) revealed that there is a strong but negative association between ethnicity and the reported number of victims (r(58) = −.657 p = .00); therefore, the null hypothesis ($H0_c$) is rejected.

Kazani

Table 2.40 Indicator III (Kazani)

Ethnicity	Number of victims mentioned			
	No victims	*1–100 killed and wounded*	*Over 100 killed and wounded*	*Total*
Bosniak from Sarajevo	12 63.2%	7 36.8%	0 0.0%	19 100.0%
Serb from Sarajevo	0 0.0%	19 90.5%	2 9.5%	21 100.0%
Serb from East Sarajevo	11 55.0%	9 45.0%	0 0.0%	20 100.0%
Total	23 38.3%	35 58.3%	2 3.3%	60 100.0%

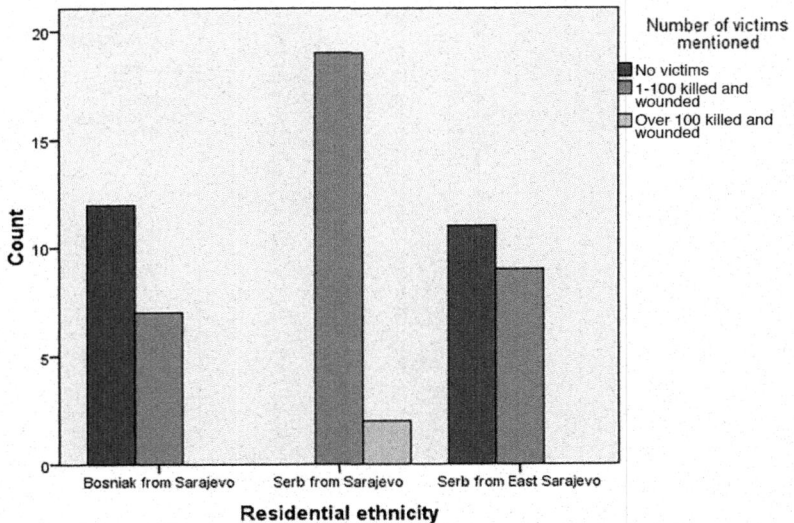

Chart 2.34 Indicator III (Kazani)

The results of the chi square test (X^2 (4, N = 60) = 22.1 p = .00) showed that there is a weak and negative association between ethnicity and the reported number of victims (r(58) = −.152 p = .245); therefore, the null hypothesis ($H0_c$) is rejected.

Vase Miskina

Table 2.41 Indicator III (Vase Miskina)

Ethnicity	Number of victims mentioned			
	No victims	*1–100 killed and wounded*	*Over 100 killed and wounded*	*Total*
Bosniak from Sarajevo	9 47.4%	7 36.8%	3 15.8%	19 100.0%
Serb from Sarajevo	8 38.1%	11 52.4%	2 9.5%	21 100.0%
Serb from East Sarajevo	17 85.0%	3 15.0%	0 0.0%	20 100.0%
Total	34 56.7%	21 35.0%	5 8.3%	60 100.0%

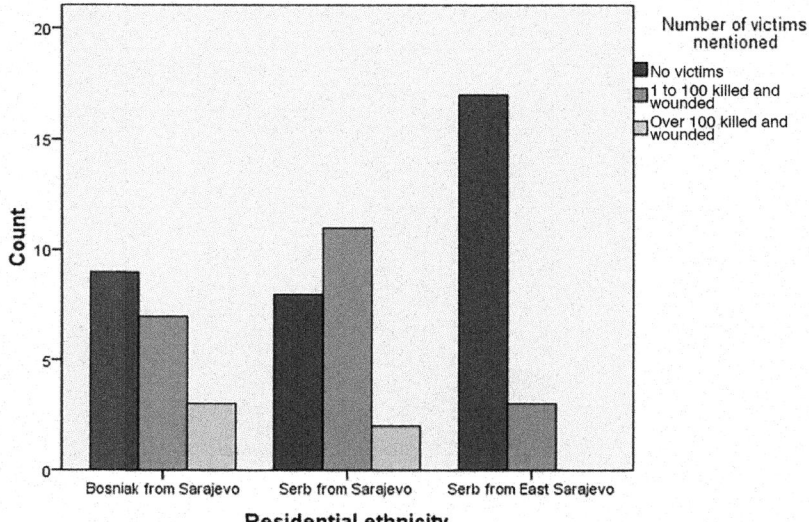

Chart 2.35 Indicator III (Vase Miskina)

The results of the chi square test (X^2 (4, N = 60) = 11.49 p = .022) revealed that there is a moderate negative association between ethnicity and the reported number of victims (r(58) = −.391 p = .002); therefore, the null hypothesis ($H0_c$) is rejected.

NATO

Table 2.42 Indicator III (NATO)

Ethnicity	Number of victims mentioned			
	No victims	*1–100 killed and wounded*	*Over 100 killed and wounded*	*Total*
Bosniak from Sarajevo	19 100.0%	0 0.0%	0 0.0%	19 100.0%
Serb from Sarajevo	4 19.0%	11 52.4%	6 28.6%	21 100.0%
Serb from East Sarajevo	2 10.0%	16 80.0%	2 10.0%	20 100.0%
Total	25 41.7%	27 45.0%	8 13.3%	60 100.0%

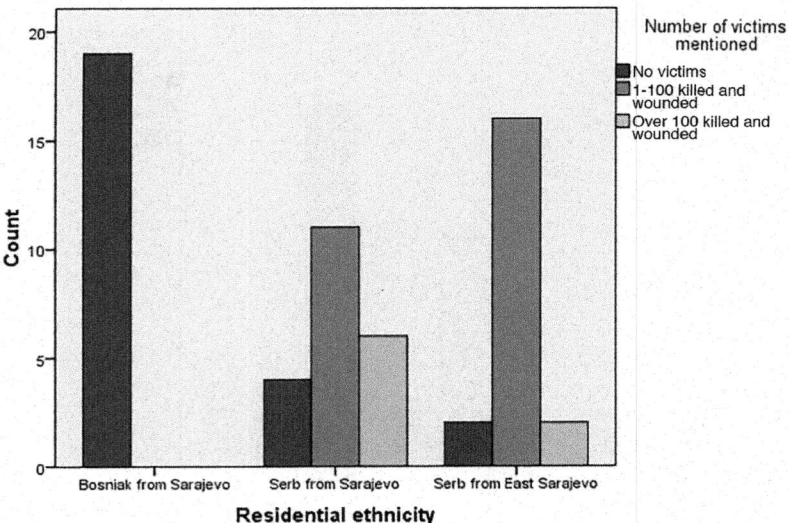

Chart 2.36 Indicator III (NATO)

The results of the chi square test (X^2 (4, N = 60) = 43.51 p = .00) showed that there is a moderate association between ethnicity and the reported number of victims for this event (r(58) = .411 p = .011); therefore, the null hypothesis ($H0_c$) is rejected.

d   Attribution of guilt

The responses to this indicator are given in the tables and charts below (for each of the four events).

Markale

Table 2.43 Indicator IV (Markale)

Ethnicity	Attribution of guilt								
	Guilt is not mentioned and other group is not guilty	Other group is guilty	Other group is guilty but with several justifications	Both groups are guilty	Third party is guilty	My group is guilty	My group is guilty but with several justifications	My group is not guilty	Total
Bosniak from Sarajevo	0	17	2	0	0	0	0	0	19
	0.0%	89.5%	10.5%	0.0%	0.0%	0.0%	0.0%	0.0%	100.0%
Serb from Sarajevo	0	0	5	0	9	0	7	0	21
	0.0%	0.0%	23.8%	0.0%	42.9%	0.0%	33.3%	0.0%	100.0%
Serb from East Sarajevo	0	13	0	0	7	0	0	0	20
	0.0%	65.0%	0.0%	0.0%	35.0%	0.0%	0.0%	0.0%	100.0%
Total	0	30	7	0	16	0	7	0	60
	0.0%	50.0%	11.7%	0.0%	26.7%	0.0%	11.7%	0.0%	100.0%

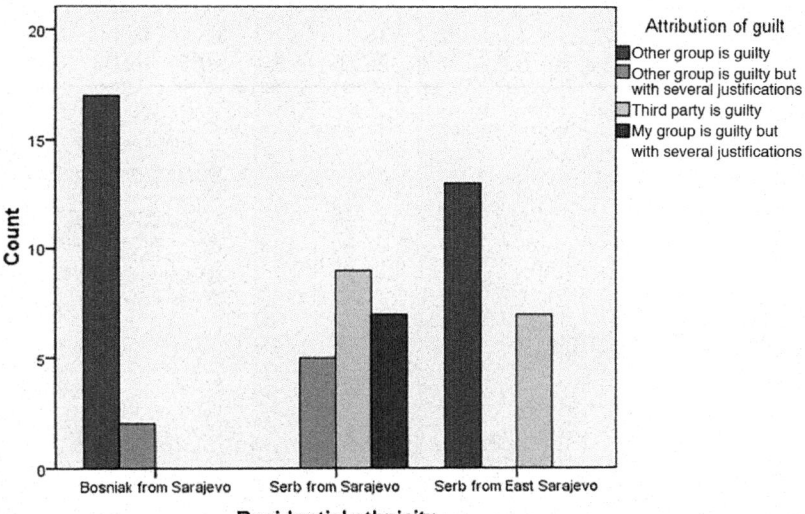

Chart 2.37 Indicator IV (Markale)

The results of the chi square test (X^2 (4, N = 60) = 42.98 p = .00) showed that there is a very weak association between ethnicity and the reported attribution of guilt for this event (r(58) = −.041 p = .754); therefore, the null hypothesis ($H0_d$) is rejected.

Kazani

Table 2.44 Indicator IV (Kazani)

Ethnicity	Attribution of guilt								
	Guilt is not mentioned and other group is not guilty	Other group is guilty	Other group is guilty but with several justifications	Both groups are guilty	Third party is guilty	My group is guilty	My group is guilty but with several justifications	My group is not guilty	Total
Bosniak from Sarajevo	1 5.3%	0 0.0%	0 0.0%	0 0.0%	2 10.5%	3 15.8%	3 15.8%	10 52.6%	19 100.0%
Serb from Sarajevo	0 0.0%	5 23.8%	4 19.0%	0 0.0%	12 57.1%	0 0.0%	0 0.0%	0 0.0%	21 100.0%
Serb from East Sarajevo	1 5.0%	17 85.0%	0 0.0%	0 0.0%	2 10.0%	0 0.0%	0 0.0%	0 0.0%	20 100.0%
Total	2 3.3%	22 36.7%	4 6.7%	0 0.0%	16 26.7%	3 5.0%	3 5.0%	10 16.7%	60 100.0%

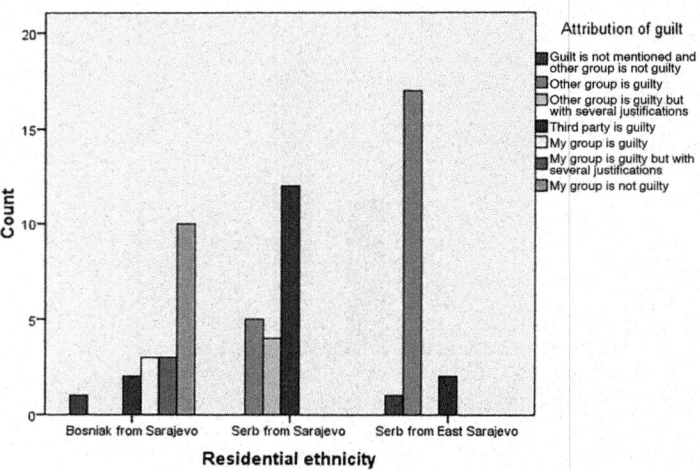

Chart 2.38 Indicator IV (Kazani)

The results of the chi square test (X^2 (4, N = 60) = 74.94 p = .00) showed that there is a strong negative association between ethnicity and the reported attribution of guilt for this event (r(58) = −.709 p = .00); therefore, the null hypothesis (H0$_d$) is rejected.

Vase Miskina

Table 2.45 Indicator IV (Vase Miskina)

Ethnicity	Attribution of guilt									
	Guilt is not mentioned and other group is not guilty	Other group is guilty	Other group is guilty but with several justifications	Both groups are guilty	Third party is guilty	My group is guilty	My group is guilty but with several justifications	My group is not guilty	Total	
Bosniak from Sarajevo	3 15.8%	12 63.2%	0 0.0%	0 0.0%	2 10.5%	0 0.0%	0 0.0%	2 10.5%	19 100.0%	
Serb from Sarajevo	0 0.0%	0 0.0%	0 0.0%	1 4.8%	9 42.9%	2 9.5%	6 28.6%	3 14.3%	21 100.0%	
Serb from East Sarajevo	0 0.0%	15 75.0%	0 0.0%	0 0.0%	5 25.0%	0 0.0%	0 0.0%	0 0.0%	20 100.0%	
Total	3 5.0%	27 45.0%	0 0.0%	1 1.7%	16 26.7%	2 3.3%	6 10.0%	5 8.3%	60 100.0%	

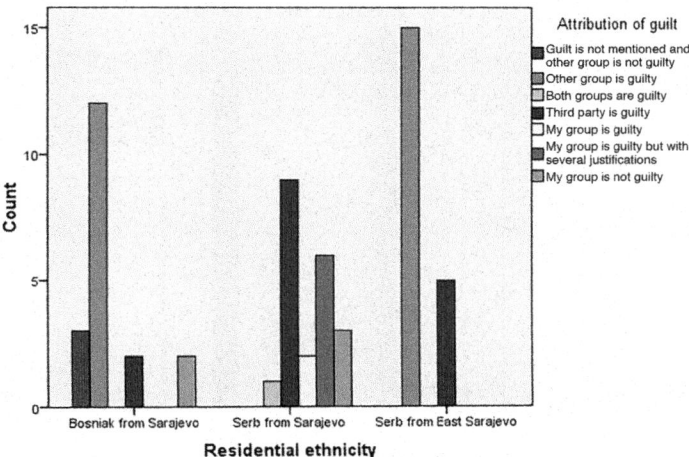

Chart 2.39 Indicator IV (Vase Miskina)

The results of the chi square test (X^2 (4, N = 60) = 44.64 p = .00) showed that there is a negative association between ethnicity and the reported attribution of guilt for this event (r(58) = −.253 p = .051); therefore, the null hypothesis ($H0_d$) is rejected.

NATO

Table 2.46 Indicator IV (NATO)

Ethnicity	Attribution of guilt								
	Guilt is not mentioned and other group is not guilty	Other group is guilty	Other group is guilty but with several justifications	Both groups are guilty	Third party is guilty	My group is guilty	My group is guilty but with several justifications	My group is not guilty	Total
Bosniak from Sarajevo	5 26.3%	0 0.0%	0 0.0%	0 0.0%	3 15.8%	0 0.0%	0 0.0%	11 57.9%	19 100.0%
Serb from Sarajevo	1 4.8%	1 4.8%	4 19.0%	0 0.0%	15 71.4%	0 0.0%	0 0.0%	0 0.0%	21 100.0%
Serb from East Sarajevo	0 0.0%	7 35.0%	0 0.0%	0 0.0%	13 65.0%	0 0.0%	0 0.0%	0 0.0%	20 100.0%
Total	6 10.0%	8 13.3%	4 6.7%	0 0.0%	31 51.7%	0 0.0%	0 0.0%	11 18.3%	60 100.0%

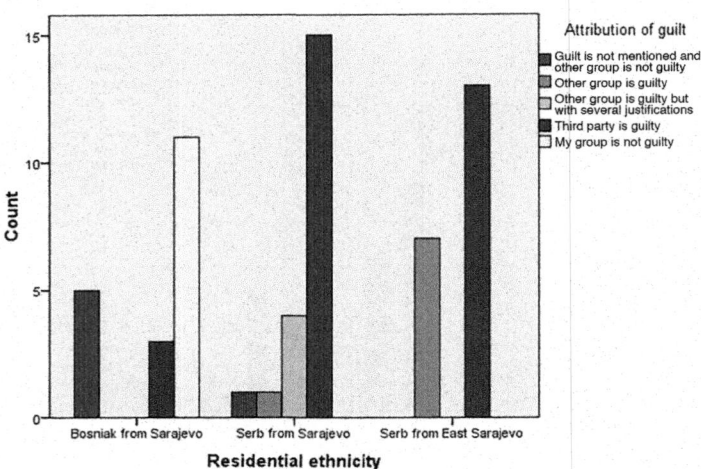

Chart 2.40 Indicator IV (NATO)

The results of the chi square test (X^2 (4, N = 60) = 56.54 p = .00) showed that there is a negative association between ethnicity and the reported attribution of guilt for this event (r(58) = −.267 p = .039); therefore, the null hypothesis ($H0_d$) is rejected.

e   Attribution of the role of victim

The responses to this question are given in the tables and charts below (for each of the four events).

Markale

Table 2.47 Indicator V (Markale)

Ethnicity	Members of my group are victims	Members of the other group are victims	Both groups are victims	Neither my nor the other group are victims	Total
Bosniak from Sarajevo	18 94.7%	1 5.3%	0 0.0%	0 0.0%	19 100.0%
Serb from Sarajevo	6 28.6%	0 0.0%	15 71.4%	0 0.0%	21 100.0%
Serb from East Sarajevo	15 75.0%	0 0.0%	4 20.0%	1 5.0%	20 100.0%
Total	39 65.0%	1 1.7%	19 31.7%	1 1.7%	60 100.0%

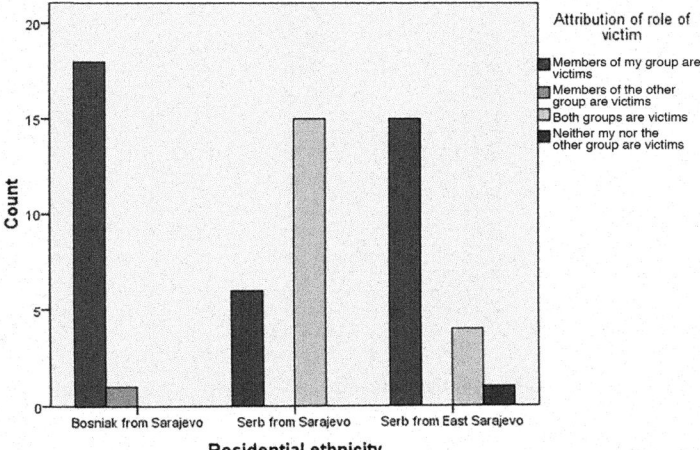

Chart 2.41 Indicator (Markale)

The results of the chi square test (X^2 (4, N = 60) = 28.69 p = .00) showed that there is a weak association between ethnicity and the reported attribution of the role of victim for this event (r(58) = .002 p = .986); therefore, the null hypothesis ($H0_e$) is rejected.

Kazani

Table 2.48 Indicator V (Kazani)

Ethnicity	Members of my group are victims	Members of the other group are victims	Both groups are victims	Neither my nor the other group are victims	Total
Bosniak from Sarajevo	0 0.0%	8 42.1%	0 0.0%	11 57.9%	19 100.0%
Serb from Sarajevo	16 76.2%	3 14.3%	2 9.5%	0 0.0%	21 100.0%
Serb from East Sarajevo	20 100.0%	0 0.0%	0 0.0%	0 0.0%	20 100.0%
Total	36 60.0%	11 18.3%	2 3.3%	11 18.3%	60 100.0%

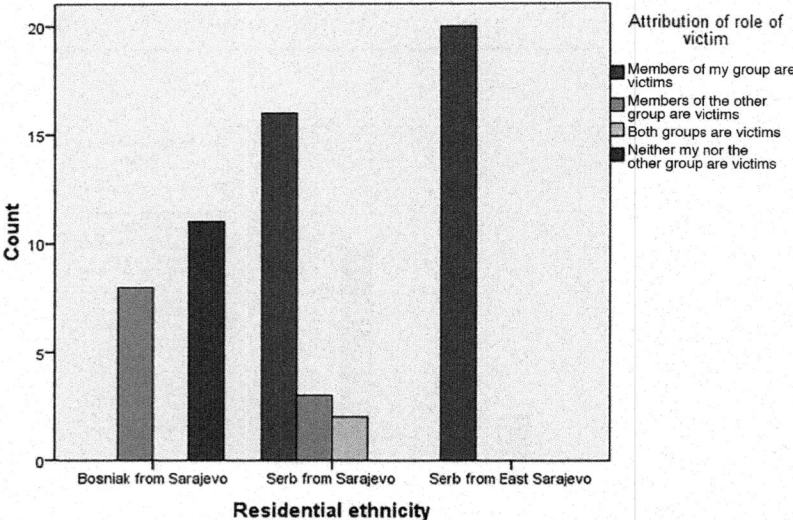

Chart 2.42 Indicator V (Kazani)

The results of the chi square test (X^2 (4, N = 60) = 54.81 p = .00) showed that there is a strong negative association between ethnicity and the reported attribution of the role of victim for this event (r(58) = −.605 p = .000); therefore, the null hypothesis ($H0_e$) is rejected.

Vase Miskina

Table 2.49 Indicator V (Vase Miskina)

Ethnicity	Members of my group are victims	Members of the other group are victims	Both groups are victims	Neither my nor the other group are victims	Total
Bosniak from Sarajevo	11 57.9%	0 0.0%	5 26.3%	3 15.8%	19 100.0%
Serb from Sarajevo	1 4.8%	1 4.8%	15 71.4%	4 19.0%	21 100.0%
Serb from East Sarajevo	15 75.0%	0 0.0%	2 10.0%	3 15.0%	20 100.0%
Total	27 45.0%	1 1.7%	22 36.7%	10 16.7%	60 100.0%

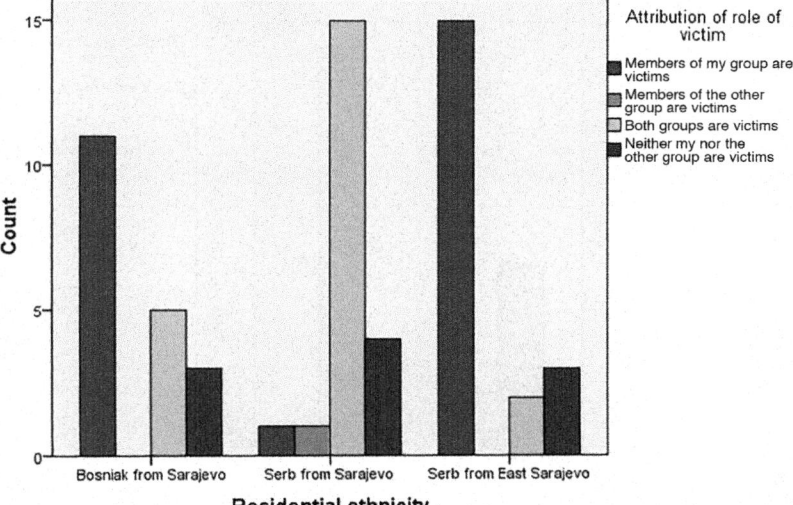

Chart 2.43 Indicator V (Vase Miskina)

The results of the chi square test (X^2 (4, N = 60) = 25.58 p = .00) showed that there is a weak and negative association between ethnicity and the reported attribution of the role of victim for this event (r(58) = −.281 p = .029); therefore, the null hypothesis ($H0_e$) is rejected.

NATO

Table 2.50 Indicator V (NATO)

Ethnicity	Members of my group are victims	Members of the other group are victims	Both groups are victims	Neither my nor the other group are victims	Total
Bosniak from Sarajevo	0 0.0%	0 0.0%	0 0.0%	19 100.0%	19 100.0%
Serb from Sarajevo	10 47.6%	0 0.0%	4 19.0%	7 33.3%	21 100.0%
Serb from East Sarajevo	20 100.0%	0 0.0%	0 0.0%	0 0.0%	20 100.0%
Total	30 50.0%	0 0.0%	4 6.7%	26 43.3%	60 100.0%

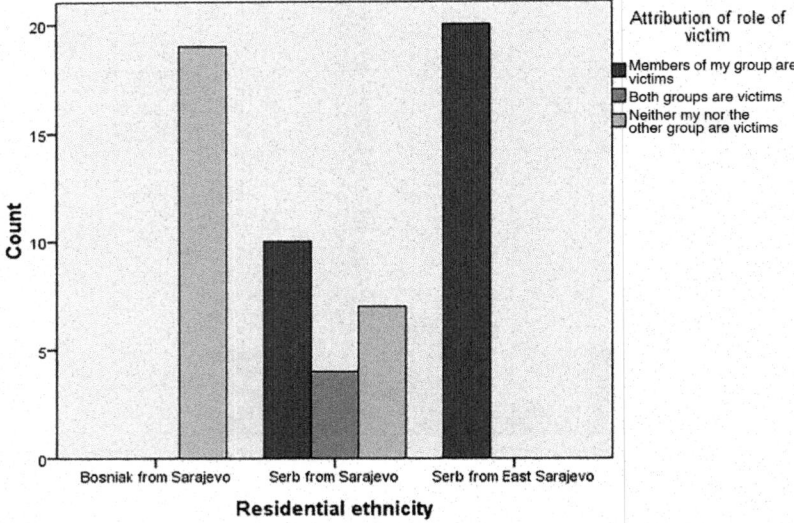

Chart 2.44 Indicator V (NATO)

The results of the chi square test (X^2 (4, N = 60) = 50.18 p = .00) showed that there is a negative association between ethnicity and the reported attribution of the role of victim for this event (r(58) = −.771 p = .00); therefore, the null hypothesis ($H0_e$) is rejected.

f   Should the event be commemorated?

The responses to this question are given in the tables and charts below (for each of the four events).

Markale

Table 2.51 Indicator VI (Markale)

Ethnicity	Yes	No	I do not know	Total
Bosniak from Sarajevo	18 94.7%	1 5.3%	0 0.0%	19 100.0%
Serb from Sarajevo	10 47.6%	2 9.5%	9 42.9%	21 100.0%
Serb from East Sarajevo	1 5.0%	7 35.0%	12 60.0%	20 100.0%
Total	29 48.3%	10 16.7%	21 35.0%	60 100.0%

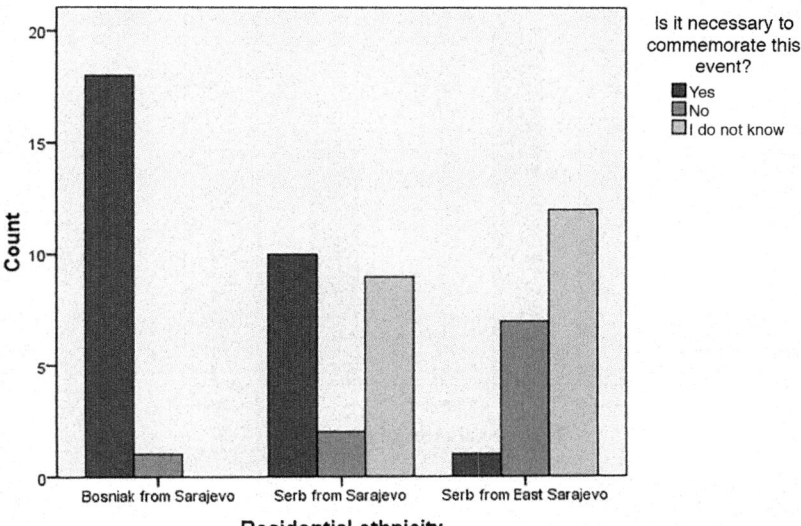

Chart 2.45 Indicator VI (Markale)

The results of the chi square test (X^2 (4, N = 60) = 32.99 p = .00) showed that there is a strong association between ethnicity and the reported necessity to commemorate the victims of this event (r(58) = .602 p = .00); therefore, the null hypothesis ($H0_f$) is rejected.

Kazani

Table 2.52 Indicator VI (Kazani)

Ethnicity	Yes	No	I do not know	Total
Bosniak from Sarajevo	5 26.3%	2 10.5%	12 63.2%	19 100.0%
Serb from Sarajevo	16 76.2%	0 0.0%	5 23.8%	21 100.0%
Serb from East Sarajevo	11 55.0%	1 5.0%	8 40.0%	20 100.0%
Total	32 53.3%	3 5.0%	25 41.7%	60 100.0%

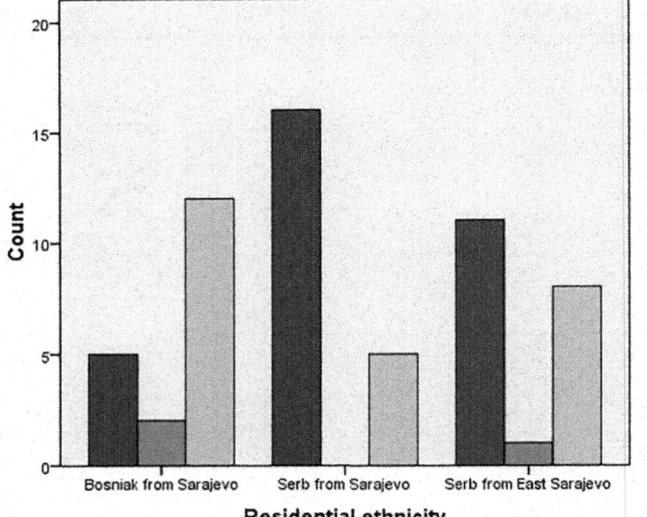

Chart 2.46 Indicator VI (Kazani)

The results of the chi square test (X^2 (4, N = 60) = 10.61 p = .031) showed that there is an association between ethnicity and the reported necessity to commemorate the victims of this event (r(58) = −.095 p = .469); therefore, the null hypothesis ($H0_f$) is rejected.

Vase Miskina

Table 2.53 Indicator VI (Vase Miskina)

Ethnicity	Yes	No	I do not know	Total
Bosniak from Sarajevo	12 63.2%	0 0.0%	7 36.8%	19 100.0%
Serb from Sarajevo	12 57.1%	1 4.8%	8 38.1%	21 100.0%
Serb from East Sarajevo	3 15.0%	9 45.0%	8 40.0%	20 100.0%
Total	27 45.0%	10 16.7%	23 38.3%	60 100.0%

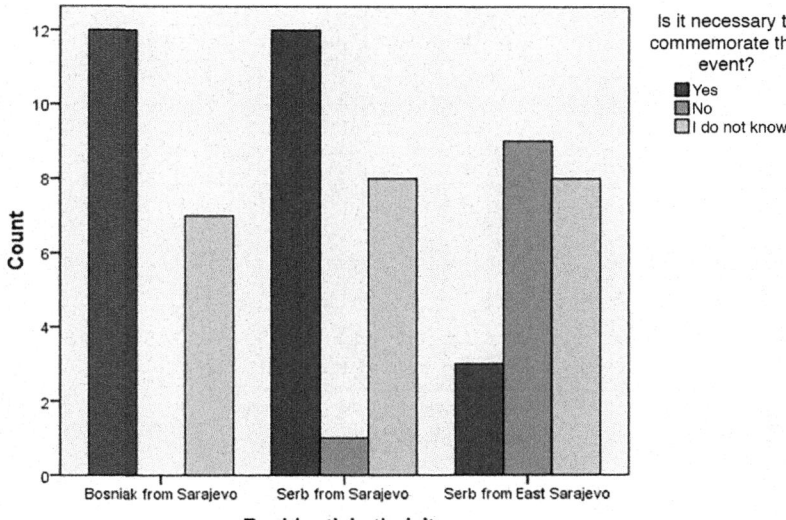

Chart 2.47 Indicator VI (Vase Miskina)

The results of the chi square test (X^2 (4, N = 60) = 20.69 p = .000) showed that there is a weak association between ethnicity and the reported necessity to commemorate the victims of this event (r(58) = .248 p = .056); therefore, the null hypothesis ($H0_f$) is rejected.

NATO

Table 2.54 Indicator VI (NATO)

Ethnicity	Yes	No	I do not know	Total
Bosniak from Sarajevo	5 26.3%	5 26.3%	9 47.4%	19 100.0%
Serb from Sarajevo	9 42.9%	3 14.3%	9 42.9%	21 100.0%
Serb from East Sarajevo	15 75.0%	1 5.0%	4 20.0%	20 100.0%
Total	29 48.3%	9 15.0%	22 36.7%	60 100.0%

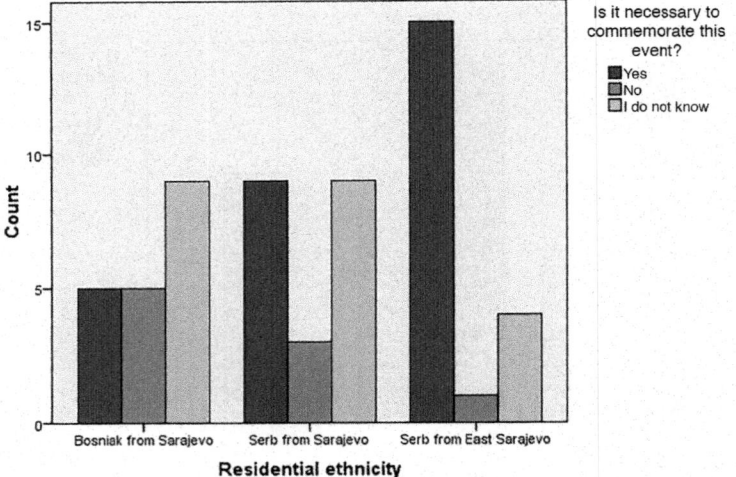

Chart 2.48 Indicator VI (NATO)

The results of the chi square test (X^2 (4, N = 60) = 10.27 p = .003) showed that there is a weak association between ethnicity and the reported necessity to commemorate the victims of this event (r(58) = −.347 p = .007); therefore, the null hypothesis ($H0_f$) is rejected.

Brief discussion

The null hypothesis was rejected in all cases but one – Indicator II (Kazani event). While the same situation happened in the first generation, one can conclude that the main reason was the lack of knowledge of the particular event and the lack of information on that event being given through personal narratives, media and education. It is important to notice that the Kazani event came to light by the end of the data collection process; therefore, the first generation still has their own memories/stories/recollections of it, but the second generation was in most cases deprived of such stories (parents were not talking about it; media and schools did not include it). In a similar way as with the first generation, we may say that Serbs from Sarajevo (second generation) developed their own narrative which resembled neither the narrative of Bosniaks (assumed due to their geographic proximity and everyday exposure to each other through school and other social networks) nor the narrative of Serbs from East Sarajevo (assumed due to their ethnicity).

Narratives of Serbs from Sarajevo (I and II generation)

The second hypothesis (H2) predicted that the narratives of Serbs from Sarajevo (both generational cohorts) would resemble the narratives of Bosniaks more closely due to their geographic proximity and cohesion formed during the war (I generation), or due to their everyday exposure through school and other social activities (II generation). However, as previously stated during the analysis of each indicator, such a connection was not found (not even when the case of Kazani was taken into consideration). It seems as though Serbs from Sarajevo (both generations) formed their own narrative independently from their Bosniak neighbours and Serbs from East Sarajevo (with whom they share an ethnicity). Therefore, the second hypothesis (H2) can be rejected as there was not enough evidence to support it.

In this research, bias was analyzed in terms of comparison; therefore, we can only say that participants were biased in cases where a strong association between ethnicity and responses to the question was found among all three groups. It is important to mention that a historical narrative of any kind was used neither as a model for bias nor as an important imperative for historical truth. Therefore, the rejection/acceptance of both the first and second hypotheses was based on a comparison and analysis of the association between ethnicity and the responses, and never as a deviation from a particular historical narrative.

Part II Readiness for Reconciliation

Part IIa Readiness for reconciliation (H3) – I generation

The readiness for reconciliation was measured by four subscales. The results are provided in the tables below.

Table 2.55 Readiness for reconciliation – subscale cooperation

(I) Residential ethnicity	(J) Residential ethnicity	Mean difference (I-J)	Std. error	Sig.
Bosniak from Sarajevo	Serb from Sarajevo	.29398	.17828	.308
	Serb from East Sarajevo	−.16253	.18127	1.000
Serb from Sarajevo	Bosniak from Sarajevo	−.29398	.17828	.308
	Serb from East Sarajevo	−.45651*	.17983	.039
Serb from East Sarajevo	Bosniak from Sarajevo	.16253	.18127	1.000
	Serb from Sarajevo	.45651*	.17983	.039

* The mean difference is significant at the 0.05 level.

Table 2.56 Confidence interval

(I) Residential ethnicity	(J) Residential ethnicity	95% Confidence interval	
		Lower bound	Upper bound
Bosniak from Sarajevo	Serb from Sarajevo	−.1412	.7292
	Serb from East Sarajevo	−.6050	.2800
Serb from Sarajevo	Bosniak from Sarajevo	−.7292	.1412
	Serb from East Sarajevo	−.8955	−.0175
Serb from East Sarajevo	Bosniak from Sarajevo	−.2800	.6050
	Serb from Sarajevo	.0175	.8955

The results show a significant difference (at the 0.05 level) in readiness to cooperate between Serbs from Sarajevo and Serbs from East Sarajevo.

Table 2.57 Readiness for reconciliation – subscale distrust

(I) Residential ethnicity	(J) Residential ethnicity	Mean difference (I-J)	Std. error	Sig.
Bosniak from Sarajevo	Serb from Sarajevo	.92839*	.30474	.009
	Serb from East Sarajevo	.46621	.30987	.408
Serb from Sarajevo	Bosniak from Sarajevo	−.92839*	.30474	.009
	Serb from East Sarajevo	−.46218	.30740	.409
Serb from East Sarajevo	Bosniak from Sarajevo	−.46621	.30987	.408
	Serb from Sarajevo	.46218	.30740	.409

* The mean difference is significant at the 0.05 level.

Table 2.58 Confidence interval

(I) Residential ethnicity	(J) Residential ethnicity	95% Confidence interval	
		Lower bound	Upper bound
Bosniak from Sarajevo	Serb from Sarajevo	.1845	1.6723
	Serb from East Sarajevo	−.2902	1.2226
Serb from Sarajevo	Bosniak from Sarajevo	−1.6723	−.1845
	Serb from East Sarajevo	−1.2126	.2882
Serb from East Sarajevo	Bosniak from Sarajevo	−1.2226	.2902
	Serb from Sarajevo	−.2882	1.2126

The results show a significant difference (at the 0.05 level) in readiness to trust between Serbs from Sarajevo and Bosniaks from Sarajevo.

Table 2.59 Readiness for reconciliation – subscale forgiveness

(I) Residential ethnicity	(J) Residential ethnicity	Mean difference (I-J)	Std. error	Sig.
Bosniak from Sarajevo	Serb from Sarajevo	.08892	.19776	1.000
	Serb from East Sarajevo	−.29161	.20109	.452
Serb from Sarajevo	Bosniak from Sarajevo	−.08892	.19776	1.000
	Serb from East Sarajevo	−.38053	.19949	.179
Serb from East Sarajevo	Bosniak from Sarajevo	.29161	.20109	.452
	Serb from Sarajevo	.38053	.19949	.179

Table 2.60 Confidence interval

(I) Residential ethnicity	(J) Residential ethnicity	95% Confidence interval	
		Lower bound	Upper bound
Bosniak from Sarajevo	Serb from Sarajevo	−.3938	.5717
	Serb from East Sarajevo	−.7825	.1993
Serb from Sarajevo	Bosniak from Sarajevo	−.5717	.3938
	Serb from East Sarajevo	−.8675	.1064
Serb from East Sarajevo	Bosniak from Sarajevo	−.1993	.7825
	Serb from Sarajevo	−.1064	.8675

There were no significant differences on this subscale.

Table 2.61 Readiness for reconciliation – subscale rehumanization

(I) Residential ethnicity	(J) Residential ethnicity	Mean difference (I-J)	Std. error	Sig.
Bosniak from Sarajevo	Serb from Sarajevo	.34946	.19051	.210
	Serb from East Sarajevo	−.16322	.19371	1.000
Serb from Sarajevo	Bosniak from Sarajevo	−.34946	.19051	.210
	Serb from East Sarajevo	−.51268*	.19217	.027
Serb from East Sarajevo	Bosniak from Sarajevo	.16322	.19371	1.000
	Serb from Sarajevo	.51268*	.19217	.027

* The mean difference is significant at the 0.05 level.

Table 2.62 Confidence interval

(I) Residential ethnicity	(J) Residential ethnicity	95% Confidence interval	
		Lower bound	Upper bound
Bosniak from Sarajevo	Serb from Sarajevo	−.1156	.8145
	Serb from East Sarajevo	−.6361	.3097
Serb from Sarajevo	Bosniak from Sarajevo	−.8145	.1156
	Serb from East Sarajevo	−.9818	−.0436
Serb from East Sarajevo	Bosniak from Sarajevo	−.3097	.6361
	Serb from Sarajevo	.0436	.9818

The results show a significant difference (at the 0.05 level) in rehumanization between Serbs from Sarajevo and Serbs from Sarajevo.

Part IIb Readiness for reconciliation (H3) – II generation

The results on readiness for reconciliation in the second generation of participants are presented in the tables below. However, significant differences were not found for any of the subscales or between ethnicities.

Table 2.63 Readiness for reconciliation – subscale cooperation

(I) Residential ethnicity	(J) Residential ethnicity	Mean difference (I-J)	Std. error	Sig.
Bosniak from Sarajevo	Serb from Sarajevo	.30977	.25379	.682
	Serb from East Sarajevo	.08263	.25678	1.000
Serb from Sarajevo	Bosniak from Sarajevo	−.30977	.25379	.682
	Serb from East Sarajevo	−.22714	.25043	1.000
Serb from East Sarajevo	Bosniak from Sarajevo	−.08263	.25678	1.000
	Serb from Sarajevo	.22714	.25043	1.000

Table 2.64 Confidence interval

(I) Residential ethnicity	(J) Residential ethnicity	95% Confidence interval	
		Lower bound	Upper bound
Bosniak from Sarajevo	Serb from Sarajevo	−.3162	.9358
	Serb from East Sarajevo	−.5508	.7160
Serb from Sarajevo	Bosniak from Sarajevo	−.9358	.3162
	Serb from East Sarajevo	−.8449	.3906
Serb from East Sarajevo	Bosniak from Sarajevo	−.7160	.5508
	Serb from Sarajevo	−.3906	.8449

Table 2.65 Readiness for reconciliation – subscale distrust

(I) Residential ethnicity	(J) Residential ethnicity	Mean difference (I-J)	Std. error	Sig.
Bosniak from Sarajevo	Serb from Sarajevo	.32556	.29729	.834
	Serb from East Sarajevo	.09342	.30080	1.000
Serb from Sarajevo	Bosniak from Sarajevo	−.32556	.29729	.834
	Serb from East Sarajevo	−.23214	.29336	1.000
Serb from East Sarajevo	Bosniak from Sarajevo	−.09342	.30080	1.000
	Serb from Sarajevo	.23214	.29336	1.000

Table 2.66 Confidence interval

(I) Residential ethnicity	(J) Residential ethnicity	95% Confidence interval	
		Lower bound	Upper bound
Bosniak from Sarajevo	Serb from Sarajevo	−.4077	1.0589
	Serb from East Sarajevo	−.6485	.8354
Serb from Sarajevo	Bosniak from Sarajevo	−1.0589	.4077
	Serb from East Sarajevo	−.9558	.4915
Serb from East Sarajevo	Bosniak from Sarajevo	−.8354	.6485
	Serb from Sarajevo	−.4915	.9558

Table 2.67 Readiness for reconciliation – subscale forgiveness

(I) Residential ethnicity	(J) Residential ethnicity	Mean difference (I-J)	Std. error	Sig.
Bosniak from Sarajevo	Serb from Sarajevo	−.11278	.24752	1.000
	Serb from East Sarajevo	−.31921	.25044	.623
Serb from Sarajevo	Bosniak from Sarajevo	.11278	.24752	1.000
	Serb from East Sarajevo	−.20643	.24425	1.000
Serb from East Sarajevo	Bosniak from Sarajevo	.31921	.25044	.623
	Serb from Sarajevo	.20643	.24425	1.000

Table 2.68 Confidence interval

(I) Residential ethnicity	(J) Residential ethnicity	95% Confidence interval	
		Lower bound	Upper bound
Bosniak from Sarajevo	Serb from Sarajevo	−.7233	.4978
	Serb from East Sarajevo	−.9370	.2985
Serb from Sarajevo	Bosniak from Sarajevo	−.4978	.7233
	Serb from East Sarajevo	−.8089	.3961
Serb from East Sarajevo	Bosniak from Sarajevo	−.2985	.9370
	Serb from Sarajevo	−.3961	.8089

Table 2.69 Readiness for reconciliation – subscale rehumanization

(I) Residential ethnicity	(J) Residential ethnicity	Mean difference (I-J)	Std. error	Sig.
Bosniak from Sarajevo	Serb from Sarajevo	.47594	.27540	.268
	Serb from East Sarajevo	.02737	.27865	1.000
Serb from Sarajevo	Bosniak from Sarajevo	−.47594	.27540	.268
	Serb from East Sarajevo	−.44857	.27176	.313
Serb from East Sarajevo	Bosniak from Sarajevo	−.02737	.27865	1.000
	Serb from Sarajevo	.44857	.27176	.313

Table 2.70 Confidence interval

(I) Residential ethnicity	(J) Residential ethnicity	95% Confidence interval	
		Lower bound	Upper bound
Bosniak from Sarajevo	Serb from Sarajevo	−.2034	1.1553
	Serb from East Sarajevo	−.6600	.7147
Serb from Sarajevo	Bosniak from Sarajevo	−1.1553	.2034
	Serb from East Sarajevo	−1.1189	.2218
Serb from East Sarajevo	Bosniak from Sarajevo	−.7147	.6600
	Serb from Sarajevo	−.2218	1.1189

Brief discussion

The Readiness for Reconciliation Scale was designed by Petrović (2005) in order to measure reconciliation on four subscales: cooperation, distrust, forgiveness and rehumanization. While the first three subscales are self-evident (even by their titles), the last one refers to the opposite of *dehumanization* – readiness to dehumanize the opponent and to perceive them as someone/something that does not require to be treated in a humane way.

The hypothesis H3 was not proved fully because different results were obtained on different subscales, and for the two generational cohorts.

Significant differences at the 0.05 level were found on the subscales cooperation (between Serbs from Sarajevo and Serbs from East Sarajevo, which partially proved the third hypothesis), distrust (between Bosniaks and Serbs from Sarajevo, which is not in line with the third hypothesis) and rehumanization (between Serbs from Sarajevo and Serbs from East Sarajevo, which, again, partially proves the third hypothesis). However, significant differences were not found in the second generation on any of the four subscales.

Keeping in mind the complexity of the responses and the fact that independent evaluators were included in the quantitative part of the analysis, it is important to emphasize the importance of qualitative analyses of pure narratives that will be described in the following sections. Given the inability of statistics to grasp all data at once, as well as to describe each "no" and/or "yes" in line with the broader narrative each person provided, it is extremely important to provide the deeper insight into both narratives but also the ways in which they were retold, explained and transmitted.

Narrative (in)coherence and traumatic experiences

Traumatic narratives are characterized by incoherence; however, in this research that incoherence corresponds to participants' inability to produce a consistent story with a general framework (*where, when, how did the event happen*). On the contrary, their stories were mostly related to where they were and what they were doing (and how they felt) when the event happened. The closer (geographically speaking) they were to the place, the less coherent their story was, but at the same time, it was very emotionally saturated. Also, the more attached they felt towards a particular event (in most cases either they or someone close to them was involved in the event), the less structured narratives they produced; for example:

> Serb, 59, East Sarajevo: *A lot of people were killed at Markale bazaar. I remember it well. My friend was there . . . He survived, but lost both of his legs. I went to the hospital to visit him . . . I still remember that scene, seeing him in his hospital bed, covered completely by a white blanket. He saw me, smiled, and asked: "Did you bring me socks?"*

However, these incoherent stories range from emotionally saturated narratives to factual and reserved narratives:

> Serb, 63, East Sarajevo: *I think the NATO bombing of the Republic of Srpska was planned and financed by someone. Those who paid were really rich and well informed. The only reason was to put the blame on Serbs. Nothing else.*
>
> *Markale . . . Grenade was there . . . Or maybe it was not. What can someone like me, an ordinary* man, tell about it? I can only say that I feel sorry for the victims.

Serb, 59, East Sarajevo: *I am not interested to talk about Markale. There are people out there who should think about it. Our politicians. I can only feel sorry for the victims and their families.*

Bosniak, 60, Sarajevo: *Commemorations should not be organized for any event. Whenever they organize it they spread hatred.*

Bosniak, 45, Sarajevo: *I blame Serbs for this war. I blame them for most of the things related to the war. They always had aspirations to occupy huge territory, and they did not have a problem with killing people in order to achieve their goal.*

Serb, 47, Sarajevo: *I was so happy when I heard about the NATO bombing of the Republic of Srpska. I wanted to see that, wanted to sing and dance . . . They kept me under siege for four years. That was the end of that terror.*

Narrative accounts are not told in a vacuum, but are shaped and encouraged by a specific context (Murray, 2003, p. 116). There is usually a large layer outside the story that represents the socio-political context in which that story is told, which influences what, how and why elements within the story are seen as important and relevant (Murray, 2003). It is important to emphasize that this field research did not occur in a laboratory setting, and participants were neither deprived of media sources nor kept in a specific type of isolation. Therefore, the political context before the field research took place, as well as the ongoing political debate (Hague tribunal cases, trial of Naser Orić, a former Bosnian Army officer who was accused of mistreatment of Bosnian Serb detainees in the region of Srebrenica in late 1992 and early 1993) and the regular commemorations of these and other events, has influenced and shaped the responses of participants (for instance, during Naser Orić's trial they were more likely to include it in each narrative regardless of it not being directly related to the question). In such circumstances a narrator is regarded as a complex psychosocial subject who is an active agent in a social world, and it is through the narrative analyses that we can understand both narrators and their worlds (Murray, 2003, p. 116).

Analysis of narratives in this research reveals the great impact of social context on the formation of memories and also the fact that individual memories formed under the influence of such contact in one group can be combined to make a collective narrative. In saying that, one does not think of a pure collection of individual narratives, but of the process of extracting one dominant narrative for each group. Such a narrative is usually the most frequently mentioned, retold and/or emphasized story among all or the majority of members of one group. That can also be supported through the analysis of the first associations of participants for each of the four events. The associations in the following tables represent the first words and/or sentences participants said when each of the four events was mentioned.

Table 2.71 First association(s) (Vase Miskina Street event)

Bosniaks, older generation	Bosniaks, younger generation	Serbs, East Sarajevo, younger generation	Serbs, East Sarajevo, older generation	Serbs, older generation, Sarajevo	Serbs, younger generation, Sarajevo
Burned tram at Skenderija, shooting	I hardly remember	Huge tragedy, result of war	I feel sorry	War	I do not remember
shelling	queue, bread, civilians	I hardly remember	Dead soldiers, street, children	terror, human stupidity, grief	That is Ferhadija street now
many people wounded, blood, screams	murder, crime, killing	unknown . . .	shelling, victims, blood	I was 100 metres away	crime
terrible, horrible	blood, death, sadness	tama	shelling	pain, cramp, fear	killing of innocent people
amoral and terrible act	unknown event	Army of FBiH[1] has bombed	horrors	killing of innocent civilians	uninvestigated
terrible act	crime	Yugoslav National Army	politicians wanted war	I never tried to analyze it	massacre
sad, terrible, horrible	war, blood, pain	Sick Muslim	there are people to think about it	Horror, fear, insecurity	fear
sadness, death, misery	sadness	terror	journalists ready to document	Each one of us could have been a victim	pain, red
blood, screams	aggression on Bosnia	I hardly remember	horror	Terrible event, innocent people	war
sadness, fear	war in BiH[2]	Operation under a false flag	stradanje	Horror, sadness	I do not remember accurately
crime	killings, hunger, poor citizens	Set-up event	killing of two colleagues	blood, fear	hunger
anger, sadness, grief	I do not have association	I do not have association	I do not have association	I do not want to recall	I do not know anything about this
terrible	I do not have association	Set-up event	Innocent people terrible	Huge sadness	Happened in the wartime
explosion, destroyed bodies		Never described till the end	death, killing, innocent people	Bread, blood	I do not know . . . fear . . .
		Operation under a false flag			underinvestigated, unknown

(Continued)

Table 2.71 (Continued)

Bosniaks, older generation	Bosniaks, younger generation	Serbs, East Sarajevo, younger generation	Serbs, East Sarajevo, older generation	Serbs, older generation, Sarajevo	Serbs, younger generation, Sarajevo
wartime Sarajevo	sadness	Serbs accused by Bosniaks	bread, diversion	Bread queue	killings
walks while I was young	unknown	People said that Serbs were guilty	leader	Unbelievable	I do not have association
blood I saw on TV	death, sadness, pain	accused not explained	set-up event, shameful, misery	sadness	war
I do not have association	massacre	I do not have association	crime against civilians	fear, death	1992
Act of crime	I do not have association	I do not know what to say, there is too much information about that event out there	I feel sorry for people	first killing	Bread queue, shell
Beasts killed innocent people	I do not have association		War consequences exaggerated	bread, queue, hunger	
blood, pieces of body, cry	bread, children, shell		there were a lot of stories out there	war does not choose	
It is going to end soon			I do not have association	killings	
innocent, scream, pieces of body			war, killings, innocent people	why?	
blood, death, fear			innocent people were killed	Cannot understand that	
red			innocent people were killed	Horror, horror	
War, queue, bread			horror	disbelief	
horrible			crime	innocent people	
beginning				innocent people are killed in every war	
fear				victims, war, killings	
beginning of war				blood, bread, horror	
				sadness	

Table 2.72 First association(s) (Kazani event)

Bosniaks, older generation	Bosniaks, younger generation	Serbs, East Sarajevo, younger generation	Serbs, East Sarajevo, older generation	Serbs, older generation, Sarajevo	Serbs, younger generation, Sarajevo
murder of Serb population	I have no association	the tragedy of a nation in one city	aggression against the Serbs	I should have been liquidated	I do not remember
unreliable crime	crime, Caco[3], Serbs	I do not remember well	innocent victims	responsibility of authority, horror, tragedy	Caco
crime	I have no association	uncleared	the hate created for the Serbs	people are beasts	pit
it's insane	death, providence, war	incomprehensible	criminals and paramilitaries	disbelief, fear, crap	murder
loathing	unknown	has not yet been explained	The Serbs fired	I could have been killed	I do not know much about it
a vicious crime	misunderstanding, no control	I have no association	Serbs grabbed by Sarajevo	taking civilians to death	vaguely
conviction for a crime	I have no association	I have no association	bloodshed	sadness, concern	I have no association
bitterness ("čemer"), death and misery	I have no association	killing Serbs	it only knows who has lost someone there	the suffering of innocent civilians	I have no association
crime, shame	the crimes of the Army of BiH against Serb civilians	death and death	they throw people into a pit they cannot get into	civilians	Army of BiH
sorry, revenge		I have no association	simple juxtaposition	innocent citizens of Sarajevo	murder
crime	Caco	death	crime	innocent	I do not know
unnecessary happening		murder	I have no association	innocent, innocent civilians	I have no association
passionately		I have no association	horror	dirty war	I'm not sure
a crime against the Serbs		death in the pit			unknown to the end
suffering on Trebevic		pit, mountain			
the Serbs' suffering		pit			

(Continued)

Table 2.72 (Continued)

Bosniaks, older generation	Bosniaks, younger generation	Serbs, East Sarajevo, younger generation	Serbs, East Sarajevo, older generation	Serbs, older generation, Sarajevo	Serbs, younger generation, Sarajevo
a vicious fool	I have no association	death in the pit	death	war, horror	vaguely remembered
criminal act	I have no association	aggression against the Serbs	terrible	fear	war
pits, rocks, cry			I have no association	bad road	chasm
horrible			I have no association	the suffering of Sarajevo Serbs	I do not know . . .
Killed Serbian civilians			I have no association	war, blood, pit	unclear event
The raid of innocent Serb civilians			sadness, sorrow	throwing the body into a pit	crime
uncleared			a crime against civilians	Caco	
killing, pit			many Serbs have been killed	Mušan Topalović Caco	
pit			prisoners	paramilitary units of the Army of BiH	
retaliation			I have no association	everyone could suffer	
ghastly			I have no association	horror, siege	
invented			horrors	war, horror, killings	
			the suffering of innocent civilians	pit	
			the suffering of innocent citizens	Serbs from Sarajevo were killed	
			the crime of the Serbs	pit, murder, innocent	
			human nonsense from the war	crime	
			I'm terrified		

Table 2.73 First association(s) (Markale bazaar event)

Bosniaks, older generation	Bosniaks, younger generation	Serbs, East Sarajevo, younger generation	Serbs, East Sarajevo, older generation	Serbs, older generation, Sarajevo	Serbs, younger generation, Sarajevo
I was in the bazaar circle ten minutes earlier … I could have been killed when the grenade was fired.	massacre, suffering, victims	the suffering of the innocent people during the war	the grenade fell or not	way round, Markale in front of me	murder
again	marks, massacres, civilians, bodies	I can hardly remember	staged	bitterness ("čemer"), sorrow, human stupidity	grenade
crime	blood, death, scream	unknown	staged	the market of human flesh	blood, murder
horror, horror, horror	massacre, blood, death, war	vaguely	different interpretations	bitterness	massacre
horror and feeling of being lost	genocide against mankind	changeling	furnished	("čemer"), fear, sadness	unclear event
a vicious crime	crime	changeling	say it was a grenade	horror, catastrophe	death
astonishing, miserable, immoral	a large number of victims, blood	they lie	I do not think about it	I do not want to remember	lots of casualties
sadness, death, bitterness ("čemer")	death	I have no association	Izetbegović in the opera	sorrow, sorrow, wrath	grenade
man lies across the fence	shelling of the civilian position from the Army of the Republic of Srpska and the Yugoslav People's Army	Bosniaks committed a crime against their people and blamed the Serbian people for that	again!	weird, fear, panic	market
horror, horror, horror		a complicated case	crime	a vicious event	war
massacre	bazaar, grenade, morgue	set-up event	I have no association	sorrow, pain, tragedy	nineties
pain, sorrow, bitterness ("čemer")		construct	disbelief	sadness	victims
massacre, scream, dead bodies		construction, unclear	death of innocent people	blood, fear	grenades
			horror	blood	siege
			innocent victims		killing
			mining of peace negotiations		sadness
			mining of negotiations		murder
					casualty
					vaguely remembered

(Continued)

Table 2.73 (Continued)

Bosniaks, older generation	Bosniaks, younger generation	Serbs, East Sarajevo, younger generation	Serbs, East Sarajevo, older generation	Serbs, older generation, Sarajevo	Serbs, younger generation, Sarajevo
going to Markale	war, fear	The Bosniaks blamed the Serbian troops for the attack they themselves carried over the Bosniaks	horror, sadness	blood, lesions	attacks, nineties, war in BiH
tables and chairs	a lot of innocent victims		setup	terrible, inhumane	
blood			I'm sorry for the people	corpses	
I have no association	the bomb was thrown at civilians	setup	massacre	massacre	
criminal procedure, fascism	the extinction of innocent life	blaming Serbs	I have no association	fear, panic	
I'm worried that my husband is in that place	many dead and injured in one place	game	directed	there were two times	
body pieces, blood	evil, sadness, pain	uncleared	horrors	the suffering of the innocent people	
horror	massacre	vaguely	the suffering of innocent people, the consequence of the war	people are the means	
Shattered body, strong, smell of blood and gunpowder	blood, sadness, fear	unreasonable case		again	
Death, despair, fear	a lot of dead, innocent victims,		the suffering of innocent citizens	is that so possible?	
massacre	blood, wounded, people who help		a crime against innocent citizens	unclear, unclear	
broken body	bombing, chetniks,[4] murder		political turmoil	innocent	
fear			West	different price	
the suffering of the innocent				victims for the second time	
murder				unclear case	
horror, horror, beast act				two massacres at the bazaar	
				bazaar, blood, killings, grenade	
				innocent	

Table 2.74 First association(s) (NATO event)

Bosniak, older generation	Bosniaks, young generation	Serbs, East Sarajevo, younger generation	Serbs, East Sarajevo, older generation	Serbs, older generation, Sarajevo	Serbs, younger generation, Sarajevo
we finally got rid of shelling	I have no association	action of Western countries directed against one side (against Serbs)	in every war Serbs suffer the most	Smoke above Jahorina	end of war
the beginning of the end of the war	bombing, NATO, RS[5]	innocent people	striking bombardment	it was the only way to end the war and the siege of Sarajevo	NATO
conscience	I have no association	innocent people	I survived it	if you are not good, we will introduce democracy	war
that's what it takes	stopping the war in BiH	innocent people	Survived	you deserve – you feel 14-year-old fear	bombs
satisfaction over the end of the war	attempt to end the war in BiH	I have no association	NATO beat the Serbs	could be expected when-then	bombing of Serbs
finally	justice, late	I have no association	that the war was over	I do not want to remember	America
end of the war	I have no association	aggression, injustice, terror	horrible	I was expecting it	NATO
deserved punishment for crimes	late reaction of NATO's	bombardment by the United States	the war did not repeat itself	he talked about it, so it happened	airplanes
relief	after Markale	the suffering of a large number of Serbs	not repeated anywhere	could be expected to happen	bombing
disbelief	aircraft, end of war	attack on one side	I have no association	so it is ordered	war
righteousness	I have no association	the suffering of the innocent	the biggest crime	justifiably	during the war in BiH
deserved, justified	I have no association	bombing Serbian positions by NATO	fear, suffering	expected	I have no association
passionately	I have no association	innocent on the road	banging in the back, bang	end of the war	I do not know exactly
reaction to the siege of Sarajevo	I have no association	exhorting us over our people	disaster	it's over	I do not have a lot of information
surrounded by Sarajevo	I have no association	innocent blood	fear, trouble	International community	I do not know …
ghastly	I have no association		we're guilty of everything		Airplane, bomb
I have no association	I have no association		innocent people		Bombing
I have no association	freedom				Bombs all around
					NATO
					America
					America, war

(Continued)

Table 2.74 (Continued)

Bosniak, older generation	Bosniaks, young generation	Serbs, East Sarajevo, younger generation	Serbs, East Sarajevo, older generation	Serbs, older generation, Sarajevo	Serbs, younger generation, Sarajevo
satisfaction	NATO airplanes were bombarding	innocent	fear, sadness	America	
disabling the superior enemy	NATO, Markale, destruction	aggression	injustice	Americans break down BiH	
NATO aircraft, explosions		aggression, death	expected	destruction	
What goes around, comes around		war	I have no association	bombs, uranium	
end of the war, relief		attack on Serbs	I'm trying to bomb your home from a plane so you cannot live where to live	the end	
aircraft sound, hope, uncertainty			I have no association	horror	
the end			fear, panic, pain, anger	relief	
revenge			unjust bombardment	I have no association	
finally			NATO aggression	injustice	
retaliation for Markale			an attack on the Serbian side was planned	America	
bombs and smoke			damaged windows	America, collapse unfairly	
happiness			forced into the negotiations	America, injustice	
				Americans, an attempt of peace	
				America breaks down BiH	
				I have no association	

1 Federation of Bosnia-Herzegovina
2 Bosnia-Herzegovina
3 Mušan "Caco" Topalović was commander of the 10th Mountain brigade in the Army of the Republic of Bosnia-Herzegovina. According to some sources, he is believed to be responsible for the killings of Serbs in Kazani.
4 Members of a Serbian nationalist guerrilla force in the Balkans, active during the 1992–1995 war in Bosnia-Herzegovina.
5 Republic of Srpska

Even though they were asked to say up to three words, most participants either were unable to do so (so they said one or two words) or reacted with a full sentence (a shorter one). It is evident that these associations are also grouped in a way that can result in a "collective association" for each of the three groups while at the same time such collective associations correspond to the three collective narratives extracted from participants' stories.

While Bosniaks and Serbs from Sarajevo mostly used words such as "blood", "pain", "bread", "innocent civilians" and "death", the dominant associations among Serbs from East Sarajevo were "unclear", "unknown", "construct" and "constructed". However, one can notice that Serbs from Sarajevo in their associations emphasize the words "fear", "death" and "innocent", while some of them use the fact that "I was 100 metres farther". In terms of the phenomenological characteristics of these associations, one can notice that some participants referred to colours, such as red (instead of saying blood), and some of them said that they "can still smell the grenade". One of the very frequent words was "čemer", which, when translated into English, corresponds to a combination of several emotions and feelings: sadness, sorrow, bitterness, despondency and grief. That word is often used in Bosnian poetry and literature in general, as it corresponds to the specific type of emptiness, sadness and bitterness that results from a traumatic event. Therefore, its presence here gives a much better picture of how participants understood the world around them during the specific war events. It is also interesting to notice that only one participant (a Bosniak from Sarajevo while telling her/his associations with the event in Vase Miskina street) said: "Walks when I was young". It seems as though some people are still trying to embrace the old, pre-war picture of areas (streets) largely affected by the war later. This can also give some space to the formation of reconciliation models and also healing, all of which will be analyzed in the last two chapters. The greater elaboration of critical details and the focus being put on the boundaries, as well as the superior recognition and recall of central, emotion-arousing details in a traumatic event, is a special phenomenon in cognitive psychology called tunnel memories (Safer, Christianson, Autry, & Osterlund, 1998). Such emotion-loaded narratives (as well as first associations with the events) are characteristic of the stories given by participants in this research, and this also helps us understand their incoherence and inability to follow a particular structure. Even though the interview questions were very structured, participants simply avoided providing a coherent, well-organized narrative and "describing" the event in the way they think or know it happened. In most of the cases they were reacting in line with their first associations, either starting to blame the other side, or trying to emphasize their in-group victimization, or their in-group suffering. While this is in line with present theories of the formation of traumatic narrative, incoherence should be analyzed within the social context in which it occurs, but also within cognitive theories of memory association with trauma.

Traumatic narratives are characterized by incoherence, defragmentation and sensory experiences. Janet (1909) was among the first scientists analyzing dissociated and fragmented narrative as well as threatening vivid flashbacks in traumatic memory. Until now, his research has been strongly appreciated in neuroscience. Brewin, Dalgleish, and Joseph (1996) suggested two types of memory that are associated with trauma, and they described them as verbally accessible memory (VAM), responsible for the narrative aspect of the traumatic memory and partially integrated into autobiographical memory, while it partially gives rise to a fragmented and dissociated narrative that can be accessed deliberately when required. Situationally accessible memory (SAM) is responsible for flashbacks, which are vivid memories that are triggered automatically and involuntarily and result in emotionally threatening but richly detailed memories (Burnell, Coleman, & Hunt, 2010, p. 59).

Integration of traumatic memories into a coherent narrative is one of the preconditions for their reconciliation (Brewin et al., 1996). However, over time traumatic narrative can become an explicit and integrated personal narrative (van der Kolk & Fisler, 1995), which was proved in this research on Sarajevo and East Sarajevo as well. Most of the narratives were recalled in the form of dissociated mental imprints of sensory and affective elements of the traumatic experience (as visual, affective, auditory and kinaesthetic experience), after which a personal narrative appears (van der Kolk & Fisler, 1995). In the present research all participants struggled to form coherent and structured narratives of what happened, while those who were either geographically closer to the event or somehow involved (either they were there, or a family member or close friend was there) started describing the events by explaining what they were doing, where they were or how they felt at that point of time. However, none of the participants in this research actually specifically pointed out the ways through which he/she tried to cope with such incoherent traumatic narratives of the past. Most of what I as a researcher was able to get was associated with the reluctance to talk and fear of being judged; one Serb from East Sarajevo (older generation) said he/she was "afraid of being labelled as nationalist".

Hunt and Robbins (2001) identified two coping strategies that influence how war veterans cope with traumatic narratives: avoidance and processing. Avoidance can be defined as staying out of situations or away from people that can trigger traumatic memories, while processing involves actively seeking people who can support the recall of traumatic memories and who can provide the opportunity to both narrate and make sense of the traumatic past (Burnell et al., 2010, p. 60). In their research conducted on British

World War II and Korean War veterans Hunt and Robbins (2001) found that the veterans processed their memories at veterans' associations with comrades of the same war or with others who served with them, while family members were used as a safe space where they were not supposed to talk about war and traumatic experiences at all. It is assumed that war veterans (as well as other survivors of traumatic experiences) will try to find meaning in their memories of those events. In order to explore the coherence of narratives and representations of "my-their" memories of a second generation, a qualitative narrative analysis was conducted in the present research.

A definition of coherent narrative was taken from Burnell et al.'s (2010, p. 62) research on World War II veterans' experiences of social support in relation to the narrative coherence of war memories; therefore, the coherent narrative was defined as "one that is structured, affectually consistent, and is fully integrated". It was really hard to determine that type of coherence in narratives obtained from the first generation of Sarajevans and East Sarajevans. However, the narratives of the second generation mostly resembled history textbooks (even though they did not learn about the 1992–1995 war in school). This can be explained by the fact that the second generation did not hear a lot about these events from their parents directly, but they found and read some facts on Internet forums or heard about them on television. The fact that they did not show their own emotions but a so-called learnt emotional response that was highly dependent on their in-group belonging explains why their narratives were characterized by factuality. However, it was interesting to see how that factuality developed into a "collective factuality" that embraced the major grand narrative of their in-group:

PARTICIPANT (BOSNIAK, SARAJEVO, 19 YEARS OLD): You are asking me about the event that happened in Vase Miskina street? Where is that street in Sarajevo? I never heard of it.

RESEARCHER: It is called Ferhadija street now. Before it was Vase Miskina street.

PARTICIPANT (BOSNIAK, SARAJEVO, 19 YEARS OLD): Oh, yes . . . I remember it now. Or, let's say, I cannot recall it in a way a survivor can. I was born after the war . . . I do not have that type of memory . . . As survivors have . . . You know, they can tell it more accurately, I guess. But I saw the plaque. I realized that people were killed there while waiting in a bread queue . . . But it happened because Serbs wanted to cleanse Sarajevo of all Muslims. That was the only reason.

What is seen in the previous excerpt from an interview with a 19-year-old Bosniak from Sarajevo is that, at the very beginning, he seemed to be pretty unaware of the change in street name (the names of the streets were changed after the war, mostly in cases when some of them reflected previous regimes, either World War II or the 1992–1995 war); however, when reminded, he was not able to produce a coherent narrative and describe what happened, but instead tried to explain that his recall is not the same as the recall of the survivors. Nevertheless, he did not describe the event by itself, but gave some sort of opinion on what happened (which, at the same time, included both putting guilt and blame on one group, and using it as a reason for the event occurrence – without clearly describing it and letting us know if he has some knowledge about it, if not memory).

We can say that memory for traumatic events has two poles: on one side there are the autobiographical memories of the direct victims, while on the other side there are the collective memories of second, third and many new generations. Between these two poles are so-called "my-their" memory images, which lie somewhere between personal memories and images younger generations could not have. They differ from collective memories in that they are experienced by the person as very personal and they elicit highly emotional feelings (Hirsch, 2008; Landsberg, 2004). That is significantly more likely to occur in situations that have certain indications of traumatic events from the past (e.g., when a person needs to visit a concentration camp in Poland) (Chaitin & Steinberg, 2014). According to Tulving (1993), the person can mentally travel to the traumatic event.

According to Chaitin and Steinberg (2014) "my-their" memories differ from the individual memories in several aspects:

1   the person senses that she/he possesses individual memories, although she/he could not possibly have experienced those events or it is very unlikely that a person actually survived and remembered those events;
2   it is a reconstructed memory, based on interpretations of the memories of older generations and longer exposure to collective memories;
3   such memories lack the vivid details of long episodic memories and are therefore more generic;
4   memories oscillate between the perspective of the first and third persons;
5   memories are "learned", implanted from the outside by the older generation.

Some of the mentioned characteristics were found in the narratives of younger generations of Sarajevans and East Sarajevans, especially when they were trying to describe when and how certain events happened. For instance, when asked about the event in Vase Miskina street, a 19-year-old Serb from East Sarajevo said: "*I heard about that event from my professor of political economy and EU integration. He told us that the Serbs were unfairly accused and that Bosniaks were supposed to be blamed for that*". However, when asked about the NATO bombing, he responded: "*Bosniaks are responsible for that event as well. Do not ask me why, because I do not really know. I probably think this way because I am a patriot*". What is obvious here is the presence and incorporation of the elements of emotions (according to Hirsch, 2008; Landsberg, 2004), collective identity, and issues of intergenerational transmission of massive social trauma, all of which are part of the content of "my-their" memories.

The elements of transgenerational transmission of social trauma as well as the influence of collective identity on "my-their" memories are seen in the following excerpts as well:

> Bosniak, 19, Sarajevo: *Somebody's hatred towards Muslims caused all these war events, including the one in Vase Miskina street . . .*
>
> *The most responsible person for Kazani is the late president Alija. He ordered those terrible crimes. I would not know why. There is no response to that, besides hatred.*
>
> *NATO is responsible for bombing of the Republic of Srpska. It happened as some sort of revenge for Markale . . .*
>
> Serb, 19, East Sarajevo: *Bosniaks set up all those events. They victimized their own people, their own civilians, in order to accuse the Serbs.*
>
> *We should not commemorate Markale . . . Why would we? It was all constructed.*
>
> *The NATO bombing was a terror. They were attacking us with no reason.*
>
> Serb, 17, Sarajevo: *I do not know a lot about war in general, as that is something we do not learn in school. However, I heard about Markale, it was a terrible attack. So many innocent people killed. It should never happen again to anyone.*
>
> Bosniak, 19, Sarajevo: *What happened in Vase Miskina street is the result of Serbs' desire to exterminate Muslims and take over Sarajevo . . .*
>
> *The NATO bombing represents freedom . . . Because Serbs would not have stopped the war anyway.*
>
> Serb, 18, East Sarajevo: *I think Bosniaks are to be held responsible for Markale. Serbs could not have done this.*
>
> *I have never heard of Kazani.*
>
> *Vase Miskina was set up as well. Bosniaks did it.*
>
> Bosniak, 18, Sarajevo: *People keep retelling different stories from wartime. Also, history classes contribute to it . . . In my opinion, Markale happened because Serbs wanted to kill all Muslims, which is a very immoral and unethical act. Their desire to kill exceeded all expectations . . .*

Serb, 17, East Sarajevo: *There are a lot of stories about the event in Miskina street. One of them says that it was constructed by Bosniaks. However, I am not sure that I can believe that one . . .*

Serb, 16, Sarajevo: *My parents were in Sarajevo when that (Markale) happened. They told me it was a horrible event. My mum also told me they felt relief during and after the NATO bombing. Because they knew that the war was over.*

Bosniak, 19, Sarajevo: *I saw the massacre in Vase Miskina street on TV. I do not wish something like that on even my worst enemy. However, I do not wish to judge. I am not here to judge. God is the only judge, and he will evaluate all their bad intentions.*

Serb, 16, East Sarajevo: *Members of one group (Bosniaks) committed wrongdoings towards their own group and then accused the other group (Serbs) of committing it. Everything was constructed.*

Serb, 15, Sarajevo: *I read about these events on the Internet. So many things can be found on portals. I know that there are a lot of different interpretations of what has happened; however, that does not justify the level of hatred towards the other group. Reading comments full of hatred makes me feel anxious about my future here.*

Bosniak, 19, Sarajevo: *Serbs were not happy with the fact that Bosniaks wanted to have their own country.*

Serb, 17, Sarajevo: *What happened in Vase Miskina street happened due to the wrong ideology. It happened because of the hatred of one group (Serbs) towards the other group (Bosniaks). Serbia had a desperate desire to become a huge country while at the same time it was destroying the other country (Bosnia) and Bosnians.*

I do not think we should mark or commemorate the NATO bombing of the Republic of Srpska. Maybe they can write about it in history textbooks, but just in the form of a historical fact, nothing else.

The presented excerpts from narratives reveal the ways in which these memories were formed, and that includes both transgenerational transmission and also the influence of in-group identity and the collective memories of the in-group. We can say that individual memories and collective memories are mutually very connected, and this connection is very noticeable when we consider the traumatic events of the past relevant to one group (wars, violence, genocide, etc.). However, it looks as if "my-their" memories can also be connected to and influenced by the other types of memories, which, according to Chaitin (2014), are not fixed, but are strong when they arise in the moment. They have three main functions: intrapersonal, interpersonal and directive (Bluck et al., 2005). Chaitin and Stenberg (2014) in their study of descendants of survivors of Holocaust victims and descendants of Palestinians who survived al Naqba come to the conclusion that the younger generation (which did not experience the traumatic events) adopts and internalizes the narratives of the older generation, which causes them to become imprisoned in those memories and traumas. The authors did not specify in what way these memories would help or hinder a reconciliation process, but emphasized that even those who possess "my-their" memories can demonstrate a high willingness for reconciliation if they are in situations that require cooperation and dialogue with members of the other ("enemy") group. Albeck et al. (2002) in their research showed that personal narratives can help Germans and Jews as well as Israelis and Palestinians to move closer to reconciliation, especially when they take place in a "safe" environment that encourages active listening, dialogue and reflection.

If we apply that to the Bosnian context and the results of this research, we can say that the younger generation has developed "my-their" memories in such a way that they embrace both the narratives of the older generation and the narratives of their surroundings (peers, professors, friends, media/ Internet). Even though there were no statistically significant differences in readiness to reconcile among the three groups (in the younger generation), while going through all the narratives (and also first associations) we can notice the formation of three grand or major narratives that somehow flow above all lower, single-individual narratives. If we take into consideration that there are different approaches to collective memories as well as different definitions, we can say that those "floating" narratives can be understood not as a pure most frequent word or a sentence each group member used, but as a combination of similar/same constructs used while describing events. It is also interesting to understand how these constructs were acquired and later shared among members of the same group, and also transgenerationally transmitted.

Table 2.75 represents the major information sources participants mentioned as important for them when getting to know more about these events. Even though media are mentioned as the most frequent source, it should be taken into consideration that the lack of electricity during the 1992–1995 war in Bosnia-Herzegovina deprived almost all people of television and radio (the Internet was not a source at that time in this region). Therefore, in most of the cases when a participant mentioned media he/she added: "It was in those rare situations when we got electricity for two hours per night, and then you turned on the TV and watched whatever could be watched". However, participants were exposed to different TV programmes depending on where they were, but the fact that electricity was scarce meant they were mostly deprived of it. Most of the information was retold in the form of stories among family members, neighbours and friends.

Table 2.75 Source(s) of information

	Number	Percent
I happened to be there	1	0.7
TV	1	0.7
Survived	1	0.7
Historical documents, documentary movies	2	1.3
Internet	1	0.7
Eyewitness testimonies and court	1	0.7
Colleagues	1	0.7
Neighbour	1	0.7
Neighbours	9	6.0
Neighbours and friends	2	1.3
Media	69	46.0
Media and history classes	1	0.7
Neighbours and media	2	1.3
Media and neighbour who was nurse in clinical centre Vrazova	1	0.7
Media and people from the city, friend who was wounded at Markale	1	0.7
Media and people who survived it	1	0.7
Media was informing, but media is guilty as well	1	0.7
Controversial media	1	0.7
Media that was leading this war	1	0.7
Media, neighbour	6	4.0
Media, neighbour, friends	1	0.7
Media, my friend lost his daughter during this event	1	0.7
Media, acquaintances	1	0.7
Media, survivors, neighbours	3	2.0
Media, newspapers	1	0.7
Media, Wikipedia, documentary movies, communication with the elderly	1	0.7
I was 400 metres away, my friend was wounded; also, colleagues and teachers from the Institute Svjetlost told me about it because they were advised to leave the workplace in advance	1	0.7
Cousins	1	0.7
Friends who lived nearby	1	0.7
Neighbour who survived	1	0.7
Survivors	9	6.0
Survivors and history classes	1	0.7
Survivors and media	4	2.7
Friends	1	0.7
Colleagues	3	2.0
Friends who were nearby	1	0.7
Friends who lived in Vase Miskina	1	0.7
I was walking along that street before the accident happened	1	0.7
Friend's sister	1	0.7
Older colleagues	1	0.7
Older people who survived the war	1	0.7

	Number	Percent
I witnessed this event	4	2.7
TV	3	2.0
TV and radio	1	0.7
In school	1	0.7
Wikipedia	1	0.7
Total	150	100.0

Speakers and listeners often influence each other's memories during conversation and, in doing so, promote the formation of a shared, or collective, memory (Coman & Hirst, 2015). That process or a moment during which such mnemonic consensus occurs is called socially shared retrieval-induced forgetting (SSRIF). In situations when listeners attend to speakers' selective retrieval of previously encountered events, they forget unmentioned but related information more than they forget unrelated, unmentioned previously studied information (Coman & Hirst, 2015). Due to such a process, both of them remember and forget the event in a similar way. In their study of SSRIF, Coman and Hirst (2015) concluded that group membership plays a role in SSRIF, because Princeton students listening to a speaker selectively recall previously studied material showed SSRIF when the speaker was identified as a fellow Princeton student, but not when he or she was identified as a Yale student. Also, similar patterns of selective forgetting are more likely to occur between speakers and listeners if they belong to the same social group. In other research on memories of the 11 September terrorist attack, Coman, Manier, and Hirst (2009) concluded that conversations can alter the memories of speakers and listeners in similar ways, even when the memories differ, which implies that SSRIF could be one of the mechanisms for the formation of collective memories.

Following the SSRIF theory, we can conclude that the basic mnemonic mechanisms are adapted to promote the emergence of shared mnemonic representations that preserve group membership and group identity in a way that we could see in the present research. The fact that memories are not formed in a vacuum, and that members of the same group interact with each other more than they interact with members of the other group, contributes to the formation of three "floating" narratives in these three groups.

While responding to the question related to the sources of information some members of the younger generation mentioned their family members, teachers and peers. Even though in this research two generational groups were interviewed, there was no connection between them; therefore, it is impossible to draw conclusions on the basis of transgenerational transmission of memories and trauma. However, it is possible to speak about indirect transmission, while keeping in mind that members of the younger generation were under the influence of the memories of their parents, grandparents and other older relatives.

According to Volkan (2001), a large group "chooses" to dwell on a past traumatic event and make it a major design to be stitched on the canvas of a large-group tent. While doing so, the same group also chooses the trauma which can further be transmitted to their children. Such chosen trauma can be reactivated through ideology, enhancement of leader-follower interaction, time, feelings of victimization, prejudice and conflict, which all leads to irrational decision making and destructive large-group activities (Volkan, 2001). Transmission of different chosen traumas and difficult memories is still taking place in post-war Bosnia-Herzegovina (Mušić, Jeftić, & Draganović, 2014). Kalina Yordanova (2015) argues that memories of war violence are being preserved not only in narratives, but also in acts and objects, such as developing an illness, producing war-related art or visiting places that link back to the war. According to her findings, the war generation from Bosnia-Herzegovina is not able to recall coherent war narratives due to four reasons: at the onset of the war people denied many of the warning signs, making the war seem an overwhelming and surreal event which is impossible to describe to someone without such experience; the ambiguity of the parents' experience of war, which originates in shifts between the positions of victim, murderer and witness, complicates transmission since there is no clear-cut narrative about the war in the first person singular; the experience of extreme violence challenges the war generation's capacity to comprehend and integrate what they have lived through; and the inability to produce a war narrative in the first person is shaped by the wider context of polarization and profanization of the issue of war (Yordanova, 2015). The fact that the younger generation does not receive a coherent narrative from their parents could be one of the reasons why they were not able to produce their own story. However, one should take into consideration that most parents do not talk to their children about the war that openly, and even those who do so do not give specific information on all four events mentioned in this research. Also, one of the most important factors to mention here is that the younger generation does not learn about the 1992–1995 war in school, because it is forbidden to talk about this until a common narrative has been established.

History teaching in elementary and secondary schools in Bosnia-Herzegovina has not yet been agreed upon and has been carried out using three different curricula: the curricula of the two entities (the Federation of Bosnia-Herzegovina and the Republic of Srpska) and the Croatian curriculum followed in certain parts of Bosnia-Herzegovina (Jeftić, 2013). The 1992–1995 war in Bosnia-Herzegovina was not included in the official curriculum in most parts of the country, due to the recommendations of the Council of Europe to temporarily suspend teaching about the war years. The Parliamentary Assembly of the Council of Europe argued for the temporary suspension of teaching of the 1992–1995 period until historians in Bosnia-Herzegovina, with the support of international experts, establish a common approach to the study of this period in schools. The Council of Europe intervened in the case of the curriculum through establishing a committee and proposing guidelines, but these approaches contributed more to the formation of an intellectual vacuum and the omission of the 1992–1995 events from history textbooks. The Guidelines for the Evaluation of History Textbooks for Primary and Secondary Schools in Bosnia-Herzegovina were adopted in 2003 with the major aim of developing a balanced, comparative and multi-perspective narrative (Pingel, 2008). The guidelines specify the following: the quantity of information related to the political history that should be reduced; the writing of history textbooks, since the modern textbook is expected to educate, encourage, guide and lead the development of students; and what history textbooks should look like, from format to content (Jeftić & Joksimović, 2014). Regardless of the guidelines being there to ensure preparation of identical history textbooks for students in Bosnia-Herzegovina and regardless of the fact that the 1992–1995 war was supposed to be omitted from these textbooks, in practice this is not the case. Content analysis of three history textbooks used in the Federation of Bosnia-Herzegovina, the Republic of Srpska and the areas of Bosnia-Herzegovina that follow the Croatian curriculum revealed that the 1992–1995 war was mentioned and described in the Croatian textbook (Matković, Mirošević, Goluža & Šarac, 2003), while it was omitted in the other two (Jeftić & Joksimović, 2014). However, a detailed analysis revealed that in the preface of textbook used in the Federation of Bosnia-Herzegovina the 1992–1995 war was mentioned: "It is particularly important to note that in this period, an independent state of Bosnia-Herzegovina was established, after a long and terrible war which was led against it by all means" (Hadžiabdić, Dervišagić, Mulić, & Mehić, 2007, p. 5). Also, a textbook used in the Republic of Srpska contains interesting instructions for students/readers at the end of a chapter titled "Yugoslavia after World War II": "You can be informed of the events of our nearest past (after 1991) on the basis of interviews with contemporaries (teachers, parents, participants in events) as well as from other sources (newspapers, documents, photographs, documentaries, etc.). Information can be discussed during history class and tutorials" (Živković & Stanojlović, 2012, p. 163).

The above analysis implies why school was mentioned as a source of information about the war only once. However, during interviews, one student said that he had heard about the Markale event from his professor; therefore, one cannot be sure that the guidelines are followed in the classes and that professors really use the proposed textbooks or other sources as well. The EURO Clio project is one of the initiatives trying to empower history teachers to talk about the difficult past with their students. The biggest power of history teachers is not to teach their students the numbers of people killed and murdered, but to teach the students why such events should never happen again. Therefore, the following chapters will be related to the organization of remembrance in a way that contributes to peace and to ways to develop historical empathy within the classroom and to transmit it to the next generations.

References

Albeck, J. H., Adwan, S., & Bar-On, D. (2002). Dialogue groups: TRT's guidelines for working through intractable conflicts by personal storytelling in encounter groups. *Peace and Conflict Journal of Peace Psychology, 8*, 301–322.

Bandura, A. (1999). A social cognitive theory of personality. In: L. Pervin & O. John (Eds.), *Handbook of personality* (2nd ed., pp. 154–196). New York: Guilford Publications.

Bandura, A. (2002). Social cognitive theory in cultural context. *Applied Psychology, 51*(2), 269–290.

Bar-Tal, D. (1993). Patriotism as fundamental beliefs of group members. *Politics & the Individual, 3*(2), 45–62.

Bar-Tal, D. (1998). Societal beliefs in times of intractable conflict: The Israeli case. *International Journal of Conflict Management, 9*(1), 22–50.

Bar-Tal, D. (2000). *Shared beliefs in a society: Social psychological analysis.* Thousand Oaks, CA: Sage.

Bar-Tal, D. (2013). *Intractable conflicts: Socio-psychological foundations and dynamics.* Cambridge, UK: Cambridge University Press.

Bar-Tal, D., & Salomon, G. (2006). Israeli-Jewish narratives of the Israeli-Palestinian conflict: Evolvement, contents, functions and consequences. In R. I. Rotberg (Ed.), *Israeli and Palestinian narratives of conflict: History's double helix.* Bloomington, IN: Indiana University Press.

Baumeister, R. F., & Hastings, S. (1997). Distortions of collective memory: How groups flatter and deceive themselves. In J. W. Pennebaker, D. Paez, & B. Rime (Eds.), *Collective memory of political events: Social psychological perspectives* (pp. 277–293). Mahwah, NJ: Erlbaum.

Bilali, R. (2012). Identity centrality and in-group superiority differentially predict relations to historical victimization and harm doing. *International Journal of Conflict and Violence, 6*(2), 322–338.

Billing, M. (1995). *Banal Nationalism.* London: Sage.

Bluck, S., Alea, N., Habermas, T., & Rubin, D. (2005). A tale of three functions: The self-reported uses of autobiographical memory. *Social Cognition, 23*, 91–117.

Branscombe, N., & Doosje, B. (2004). *Collective guilt: International perspectives.* Cambridge, UK and New York, NY: Cambridge University Press.

Branscombe, N., & Miron, A. M. (2005). Interpreting the in-group's negative actions toward another group: Emotional reactions to appraised harm. In L. Z. Tiedens & C. W. Leach (Eds.), *The social life of emotions* (pp. 314–355). New York, NY: Cambridge University Press.

Brewin, C. R., Dalgleish, T., & Joseph, S. (1996). A dual representation theory of posttraumatic stress disorder. *Psychological Review, 103*(4), 670–686.

Bruner, J. S. (1990). *Acts of meaning*. Cambridge, MA: Harvard University Press.

Burnell, K. J., Coleman, P. G., & Hunt, N. (2010). Coping with traumatic war memories: Second World War veterans' experiences of social support in relation to the narrative coherence of war memories. *Ageing and Society, 30*(1), 57–78.

Cairns, E., & Darby, J. (1998). The conflict in Northern Ireland: Causes, consequences, and controls. *American Psychologist, 53*(7), 754–760.

Cameron, J. E. (2004). A three-factor model of social identity. *Self and Identity, 3*, 239–262.

Cameron, J. E., & Lalonde, R. N. (2001). Social identification and gender-related ideology in women and men. *British Journal of Social Psychology, 40*, 59–77.

Castano, E., & Giner-Sorolla, R. (2006). Not quite human: Infrahumanization in response to collective responsibility for intergroup killing. *Journal of Personality and Social Psychology, 90*(5), 805–818.

Cehajic, S., Brown, R., & Castano, E. (2008). Forgive and forget? Antecedents and consequences of intergroup forgiveness in Bosnia and Herzegovina. *Political Psychology, 29*(3), 351–367.

Chaitin, J., & Steinberg, S. (2014). "I can almost remember it now": Between personal and collective memories of massive social trauma. *Journal of Adult Development, 21*, 30–42.

Chase, S. E. (2002). Learning to listen: Narrative principles in a qualitative research methods course. In R. Josselson, A. Lieblich, & D. P. McAdams (Eds.), *Up close and personal: The teaching and learning of narrative research* (pp. 79–100). Washington, DC: American Psychological Association.

Coman, A., Manier, D., & Hirst, W. (2009). Forgetting the unforgettable through conversation: Socially shared retrieval-induced forgetting of September 11 memories. *Psychological Science, 20*(5), 627–633.

Coman, A., & Hirst, W. (2015). Social identity and socially shared retrieval induced forgetting: The role of social group membership. *Journal of Experimental Psychology: General, 144*(4), 717–722.

Connerton, P. (1989). *How societies remember*. Cambridge, UK: Cambridge University Press.

Devine-Wright, P., & Lyons, E. (1997). Remembering pasts and representing places: The construction of national identities in Ireland. *Journal of Environmental Psychology, 17*(1), 33–45.

Doosje, B., & Branscombe, N. (2003). Attributions for the negative historical actions of a group. *European Journal of Social Psychology, 33*, 235–248.

Elkins, J. (2005). *Master narratives and their discontents*. New York, NY: Routledge.

Fossion, P., Rejas, M.C., Servais, L., Pelc, I., & Hirsch, S. (2003). Family approach with grandchildren of Holocaust survivors. *American Journal of Psychotherapy, 57*(4), 519–527.

Freeman, M. (2002). Narrative unconscious. *Narrative Inquiry, 12*(1), 193–211.

Gaskell, G. D., & Wright, D. B. (1997). Group differences in memory for a political event. In J. W. Pennebaker & D. Paez (Eds.), *Collective memory of political events: Social psychological perspectives*. Hillsdale, UK: Lawrence Erlbaum.

Halbwachs, M. (1992). *On Collective Memory*. Chicago: The University of Chicago Press.

Hewer, C. J., & Roberts, R. (2012). History, culture and cognition: Towards a dynamic model of social memory. *Culture Psychology, 18*(2), 167–183.

Hirsch, M. (2008). The generation of post memory. *Poetics Today, 29*, 103–128.

Hunt, N., & Robbins, I. (2001). World War II veterans, social support, and veterans' associations. *Aging and Mental Health, 5*(2), 175–182.

Igartua, P., & Paez, I. (1997). Art and remembering collective events. In J. Pennebaker et al. (Eds.), *Collective memory of political events* (pp. 79–101). Mahwah, NJ: Lawrence Erlbaum Associates.

Irwin-Zarecka, I. (1994). *Frames of remembrance: The dynamics of collective memory*. London: Transaction Publishers.

Jackson, J. W. (2002). Intergroup attitudes as a function of different dimensions of group identification and perceived intergroup conflict. *Self and Identity, 1*, 11–33.

Janet, P. (1909). Problemes psychologiques de l'émotion. *Revista de Neurología, 17*(2), 1551–1672.

Jeftić, A. (2013). Social discourse in history teaching: A case of Bosnia-Herzegovina. In P*roceedings of I International Conference on Economic and Social Studies, 10–11 May, 2013, Sarajevo* (pp. 41–55). Sarajevo: International Burch University.

Jeftić, A., & Joksimović, J. (2014). Divided presentations in history textbooks in three ex Yugoslav states: Discussing implications for identity development. In *The IAFOR European Conference Series 2014 (Brighton, UK, July 2014) – The European Conference on Psychology and Behavioral Sciences* (pp. 47–60). Japan: The International Academic Forum (IAFOR).

Kansteiner, W. (2002). Finding meaning in memory: Methodological critique of collective memory studies. *History and Theory, 41*, 179–197.

Kellermann, N.P.F. (2013). Epigenetic transmission of Holocaust trauma: Can nightmares be transmitted? *The Israel Journal of Psychiatry and Related Sciences 50*(1):33–7.

Kosterman, R., & Feshbach, S. (1989). Toward a measure of patriotic and nationalistic attitudes. *Political Psychology, 10*(2), 257–274.

Landsberg, A. (2004). *Prosthetic memory: The transformation of American remembrance in the age of mass culture*. New York, NY: Columbia University Press.

Leach, C., van Zomeren, M., Zebel, S., Vliek, M., Pennekamp, S., Doosje, B., Ouwerkerk, J., Spears, R. (2008). Self-definition and self-investment: A multi component model of in-group identification. *Journal of Personality and Social Psychology, 95*, 144–165.

Leidner, B., & Castano, E. (2012). Morality shifting in the context of intergroup violence. *European Journal of Social Psychology, 42*(1), 82–91.

Leidner, B., Castano, E., & Ginges, J. (2013). Dehumanization, retributive and restorative justice, and aggressive versus diplomatic intergroup conflict resolution strategies. *Personality and Social Psychology Bulletin, 39*(2), 181–192.

Leidner, B., Castano, E., Zaiser, E., & Giner-Sorolla, R. (2010). Ingroup glorification, moral disengagement, and justice in the context of collective violence. *Personality and Social Psychology Bulletin, 36*(8), 1115–1129.

Leidner, B., Li, M., Petrović, N., & Orazni, S. N. (2017). The role of retributive justice and the use of international criminal tribunals in postconflict reconciliation. *European Journal of Social Psychology, 48*(2), 133–151.

Lickel, B. (2012). Retribution and revenge. In L. R. Tropp (Eds.), Oxford library of psychology. *The Oxford handbook of intergroup conflict* (pp. 89–105). New York, NY, US: Oxford University Press.

Liu, J. H. (1999). Social representations of history: Preliminary notes on content and consequences around the Pacific Rim. *International Journal of Intercultural Relations, 23*(2), 215–236.

Liu, J. H., & Hilton, D. J. (2005). How the past weighs on the present: Social representations of history and their role in identity politics. *British Journal of Social Psychology, 44*, 537–556.

Murray, M. (2003). Narrative psychology and narrative analysis. In P. M. Camic, J. E. Rhodes, & L. Yardley (Eds.), *Qualitative research in psychology: Expanding perspectives in methodology and design* (pp. 95–112). Washington, DC: American Psychological Association.

Mušić, L., Jeftić, A., & Draganović, S. (2014). Psycho-social aspects of trauma and its transmission in post-war Bosnia-Herzegovina. *Electronic Journal of Political Science, 5*(1), 41–55.

Nets-Zehngut, R., Pliskin, R. and Bar-Tal, D. (2015). Self-censorship in conflicts: Israel and the 1948 Palestinian exodus. *Peace and Conflict: Journal of Peace Psychology, 21*, 479–499.

Nora, P. (1998). La aventura de Les lieux de mémoire. In: J. Cuesta Bustillo (Eds.), *Memoria e Historia issue* 32 (pp. 17–34). Madrid: Marcial Pons.

Oren, N., Nets-Zehngut, R., and Bar-Tal, D. (2015). Construction of the Israeli-Jewish conflict-supportive narrative and the struggle over its dominance. *Political Psychology, 36*(2), 215–230.

Petrovič, N., (2005). *Psihološke osnove pomirenja između Srba, Bošnjaka i Hrvata.* Beograd: Institut za psihologiju Filozofskog fakulteta.

Phinney, J. S. (1990). Ethnic identity in adolescents and adults: Review of research. *Psychological Bulletin, 108*(3), 499–514.

Pingel, F. (2008). Can truth be negotiated? History textbook revision as a means to reconciliation. *Annals of the American Academy of Political and Social Science, 617*, 181–198.

Powell, A. A., Branscombe, N., & Schmitt, M. T. (2005). Inequality as in-group privilege or outgroup disadvantage: The impact of group focus on collective guilt and interracial attitudes. *Personality and Social Psychology Bulletin, 31*(4), 508–521.

Roccas, S., Klar, Y., & Liviatan, I. (2006). The paradox of group based guilt: Modes of conflict identification, conflict vehemence, and reactions to the in-group's moral violations. *Journal of Personality and Social Psychology, 91*(4), 698–711.

Roccas, S., Sagiv, L., Schwartz, S., Halevy, N., & Eidelson, R. (2008). Toward a unifying model of identification with groups: Integrating theoretical perspectives. *Personality and Social Psychology Review, 12*(3), 280–306.

Ross, M. H. (2001). Psychocultural interpretations and dramas: Identity dynamics in ethnic conflict. *Political Psychology, 22*(1), 157–178.

Safer, M. A., Christianson, S. A., Autry, M. W., & Osterlund, K. (1998). Tunnel memory for traumatic events. *Applied Cognitive Psychology, 12*, 99–117.

Schacter, D. (2001). *The seven sins of memory: How the mind forgets and remembers.* New York, NY: Houghton-Mifflin.

Shnabel, N., & Nadler, A. (2008). A needs-based model of reconciliation: Satisfying the differential emotional needs of victim and perpetrator as a key to promoting reconciliation. *Journal of Personality and Social Psychology, 94*(1), 116–132.

Smjernice za pisanje i ocjenu udžbenika historije za osnovne i srednje škole u BiH. (2005). *Komisija za izradu smjernica koncepcije novih udžbenika historije u BiH.*

Sutin, A.R., Robins, R.W. (2008). When the "I" looks at the "Me": Autobiographical memory, visual perspective, and the self. *Consciousness and Cognition, 17*(4), 1386–1397.

Tajfel, H. (1978). *Differentiation between social groups: Studies in the social psychology of intergroup relations.* London: Academic Press.

Tam, T., Hewstone, M., Cairns, E., Tausch, N., Maio, G., & Kenworthy, J. (2007). The Impact of Intergroup Emotions on Forgiveness in Northern Ireland. *Group Processes & Intergroup Relations, 10*(1), 119–136.

Tulving, E. (1993). What is episodic memory? *Current Directions in Psychological Science, 2*(3), 67–70.

Van der Kolk, B.A., Fisler, R. (1995). Dissociation and the fragmentary nature of traumatic memories: overview and exploratory study. *Journal of Traumatic Stress, 8*(4), 505–525.

Volkan, V. D. (2001). Transgenerational transmissions and chosen traumas: An aspect of large-group identity. *Group Analysis, 34*(1), 79–97.

Wertsch, J. V. (2002). *Voices of collective remembering.* New York: Cambridge University Press.

White, H. (1987). *Metahistory.* London, England: Johns Hopkins University Press.

Wohl, M. A., & Branscombe, N. (2005). Forgiveness and collective guilt assignment to historical perpetrator groups depend on level of social category inclusiveness. *Journal of Personality and Social Psychology, 88*(2), 288–303.

Yordanova, K. (2015). Images of war: The place of the war past of the parents in the second generation's identity. *Journal of Regional Security, 10*(1), 79–102.

Zerubavel, E. (2003). *Time Maps. Collective Memory and Social Shape of the Past.* Chicago: Chicago University Press.

Zerubavel, Y. (1994). The historic, the legendary, and the incredible: Invented tradition and collective memory in Israel. In J. R. Gillis (Eds.). *Commemorations: The politics of national identity* (pp. 105–126). Princeton, NJ: Princeton University Press.

Analyzed textbooks

Hadžiabdič, H., Dervišagič, E., Mulič, A., & Mehič, V. (2007). *Historija-Istorija-Povijest.* Tuzla: Bosanska Knjiga.

Matkovič, H., Miroševič, F., Goluža, B., & Šarac, I. (2003). *Povijest 4 – Udžbenik za četvrti razred gimnazije.* Mostar: Školska naklada i Zagreb: Školska knjiga.

Živkovič, D., & Stanojlovič, B. (2012). *Istorija za treći razred gimnazije prirodno-matematičkog i za četvrti razred gimnazije opšteg i društveno-jezičkog smjera.* Istočno Sarajevo: Zavod za udžbenike i nastavna sredstva.

3 Sins of memory

Terror of remembrance and terror of forgetting

The purpose of this chapter is to provide insight into the contemporary debate on moral aspects of remembrance. It is well known that societies urge people to remember and commemorate – even when such activities prevent us from moving forward. Keeping in mind the examples of Sarajevo and East Sarajevo this chapter does not attempt to respond to the difficult question *How much should we remember?*, but to elaborate the ways through which we should both remember and recall the traumatic past. Also, I shall try to describe how remembrance occurs within groups and between groups, and to provide recommendations on how to organize education to fight for reconciliation of divided memories (in the classroom and beyond).

When society experiences "the surplus of remembrance"

According to Jonah Lehrer (2012), we remember in the same way Marcel Proust wrote, which means that as long as we have memories, we keep trying to modify them to fit what we know now. In *Swann's Way*, Proust warned the reader of the paradox of seeking in reality the pictures that are stored in one's memory (Proust, 1998). Memories are always being distorted to correspond to our present situation, in-group belonging, expectations, wishes, desires . . . But what happens after one eats the Proustian *madeleine*? How much of one's memories will be recalled, retold, changed, distorted and saved again? Also, how much of these memories are we supposed to keep?

The present research shows that all groups mostly supported marking the events from the difficult past through commemorations. In-group belonging did influence their responses, but that influence was not very strong or significant. However, a few participants were against commemorations because they perceived them as a means for spreading hatred among people:

> Bosniak, 60, Sarajevo: *We should not be marking any of these events because it can spread even more hatred.*

Serb, 49, East Sarajevo: *Such commemorations are used to plant even more hatred. The major goal is supposed to be showing respect towards victims and their families, but it is usually not. The government in Sarajevo is organizing these commemorations in order to put even more blame on Serbs. Also, these plaques . . . Most of them consist of this text: "At this place Serbian aggressors killed citizens of Sarajevo". That is hatred.*

Also, one participant said that the role of commemorations is not just to mark the victims and show respect towards them and their families, but to remind and warn: *"Yes, we should start commemorating the day of the NATO bombing of the Republic of Srpska. It is important to show all Serbs what could happen to them if they try to attack us again"* (Bosniak, 58, Sarajevo).

The above lines can serve as a reminder of dangerous aspects of remembrance and recall by itself (through memorials and commemorations in this case). How much is it important to remember, and where should we draw a line under the past? Is there something like optimal remembrance, which is neither too much (as it hinders reconciliation) nor too little? There have been a lot of debates and different opinions on this question. Based on one viewpoint, it is of extreme importance to remember our past, because if we do not remember it well, it will haunt us and disturb our present. Nietzsche (1983) said that it is utterly impossible to live without forgetting because it will lead to a certain degree of insomnia and rumination on historical awareness, which in the end destroys all living things, whether a person, a people or a culture. On the other side, there is always a possibility that such memories, if very deep and intense, can prevent living in the present and being ready for reconciliation. Such deep and intense memories can further develop into dangerous memories, which are defined as those memories that disrupt the status quo, i.e., the hegemonic culture of strengthening and maintaining existing group identity (Zembylas & Bekerman, 2008). Most participants used the term "čemer", which represents a mixture of sadness, sorrow, bitterness and pain, as one of the first associations with the given events. That term in the Bosnian language (as well as in Serbian and Croatian) refers to one special condition when a person becomes too overwhelmed by certain negative feelings and emotions, due to which he/she becomes bitter inside and such a state destroys him/her slowly. One of the main questions that memory scholars are trying to answer is: *How can we remember the traumatic and difficult past in a way that won't turn us into its prisoners who won't be ready to reconcile and cooperate with the members of the other group?* Also, this question entails the organization of history, geography and literature classes, since all three cases involve discussion about the past and analysis of figures of the past.

Dangerous memories are those that recognize the heterogeneity of the historical narrative and, as such, can significantly affect the willingness for reconciliation. What becomes the "official" memory reflects the power of certain groups and ideologies in society to define the past according to their own interests. Each memory can become "dangerous" when it resists the prevailing historical narrative (Zembylas & Bekerman, 2008). As such, it hinders reconciliation, since each party wants to remember only their own pain and suffering during the traumatic event (war), and to build a group identity based on common suffering. In this way, memories become a source of hostility, hatred and violence that are transmitted across generations. This is especially true in post-conflict divided communities in which there is more than one historical narrative and these narratives can conflict with each another and, as such, continue to deepen the gap between the formerly warring groups while aggravating their dialogue. However, it is important to point out that most people are not capable of providing a coherent narrative; therefore, the existence of several interpretations of the traumatic past also corresponds to the existence of several different (sometimes even meaning-less) pieces of already distorted stories.

Neuroscience has offered an explanation for the inability of the brain to create meaningful stories out of traumatic memories. That also explains why the answers of most participants from the present research referred to smell – because smell and taste are processed by the hippocampus, the centre of the brain's long-term memory (Herz & Schooler, 2002). All other senses are first processed by the thalamus (the source of language and consciousness); therefore, they have less influence on remembering things past (to put it in a Proustian way). The already explained empirical research conducted in Sarajevo and East Sarajevo confirmed that state-ment, even though it was not neuroscientific in its essence. It is quite understandable that people were unable to give coherent, textbook-like narratives of what exactly happened in the four events. Also, it was evi-dent that certain elements of the individual narratives were common to the members of the same ethnic group – supporting in this way the for-mation of *floating narratives* – narratives that characterize members of a particular group and that they "take" from each other. For instance, there were some elements in common in the explanations provided for Markale and/or Kazani, as well as Vase Miskina and/or the NATO bombing; and it seems as if these groups are floating on such stories. The most important question is whether and how it is possible to change the direction of such a flow and help these groups meet and possibly listen to the other stories that are floating around them.

Such narratives have been created out of difficult memories that currently exist in post-war Bosnia-Herzegovina. The data provided by the analysis of three different history textbooks applied in three teaching curricula in Bosnia-Herzegovina serve as a good example of currently existing different narratives of the past which lead to further divisions and highly influence the transmission of difficult memories (especially those related to the dissolution of Yugoslavia and the 1992–1995 war). In cases where their own in-group committed wrongdoings, people often rely on familiarity and are usually guided by implicit prejudice and stereotypes when recalling the content of difficult memories. Therefore, we can say that the power of the human mind to both recollect and reproduce memories depends largely on its capacity, but also on social context and communication.

Prejudice and stereotypes affect the way people remember and report on the same events, but in the same way, the flow of communication directs our attention to particular words and phrases. As previously mentioned, when talking about traumatic experiences people usually cannot provide coherent narratives; therefore, the main story becomes distorted. According to Besser van der Kolk (2015), in trauma survivors the parts of the brain that have evolved to monitor for danger remain overactivated, and even the slightest sign of danger, regardless whether it is real or misperceived, can trigger an acute stress response accompanied by intense unpleasant emotions and overwhelming sensations. Due to these post-traumatic reactions survivors experience difficulties connecting with other people, while their closeness often triggers the sense of danger. The paradox of this situation is that the contact is actually what people need the most in such a situation, while they are experiencing high levels of stress and fear. However, remembering too much as well as too little can hinder the ability of an individual to overcome stress and fear. On the contrary, it is hard to estimate how much remembrance is enough and how much forgetfulness is needed for individuals to become ready to reconcile and to overcome boundaries created by a difficult past.

Pros and cons of moral amnesia

Regardless of how much one wants to remember and/or to forget, the nature of traumatic experiences prevents the brain from creating a meaningful and coherent story. Such a neuroscientific explanation of memory distortion turns into an interesting paradox based on which it becomes quite normal and usual to change the content of our memories. However, some physical sensations in terms of smell and taste do not change over time (and Proust knew that a long time ago). Therefore, it would be quite unrealistic to expect that participants from Sarajevo and East Sarajevo would produce a history textbook-like narrative while describing events they found traumatic. If we take into account that such experiences have been transmitted to the younger generation (either directly from parents or by other means such as television, radio, school and the Internet), we can easily expect more or less similar non-coherent narratives from youngsters. However, in that case it is important to notice that the level of trauma in their case largely depends on their in-group membership and commitment. In terms of "remembering things past", the ability to communicate a traumatic narrative both within and outside one's group is an important contribution to the process of reconciliation and mutual dialogue, but also an important aspect of mental health and a meaningful, safe and satisfying life.

Van der Kolk (2015) notes that the ability to feel safe is probably one of the single most important aspects of mental health in trauma survivors; however, the most pernicious effect of trauma is that it disrupts the ability to accurately read and understand others, making the trauma survivor either less able to detect danger or more likely to misperceive danger where there is none. Hence, it is hard to expect people to talk and expose their largely incoherent narratives because of lack of trust and ability to understand the other side or, even more important, ability to anticipate how the other side would react. Even participants in the present research were very likely to ask not only about the purpose of interviews, but also about the background of the researcher (position, ethnicity, beliefs etc.). Regardless of how much they remembered (and, in this case, how much their narrative was distorted and around which specific themes that distortion had happened), their internal warning signals made them quite confused, uncomfortable and also vulnerable. In situations like this, people respond either by shutting down or by going into panic, which further leads to developing a fear of fear itself, according to van der Kolk (2015). That process explains why these floating narratives rarely (or almost never) get closer to each other – they are prevented by fear of the other side, fear of the unknown and fear of inability to anticipate the development of such a situation. As such, these narratives become even more distorted around eight main themes, but also through limited communication with in-group members. In this case, remembrance largely depends on a moral imperative posed by the in-group, without taking into account the opposite opinion. As happened between Sarajevans and East Sarajevans of both generational cohorts, they formed some opinion of the "other" side as well as of how the other side "thinks" about a particular case, and they (ab)used such claims to justify their own ("they do not want to talk to us", "they have already decided on this case as if it was set up by us", etc.). In this case, what is remembered and what is forgotten largely depends on what your group members expect you to say, just as a student from East Sarajevo noticed: "*I know that there are different stories on why Markale happened, but I chose this one because it is important to be patriot today".*

The floating narrative of one group defines the "route" its members are going to take (at least in most cases). One can conclude that Bosnia-Herzegovina is also a land of different (and difficult) floating narratives that, even though hardly communicated and followed by fear in most cases, still poison the idea of mutual dialogue, understanding and cooperation. According to Michael Ignatieff (1997), in the former Yugoslavia the past is not the ordinary past but continuous together with the present in a simultaneous order while at the same time it includes a lot of fantasies, dreams, lies and myths. Therefore, the wrongdoings committed in the past remain locked in the eternal present, looking for revenge. According to Martha Minow (1999, p. 430), the way we remember must not mistakenly produce narratives of collective guilt lying ready to be ignited by manipulative demagogues. However, the imperative to remember is forcing us to act in a certain way, which in most cases means adherence to the existing floating narrative, or, as David Rieff (2011) writes, to remember Auschwitz, Rwanda, Bosnia and other moral catastrophes is to remember how little remembering does to change who we are and what we are capable of.

Memory has lots of limitations, not only in its cognitive aspects, but in its social aspect as well. In Rieff's words (2011), our inability to forget can be actively dangerous, such as in the cases of Ireland, the United States, Australia and many others, where historical memory was sliced into slogans, battle cries and ideology. It happens because, at the end of the day, it is extremely hard to reconcile what every single group has remembered, experienced, retold and sensed. If someone follows Rieff's assumptions while considering Bosnia-Herzegovina as a mnemonic community full of different floating narratives, she/he must ask: *How much of such remembrance is enough? Should there be a certain line between remembrance and forgetting? Or, to put it the other way round, are we supposed to apply some sort of measure to get to know how much we are supposed to remember as opposed to how much we are supposed to forget?*

Considering the fact that remembrance never happens in a vacuum, and that different "measures" of a socially appropriate quantity do not exist in the way that measures exist in physics and chemistry, we cannot determine how much of remembrance is harmless. However, one can always follow the effects of memorializations that happen in a particular society and draw conclusions based on people's reactions to them. It is more than clear that memorializations matter to a lot of people. To the survivors, memorials and their accompanying commemorative activism provide feelings of a certain comfort, as their purpose is to demonstrate social empathy and solidarity, closeness and understanding. But the main purpose of these memorials is to address the therapeutic needs of their makers and to promote historical consciousness towards both individuals and communities. In the aftermath of violence, memorialization in a public space can help the process of healing and recovery, but also reconciliation if it is organized in a way to send the message that such things should never happen again. The idea of pedagogy of remembrance and memorialization arises from the basic need to understand the horrible consequences of the past events and to develop a certain moral framework for why something like that should never happen again. In order to do so, memorializations and memorials by themselves have to be organized in a way to engage and to force people to think and reason – something that differs from making people either sad or furious (without the ability to develop further opinions). Memorials and commemorations that rely on the emotional side only cannot contribute to the major idea – to teaching that the terrible acts committed in the past should never happen again – because they provoke only emotional reactions (positive, negative or even mixed). Such activation hinders the emergence of higher order processes such as thinking and reasoning; therefore, the ability of individuals and/or groups to process the information is highly limited. When we turn this into the idea of "moral amnesia" and a moral imperative to remember, we can assume that what matters is *how individuals and groups remember the difficult past and what they can learn (or have learnt) from such memories*. The way in which they form and communicate their narratives, the way in which they transmit those narratives and the way in which they elaborate further on such remembrance correspond to imperatives to understand and spread the important message – that such acts should never happen again.

"Remembrance for peace" – foundations and possibilities for *Gedenkstättenpädagogik*

It is not unusual that those who engaged in violent acts as well as those who are considered to be perpetrators usually avoid facing and dealing with the past. Such cases have been documented in South Africa, where following the end of apartheid, the former government and the security forces clamoured for a blanket or general amnesty (Tutu, 1999, p. 30). However, victims and their families can never accept the idea of either a surplus of remembrance or the need to forget, because for them remembrance is the only thing that matters.

According to Ernest Renan (1995, p. 145), "to forget and . . . to get one's history wrong are essential factors in the making of a nation". However, the interplay of remembering and forgetting is something that characterizes many post-conflict nations (including Bosnia-Herzegovina as well). Even though the past is remembered in a selective way, different floating narratives do not serve the groups who follow them, but the governing political mainstream that directs their flow. Therefore, the memory becomes the art of abusive political power that shapes it and then launches it in the public space in the form of a floating narrative designed for a particular group. While some level of forgetting can be desirable in order to control the level of empathy towards victims (or the so-called surplus of empathy towards the victim group that can be harmful towards, for instance, younger generations that belong to the perpetrator group), too much forgetting can lead to total erasure of past. The example of Rwanda presents some sort of "modified forgetting" which was applied for the sake of peaceful coexistence between members of the victim and perpetrator groups. While large numbers of Hutu convicted or suspected of involvement in the 1994 genocide have returned to their communities after being released from prison and therefore had nowhere else to go but to live together alongside the survivors of the genocide they had committed, both groups chose to deliberately forget certain facts and details from the difficult past (Buckley-Zistel, 2008). According to Susanne Buckley-Zistel (2008, 138), such "chosen amnesia is a necessity for local communities emerging from atrocities". Rosalind Shaw (2007, p. 196) discovered similar activities in Sierra Leone, where she has identified a process of "directed forgetting" as a response to the work of the Truth and Reconciliation Commission.

According to Janine Natalya Clark (2013), the major issue in post-conflict societies such as Rwanda and Croatia is not whether the past is remembered or forgotten, as these are two symbiotic and mutually reinforcing processes. This is certainly the case because forgetting, as much as remembering, is part of the reconstruction of history; therefore, the major issue is what exactly is remembered and what exactly is forgotten. Just as remembrance is under the influence of politics, memorials and commemorations will be under the same influence too. While there is a common belief that one can learn from the past only by remembering and that only by learning from the past can we try to ensure that history is not replayed, the "never again" rhetoric still provides an open floor for debates on memorials and commemorations (Clark, 2013). In that process, memorials are associated with the complex process of post-conflict reconciliation; however, "it still makes intuitive sense that people's memories of traumatic events . . . will continue to affect the social fabric in some perhaps intangible but nevertheless important way" (Sorabji, 2006, p. 1).

Nevertheless, memorials and commemorations are part of the construction and framing of society's collective memory and metanarrative. However, such memorials and commemorations can sometimes hinder the reconciliation process. Clark (2013) concluded that in the case of the Croatian town Vukovar, the erection of a joint memorial for fallen Croats and Serbs would be a good solution. Such a memorial is the Resistance Memorial in Bisesero, Kibuye, in western Rwanda. The idea to create it emerged in 1998 while there were still tensions between Hutu and Tutsi (Clark, 2013). However, its main idea of necessary co-habitation won, and that memorial is probably unique. However, in the Croatian town Vukovar, just as in Sarajevo and East Sarajevo, joint memorials still do not exist. The same resistance that Clark narrates in her research conducted in Vukovar was found in both Sarajevo and East Sarajevo, and while Croats in Vukovar were stating about Serbs that "they should apologise", a similar rhetoric was expressed by Bosniaks in Sarajevo towards Serbs from East Sarajevo, and (to a lesser extent) by Serbs from East Sarajevo towards Bosniaks from Sarajevo (and, in broader cases, towards Americans).

The examples of Vukovar and Sarajevo/East Sarajevo powerfully highlight selective remembrance and the fostering of collective floating narratives that emphasize the suffering of one ethnic group and promote a memory that members of one group can both rely on and use against the other group(s). According to Clark (2013), Vukovar's war memorials are a major contributing factor to the problems of both selective memory and excess memory; therefore, they represent a fundamental obstacle to reconciliation. A similar (if not identical) situation exists in Sarajevo and East Sarajevo, where in most cases streets were named after individuals who represented a hero for one group and an aggressor for the other. Unfortunately, more than 20 years after the wars in the Balkans, memorialization has evolved into an ethnopolitical instrument for nation-building and virtue signalling that represents a conspicuous expression of moral values and serves to keep the wounds open rather than to support reconciliation and the healing process (Touquet & Milošević, 2018). One way towards "remembrance for peace" is through peace education, promotion of shared moral values and integration in schools and among youth in general. Reconciliation by itself includes several components, a very influential one being the development of shared truths (Kriesberg, 2007). However, it is extremely hard to build such trust while groups tend to justify the wrongdoings committed by their own group members and to delegitimize the opponent. Only through dialogue can the opposing parties come to common ground and accept that there are more stories than one, and that history requires patience.

In post-war countries like Bosnia-Herzegovina, however, several different "truths" hinder the possibilities for dialogue, as well as possibilities for reconciliation. Serbs and Bosniaks disagree on who started the war, who should be considered a victim and who should be considered a perpetrator, whether it was a civil war or a planned and organized aggression etc. The narratives of Serbs from East Sarajevo in this research revealed their idea of Bosniaks starting the war (and/or provoking the international community) in

124   *Sins of memory*

order to get rid of Serbs in the city of Sarajevo. A similar counter-discourse was found in the Croatian town Vukovar, where according to the rival Serb narrative, the Croats started the war in a bid to rid Vukovar of its Serb population (Clark, 2013). One can conclude that not only divisive memorials and memorializators are to be blamed for this, but also the media, politicians and different victims' organizations ready to control, frame and distribute future floating narrative(s), together with the fact that memorials often display an exclusionary logic, which means that they are likely to have significant – if often neglected – societal implications. While reconciliation is, to reiterate, seldom an explicit goal of memorials, the creation of memorials and the collective memory that they embody can critically affect relationships within a society.

Yerushalmi (1996) said that one of the problems of contemporary society was that without some moral authority people no longer knew what needed to be remembered and what could be forgotten. In that case, both the surplus of remembrance and the surplus of forgetting hinder the reconciliation process as well as the establishment of memorials and memorialization activities that would lead to "remembrance for peace". Brett, Bickford, Sevcenko, and Rios (2007) defined memorialization as the process of creating a public memorial that corresponds to a physical representation of activities related to the events of the past which are in public spaces. Therefore, memorials can be considered necessary for people to cope with the past conflict(s). They also enable the process of marking the date of death as an act of respect for the casualties, which further contributes to social identification with the fallen in-group members, group cohesiveness and a sense of belonging (Cairns & Roe, 2003). Therefore, one of the major tasks in Bosnia-Herzegovina is to ensure the organization of memorials and commemorations in a way that is not offensive to any side and that allows the memorials to serve a pedagogical and educative function for current and future generations. In the process of transitional justice, a pedagogical function is attributed to memorials which is further reflected in education, stimulating an open and broad social dialogue about their role and importance, with the aim of respecting human rights and avoiding a repetition of the traumatic past (Brett et al. 2007). Until now there has been no legislation in Bosnia-Herzegovina that deals with the educational function of memorials as well as their role in the realization of transitional justice.

The term "memorial site pedagogics" is a literal translation of the German word *Gedenkstättenpädagogik* (*Gedenkstätte* means "memorial site" in German). According to Nicolas Berg (1996, p. 131), the German terms *Erinnerungskultur* and *Gedenkkultur* refer to a "culture of remembrance", which does not refer to the commemorations and memorials only but to all social individuals. A culture of remembrance outlines the past in general and is expressed by both individual and collective remembering, which includes commemoration of extermination sites. Therefore, a memorial site should be understood as a certain topographically specified place which is in Weber's point of view "anchored in a particular manner in memory" (Weber, 2008, p. 2). However, it should not be represented in memory only but in institutions, books, works of art and other cultural artefacts and historical dates (Weber, 2008). In such a way it will have the capacity to become a memory which survives over generations and helps us orientate while understanding intergroup relations, processes and identity formation. Thus, it may serve the purposes of education in the area of memorial pedagogy, which is in line with Nora's (1998) understanding of the function of memorial sites as a space where a memory site pedagogy develops (Kończyk, 2012). Drawing on a memory for traumatic events as something that is prone to distortions that largely depend on the position of the in-group, we can conclude that memorialization reflects a necessity to defend one's own group and a moral imperative to remember and mark atrocities committed towards one's group. According to Assman (1995), structural amnesia involves forgetting those elements of the past that are no longer meaningful in relation to the present. The choice of narrative in any situation depends on several factors; however, it is clear that there are several features that characterize the narratives of Sarajevans and East Sarajevans: omitting parts of the past, "distortion" of the past and the need to preserve the past (either in its original or a modified form). Due to the presence of different discourses on the past, but also different kinds of silence about the past, memorials and memorialization in Bosnia-Herzegovina still remain divisive political issues, not a place to meet and talk about the past. Therefore, talking about the establishment of "remembrance for peace" through a pedagogy of memorials and commemorations in contemporary Bosnia-Herzegovina is not an easy task. In a similar way, discussing the possibility of erecting joint memorials in Sarajevo, East Sarajevo and/or other towns still remains a sort of taboo. However, reconciliation is a longer process that includes lots of effort and cognitive restructuring. We do not always think of ourselves as those who either deliberately or intentionally interpret the past in a certain way, just as we do not think of ourselves doing something with little or no forethought. However, there are ways and methods for how to be vigilant and teach ourselves how to spot and prevent different types of biases and distortions. Even though it is a long-term process, change can be established through the educational system and promotion of "remembrance for peace", or so-called "peace education".

The historian Jay Winter (2013, p. 24) says that war belongs in "museum(s) because they have a semi-sacred aura. They are the repositories of the stories we tell ourselves about who we are and how we have come to be who and where we are". Apart from memorialization and the establishment of joint memorials, museums can keep the past in one form or another and, in other words, can pass it on to future generations. Such museums can function as "sites of persuasion" that may be enlisted "to build public and political support for equity, fairness and justice" (Sandell, 2012, p. 197). The education promoted through such museums (for example, the Kyoto Museum for World Peace, Gernika Peace Museum, Oslo Nobel Peace Center and War Childhood Museum in Sarajevo) serves the most important function that is the essence of "remembrance for peace": it teaches visitors that war and wrongdoings from any side should never happen again.

References

Assman, J. (1995). Collective memory and cultural identity. *New German Critique*, *65*, 125–133.

Berg, N. (1996). Auschwitz und die Geschichtswissenschaft- Ueberlegungen zu Kontroversen der letzten Jahre. In N. Berg, J. Jochimsen, & B. Stiegler (Eds.), *SHOAH. Formen der Erinnerung. Geschichte, Philosophie, Literatur, Kunst* (pp. 31–52). Munich: Wilhelm Fink Verlag.

Brett, S., Bickford, L., Sevcenko, L., & Rios, M. (2007). *Memorialization and democracy: State policy and civic action*. Chile: International Centre for Transitional Justice.

Buckley-Zistel, S. (2008). We are pretending peace: Local memory and the absence of social transformation in Rwanda. In P. Clark & Z. D. Kaufman (Eds.), *After genocide: Transitional justice, post-conflict reconstruction and reconciliation in Rwanda and beyond* (pp. 125–144). London: Hurst and Company.

Cairns, E., & Roe, M. D. (2003). *The role of memory in ethnic conflict*. New York, NY: Palgrave Macmillan.

Clark, J. N. (2013). Reconciliation through remembrance? War memorials and the victims of Vukovar. *The International Journal of Transitional Justice*, *7*, 116–135.

Herz, R., & Schooler, J. (2002). A naturalistic study of autobiographical memories evoked by olfactory and visual cues: Testing the Proustian hypothesis. *American Journal of Psychology*, *115*, 21–32.

Ignatieff, M. (1997). Articles of faith, index on censorship. The elusive goal of war trials, *Harper's*, 16–17.

Konczyik, L. (2012). The pedagogy of memory sites. *Journal of Education, Culture and Society*, *1*, 15–22.

Kriesberg, L. (2007). External contributions to post-mass-crime rehabilitation. In B. Pouligny, S. Chesterman, & A. Schnabel (Eds.), *After mass crime: Rebuilding states and communities* (pp. 243–271). Tokyo: United Nations University Press.

Lehrer, J. (2012). *Proust was a neuroscientist*. London: Canongate.

Minow, M. (1999). The work of re-membering: After genocide and mass atrocity. *Fordham International Law Journal*, *23*(2), 429–439.

Nietzsche, F. (1983). *Untimely meditations* (R. J. Hollingdal, Trans.). London: Cambridge University Press.

Nora, P. (1998). La aventura de Les lieux de mémoire. In: J. Cuesta Bustillo (Eds.), *Memoria e Historia* issue 32 (pp. 17–34). Madrid: Marcial Pons.

Proust, M. (1998). *Swann's way* (Vol. 1). New York, NY: Modern Library.

Renan, E. (1995). What is a nation? In O. Dahbour & M. R. Isray (Eds.), *The nationalism reader* (pp. 143–156). Atlantic Highlands, NJ: Humanities Press.

Rieff, D. (2011). *Against remembrance*. Melbourne: Melbourne University Press.

Sandell, R. (2012). Museums and the human rights frame. In R. Sandell & E. Nightingale (Eds.), *Museums, equality and social justice* (pp. 195–216). London: Routledge.

Shaw, R. (2007). Memory frictions: Localizing the truth and reconciliation commission in Sierra Leone. *International Journal of Transitional Justice, 1*(2), 183–207.

Sorabji, C. (2006). Managing memories in post-war Sarajevo: Individuals, bad memories and new wars. *Journal of the Royal Anthropological Institute, 12*(1), 1–18.

Touquet, H., & Milošević, A. (2018). When reconciliation becomes the r-word: Dealing with the past in former Yugoslavia. In B. Krondorfer (Ed.), *Reconciliation in global context: Why it is needed and how it works* (pp. 179–199). New York, NY: CUNY.

Tutu, D. (1999). *No future without forgiveness*. London: Rider.

van der Kolk, B. (2015). *The body keeps the score: Brain, mind and body in the healing of trauma*. New York, NY: Penguin Books.

Weber, M. (2008). *On the topic of the conference "Sites of Memory in Central Europe – Experiences of the Past and Perspectives"*. Retrieved November 12, 2014 from http://enrs.eu/images/Teksty%20pdf%20ang/Weber_ang.pdf

Winter, J. (2013). Museums and the representation of war. In W. Muchitsch (Ed.), *Does war belong in museums? The representation of violence in exhibitions* (pp. 9–12). Bielefeld: Transcript Verlag.

Yerushalmi, Y. (1996). *Zakhor: Jewish history and Jewish memory*. Seattle, WA: University of Washington Press.

Zembylas, M., & Bekerman, Z. (2008). Education and the dangerous memories of historical trauma: Narratives of pain, narratives of hope. *Curriculum Inquiry, 38*(2), 125–154.

4 Memory and remembrance in divided Bosnia-Herzegovina between a "labour in vain" and perspective taking

In this chapter remembrance of the traumatic and difficult past in Bosnia-Herzegovina will be analyzed in line with contemporary social and cognitive theories of memory in order to determine the importance of empathy development for a further reconciliation process. Also, the logic behind the establishment of "remembrance for peace" will be explored based on the impact museums can have on the development of historical consciousness and experiential learning. The case study of the War Childhood Museum in Sarajevo will be provided in order to ensure deeper understanding of connections between perspective taking, empathy and development of historical consciousness.

Re-positioning of the victim-perpetrator narrative

One can say that research on divided memories in Bosnia-Herzegovina has a long history, but a relatively small number of concrete healing and/or reconciliation programmes have resulted from scholarly work. However, mental health professionals, including psychologists, are doing their best to ensure healing and therapy for those in need – those who suffer from various types of war trauma and/or post-traumatic stress disorder. However, it is not that easy to provide such assistance with scarce resources. The purpose of the research presented in this book is not to provide an instant solution for such situations; however, its purpose is to enlighten the necessity to hear and discuss different angles of the story even in situations when we find it very emotional and disturbing.

Re-positioning the victim and perpetrator categories and giving everyone the opportunity to tell his/her side of the story opens up different wounds, biases and opinions; however, it enables those ready to talk to go through the narrative once again and analyze the ways through which it was formed (even when they are convinced that there is only one correct story). The term "narrative" itself describes how people structure episodes in personal memory for the purpose of thinking about oneself in silent remembering and communicating with others to tell the events of the past (Sarbin, 1986). According to Kraft (2006), the elements of episodic memory (memory that includes recollections of our everyday activities) and the episodes themselves are formed of two separate levels of memorial representation: core memory and narrative memory. While core memory represents the original phenomenal experience in the form of perceptual, emotional and physiological experience and includes visual images, sounds, smells, tastes, emotions and bodily sensations (both explicit and implicit), narrative memory is constructed from the images in core memory, shaped in accordance with narrative conventions, and conveyed primarily in language (Kraft, 2004, 2006). It is important to understand this division between narrative and core memory as described by Kraft as both of these elements are included in the formation of difficult narratives of the past (and ways in which individuals and societies remember traumatic events from their past). The formation of difficult narratives of conflict includes several factors: core memory, which is prone to memory errors; and narrative memory, which includes (implicit) stereotypes, (implicit) prejudice, memory sins, transgenerational transmission, the ethos of conflict, (chosen) trauma and group belonging (group glorification and attachment). Such narratives are further maintained through transgenerational transmission in the family, and an existing *zeitgeist*, which includes school, peers, media and dominant politics.

While core memory is prone to memory sins, described by Schacter (2001) as transience, absent-mindedness, blocking, suggestibility, bias, persistency and misattribution, narrative memory consists of and reveals (implicit) stereotypes, (implicit) prejudice, memory sins, transgenerational transmission, ethos of conflict and (chosen) trauma together. The way in which an individual perceives conflict is highly influenced by her/his memory, while at the same time the sense of group belonging, group superiority and attachment influence to what extent conflict will be perceived as an identity threat. The narrative of conflict will be formed around one of the eight themes of conflict given by Bar-Tal (2011): goals, security, delegitimization, self-image, victimization, patriotism, unity and peace. Therefore, individual narratives will correspond to the dominant group narrative and reflect the sense of group glorification and attachment. Formed in such a way, dominant narratives accepted widely by members of one group will be maintained and become stronger. As such, they will have the potential to develop fully into floating narratives – the narratives one group is moving ("floating") on.

Floating narratives and their transmission

In contemporary Bosnia-Herzegovina floating narratives are maintained through transgenerational transmission in the family and through external factors in society such as schools and the educational system (history classes particularly), peers, the media, dominant politics and the general *zeitgeist*. Such narratives are kept within a core memory reservoir and reflected in the narrative memory of both individuals and groups. One can say that there is a circle between an individual's core and narrative memory, the dominant floating narrative and an ethos of conflict. When analyzed in such a way, those subjects reveal the extent to which they can hinder the reconciliation process and contribute to the selective remembering of in-group wrongdoings. The necessary change of scope can only begin with the intersection of individual and collective memory, and with special emphasis on the difference between core and narrative memory. It is especially important to analyze the ways in which the eight themes of conflict narrative occur (especially within family and school) in order to mediate changes in belief related to the justness of conflict goals, delegitimization of the opponent, feelings of victimhood and notions of peace. Specifically, the beliefs about contradictory goals have to be changed in order to remove the epistemic foundations of the conflict (Bar-Tal, 2000). There is a need to develop new goals and justifications for the need to resolve the conflict peacefully and live in peace with the past enemy as well as to legitimize the construction of the new relations and begin to construct a new image for the peace partner (Bar-Tal, 2000). Legitimization and personalization of the past rival-enemy should be achieved. The new beliefs should also recognize the "contribution" of one's own group to the outbreak of the conflict and its extension, and the misdeeds of one's own group in the course of the conflict, including the responsibility for various atrocities, if committed (Bar-Tal, 2013). The described changes are supposed to reduce the monopolization of feelings of victimhood, which characterizes groups in intractable conflict. In the case of Bosnia-Herzegovina a huge emphasis should be placed on both primary and secondary school education, since different approaches to history, literature and art necessarily lead to deeper division. With regard to that, special emphasis should be given to different methods of transmitting knowledge in schools, using different sources and experiential learning ("learning by doing" that includes different methods, for example, debates during history classes, in-situ learning, bringing survivors to the class, visits to museums of war crimes etc.). It is important to connect schools to other institutions and organizations that can provide more distinctive classes directed towards the problematic past.

One of the major problems related to the remembrance of the difficult past was explored in the previous chapter and related to the "ethics" of remembrance: how much we are allowed to forget, and how much we are allowed to remember. This debate influences the school system especially, because history, geography, literature and art classes are among those that can "bring" both positive and negative memories to the surface (and those memories are polarized in different ways depending on one's in-group belonging, of course). The debate is not just about whether children should be taught to remember the past, but also about how the past is interpreted (Streich, 2002). In Bosnia-Herzegovina that is still a big question that cannot be easily resolved (given the divided teaching curricula and, in some circumstances, ethnically divided schools). The issue is not whether forgetting is a "labour in vain" or something desirable in history classes. Forgetting does not imply amnesia but rather the question whether educators can use past historical traumas to re-socialize children in a manner that is not locked into predefined scripts and collective memories (Hill, 2000).

Development of empathy in "memory prisons"

Both interpretations of a difficult past and its distortions are socially conditioned. In both cases, they can lead to the formation of dangerous memories that, once formed in the younger generation particularly, can lead them being jailed in "memory prisons" (Margalit, 2002), with the small possibilities of becoming guardians of the traumatic stories (Laub, 1992). Following (Conway, 2005), one can understand how descendants of victims of trauma construct a system that combines their working self with conceptual knowledge about these social traumas. It is very important to emphasize that the self is a combination of values, schemas, beliefs and attitudes, some of them built through interaction with the environment. Psychosocial research has shown (e.g., Albeck, Adwan, & Bar-On, 2002) that using personal narratives can help move Germans and Jews, and Israelis and Palestinians, closer to reconciliation, especially when these narratives take place in a "safe space" that encourages active listening and honest dialogue and reflection (Chaitin & Steinberg, 2014). The main aspect of a "safe environment" lies in the development of perspective taking skills and empathy, both of which are crucial for our ability to listen to the narratives of other persons and to try to understand – not judge or argue in the first place. Chaitin and Steinberg (2014) argue that the descendants of the war trauma survivors hold images and "memories" in their heads, and feel them in their hearts and bodies. They do not find such memories to be purely transgenerationally transmitted recollections of their parents, but the second generation's understandings of "what has happened". By turning to the second generation and their "my-their" memories, we can gain insight into the ways in which we are living connections (Hoffman, 2004) to the traumatic past. These understandings can further be used for repairing intergroup broken relations and developing peacebuilding programmes ("remembrance for peace" being one of them). Such a pedagogy of dangerous memories can help us understand our own suffering, but can also force us to start thinking about the position of other people in the same situation. Perspective taking, as such, becomes the precondition to empathy development.

The English word "empathy" is derived from the Greek word "empatheia", which implies physical attraction or passion. This term was accepted by Herman Lotze and Robert Vischer when they coined the German word "Einfühlung", translated by psychologist Edward Titchener in 1909 as "empathy". Empathy can be defined as the ability of a person to recognize and share the emotions of another person or fictional character. This implies, above all, an attempt to see the situation of the other person from his/her perspective, as well as the ability to enjoy the emotional world of another person.

There are two kinds of empathy: emotional and cognitive. Emotional empathy, also called affective empathy or primitive empathy, is a subjective condition that is the result of an emotional infection. This is our automatic urge to react in a certain way. This type of empathy occurs automatically, and often unconsciously. Cognitive empathy is largely aware of the reaction in order to accurately recognize and share the emotional state of another person. It is also known as "perspective taking".

The cognitive and affective dimension of empathy was used as the basis for the conception of the new concept of historical empathy. Historical empathy highlights the interaction of the cognitive and affective dimensions of empathy and as such is the basis for understanding the processes through which learning history through textbooks and museums influences a change of consciousness about particular events. The way in which the concept of historical empathy is developed through the methodology of history teaching, focussing on the dialogue between teaching about historical characters and facts as well as reconstructing the evidence-based perspective provides a useful operationalization for the analysis of these cognitive and affective dimensions (Savenije & de Bruijn, 2017, p. 833).

Since it has been developed through the methodology of teaching history, the concept of historical empathy implies a perspective that the individual takes up through knowledge and understanding of the broader historical concepts, the actors in these actions, as well as the motives, beliefs and emotions that led them (Endacott & Brooks, 2013). It is believed that historical empathy should be developed through the teaching of history in order to bring events and situations closer to students from different perspectives and enable them to develop abstract thinking. Also, the ability of historical empathy needs to begin to develop in students through the teaching of history at the earliest ages, since the concept itself implies taking the perspective of actors from the past. As it is difficult to take the perspective of an alien and understand his/her emotions, the process of taking the perspective of historical personalities from the past is much more difficult.

When it comes to the teaching of history, the notion of empathy can be related to fantasy and literary fiction. Some scientists have argued that empathy is necessary only based on true historical narratives and facts (Lee & Ashby, 1987). Such a case again leads to the problem of equating conflicting narratives and finding a true narrative. In recent years, emphasis has been placed on linking the affective and cognitive components of empathy, whereby the affective involves providing an answer to the consequences that events had in the past or in the present (Barton & Levstik, 2004).

Such a perspective is consistent with the results of psychological research according to which the cognitive and affective aspects of empathy are mutually dependent, and the very definition of empathy is reduced to the process of understanding and the emotional response to the thoughts and feelings of another person (Hoffman, 1984). Also, this perspective is in line with research in the field of museology that suggests a mutual relationship between reason and emotions and the fact that emotional responses shaped by our culture should be emphasized (Watson, 2015). Smith (2011) considered that in this way visitors to the museum with different profiles and different ideologies approach each other and share their perceptions, beliefs and emotions.

Although our empathy is inherent, we are not all capable of feeling it. However, research has shown how empathy can be learnt through contact with people and events they can transmit, and as such this is the first step towards breaking prejudices. In this process, museums play a key role as they are equipped in a unique way that encourages visitors to imagine, explore and feel a rich human heritage. As such, museums have the ability to connect art, technology, science and literature and show the way in which all human beings are interconnected. They can also complement the need for empathy in the daily life of an individual.

According to Elif Gokcigdem (2016), museums and the programmes they provide encourage the development of empathy in the following ways:

- the education and design of programmes focussed on raising awareness about people, places and objects of research that are beyond our usual experience;
- experiential learning in order to increase emotional involvement towards the presented contents;
- communicating and practising empathy as a key institutional value.

Museums thus encourage the development of empathy for both adults and children, and hence the concept of the War Museum of the World is an ideal place for raising awareness of the past as told through children's stories. Gokcigdem (2016) has developed her own model by which she explains the ways in which museums can contribute to connecting with the past and developing empathy. Her model can be applied to different museums that promote peace and reconciliation in the world; however, the relatively newly opened War Childhood Museum in Sarajevo serves as a good example because, unlike other war museums, it documents the experiences of those who were not directly engaged in the war, but still suffered multiple consequences. The museum consists of the recollection of stories, objects and personal belongings of people who spent their childhood in war. At the very beginning the collection was related to Bosnia-Herzegovina only; however, later they started collecting stories and objects from children from Syria and Ukraine. Children's stories are particularly important because they have specific potential to develop and provoke empathy, which further leads to mutual understanding, which is essential for the reconciliation process. Therefore, this museum will be used as a case study to understand the schema that proposes development of empathy and historical consciousness in younger generations through their exposure to materials that require perspective taking. Schema 4.1 was developed on the basis of the Elif Gokcigdem model when applied to the case of the War Childhood Museum in Sarajevo.

Through its social and educational mission, the Museum of War Childhood provides a safe place for meetings of different perspectives, knowledge, complex histories and values. Since visitors are placed in close proximity to real children's experiences, the museum opens up various realities and perspectives around the visitors themselves. The moment the current collection includes stories from children from different geographic areas, it will come to an authentic dialogue with the Other – one that is very distant and different, but at the same time divides our space. In this way, the Museum of War Childhood poses a challenge to prejudices and stereotypes and increases the empathy of visitors.

Each individual is characterized by the ability to retain information in the form of a story. The same contents can be recalled later, with the significance and emotional colour changed to a lesser or greater extent. Research has shown that the storytelling method (used by the War Childhood Museum when collecting video records) stimulates the development of empathy and helps us to connect emotionally even with people with whom we do not share everyday life (Gokcigdem, 2016). Also, a well-designed layout of the exhibits creates the impression of a visual testimony to the story, since beside each exhibited object, the owner's short "history" is written. This

power!), or after one history class. At this stage, perspective taking, empathy and understanding are three components that have to be developed and nurtured in younger generations, those who have never experienced war themselves. Experiential learning – "learning by doing" – can help them start perceiving the world in different frameworks and options. In contemporary Bosnia-Herzegovina, remembrance represents a "labour in vain" as individuals are imprisoned in their floating narratives that are moving around endlessly while not giving the opportunity to meet the other floating figures. Encounters in a safe space (like the War Childhood Museum, in this case) can help them both meet narratives they never heard of before and expose themselves to different perspectives and opinions.

References

Albeck, J. H., Adwan, S., & Bar-On, D. (2002). Dialogue groups: TRT's guidelines for working through intractable conflicts by personal storytelling in encounter groups. *Peace and Conflict Journal of Peace Psychology, 8*, 301–322.

Bar-Tal, D. (2000). *Shared beliefs in a society: Social psychological analysis*. Thousand Oaks, CA: Sage.

Bar-Tal, D. (Ed.). (2011). *Intergroup conflicts and their resolution: Social psychological perspective*. New York, NY: Psychology Press.

Bar-Tal, D. (2013). *Intractable conflicts: Socio-psychological foundations and dynamics*. Cambridge: Cambridge University Press.

Barton, K. C., & Levstik, L. S. (2004). *Teaching history for the common good*. Mahwah, NJ: Lawrence Erlbaum.

Chaitin, J., & Steinberg, S. (2014). "I can almost remember it now": Between personal and collective memories of massive social trauma. *Journal of Adult Development, 21*, 30–42.

Conway, M. A. (2005). Memory and the self. *Journal of Memory and Language, 53*, 594–628.

Endacott, J., & Brooks, S. (2013). An updated theoretical and practical model for promoting historical empathy. *Social Studies Research and Practice, 8*(1), 41–58.

Gokcigdem, E. (2016). *Fostering empathy through museums*. London: Rowman & Littlefield Publishers.

Hill, J. (2000). *Becoming a cosmopolitan: What it means to be a human in the new millennium*. Lanham, MD: Rowman & Littlefield.

Hoffman, E. (2004). *After such knowledge: Memory, history, and the legacy of the Holocaust*. New York, NY: Public Affairs.

Hoffman, M. (1984). Interaction of affect and cognition in empathy. In C. Izard, J. Kagan, & R. Zajonc (Eds.), *Emotions, cognitions and behavior* (pp. 103–131). Cambridge: Cambridge University Press.

Kraft, R. N. (2004). Emotional memory in survivors of the Bielefeld: A qualitative study of oral testimony. In D. Reisberg & P. Hertel (Eds.), *Memory and emotion* (pp. 347–389). New York, NY: Oxford University Press.

Kraft, R. N. (2006). Archival memory: Representations of the holocaust in oral testimony. *Poetics Today, 27*(2), 311–330.

Laub, D. (1992). Bearing witness or the vicissitudes of listening. In S. Felman & D. Laub (Eds.), *Testimony, crises of witnessing in literature, psychoanalysis and history* (pp. 57–74). New York, NY: Routledge.

Lee, P., & Ashby, R. (1987). Children's concepts of empathy and understanding in history. In C. Portal (Ed.), *The history curriculum for teachers* (pp. 62–88). London: Falmer.

Margalit, A. (2002). *The ethics of memory.* Cambridge, MA: Harvard University Press.

Sarbin, T. R. (1986). The narrative as a root metaphor for psychology. In T. R. Sarbin (Ed.), *Narrative psychology: The storied nature of human conduct* (pp. 3–21). Westport, CT: Praeger Publishers/Greenwood Publishing Group.

Savenije, G. M., & de Bruijn, P. (2017). Historical empathy in a museum: Uniting contextualisation and emotional engagement. *International Journal of Heritage Studies, 23*(9), 832–845.

Schacter, D. (2001). *The seven sins of memory: How the mind forgets and remembers.* New York, NY: Houghton-Mifflin.

Smith, L. (2011). Affect and registers of engagement: Navigating emotional responses to dissonant heritages. In L. Smith, G. Cubitt, K. Fouseki, & R. Wilson (Eds.), *Representing enslavement and abolition in museums: Ambiguous engagements* (pp. 260–303). New York, NY: Routledge.

Streich, G. (2002). Is there a right to forget? Historical injustices, race, memory, and identity. *New Political Science, 24*, 525–542.

Watson, S. (2015). Emotions in the history museum. In A. Witcomb & K. Message (Eds.), *The International handbooks of museum studies* (Vol. 11, pp. 283–301). Milton, NJ: John Wiley & Sons.

Index

120, 122–126; autobiographical
100; collective 15–20, 22, 24, 31,
110, 112, 122, 124; constructed
7; distortion 118; errors 31–32;
historical 120; long-term 117;
"my-their" 102; reconstructed 102;
selective 123; sins of 30–31, 115;
site of 9; situationally accessible 100;
verbally accessible 100
mnemonic: community 120;
consensus 107; mechanisms 107;
representations 107
mnene vii, 15
Moll, N. 8–11, 14
museum 126–128, 132–138; Gernika
Peace 126; Kyoto Museum for World
Peace 126; Oslo Nobel Peace Center
126; War Childhood Museum in
Sarajevo 126, 128, 134, 136–137; of
war crimes 130
Muslim *see* Bosnian Muslim

narrative i, viii, 9, 16, 20–21,
23–34, 26–27, 31–32, 58, 83,
89–90, 99, 101–102, 104–105,
108, 111, 113, 117–121, 123–125,
127–130, 135–136, 138; analysis
30–31, 33; coherent 100–102,
108, 117–119; collective viii, 19,
90, 99; conflict 30; dominant 23,
90, 129; emotionally saturated 89,
99; fragmented 100; group 17;
historical 20, 117, 133; incoherence
89; incoherent 119; individual 90,
117, 129; metanarrative 22, 122;
multi-perspective 109; selective 20;
structured 89, 100; traumatic 31, 33,
89, 99–100, 119; unconscious 19; *see
also* conflicting narrative; conflict-
related narrative; conflict-supporting
narrative; floating narrative
nationalism 18, 127
NATO *see* NATO bombing
Nets-Zehngut, R. 23, 113
Nietzsche, F. 116, 126

Olympic Games 1, 10–11, 14; 1984
Winter 7
Orthodox 2, 28

Ottoman Empire vii, 1, 3
Ottomans 1

patriotism 18, 22, 32, 129
peace viii, 5, 8, 12, 22, 32, 95, 98,
110; education 123, 125; General
Framework for 12; remembrance for
23, 121, 123–126
perpetrator i, iii, 18, 20–21, 23, 114,
121–123, 128
phenomenological characteristics of
memories 24, 30–31
politics 1, 113, 122; dominant 129–130
prejudice 15, 108, 129, 133–135;
implicit 118, 129
Proust, M. 115, 117–118, 126–127;
hypothesis 126; madeleine 115

reconciliation i, viii, ix, x, 5, 12, 13, 15,
21, 22, 99–100, 105, 112, 113–117,
119, 121–128, 130–131, 134, 136;
readiness for i, viii, 24, 26, 33; scale
29–30, 84–88
religion 1–3
remembrance vii, 15–16, 22, 24, 110,
112, 115–116, 118–122, 126–128,
131, 137; culture of 124; ethics of
131; for peace 23, 121, 123–126,
128, 132, 135; pedagogy of 121;
selective 123; surplus of 115, 121,
124; terror of vii, 115
Republic of Srpska 5, 10–12, 22,
89–90, 103–104, 109, 116; *see also*
Army of the Republic of Srpska
responsibility 93, 111, 130; in-group 18
Rieff, D. 120, 127
Roe, M. 124, 126

Sarajevo i, vii, viii, x, 1–14, 22–24,
27–29, 90–101, 103, 112, 114–119,
123–128, 134; Bosniak from 34–89,
123; Winter Olympics 8–11
Schacter, D. 15, 24, 30–33, 113, 129, 138
security 22, 31, 91, 114, 121, 129
Serb: from East Sarajevo 34–89,
99–100; from Sarajevo 34–89,
99–100
Siege: of Sarajevo 15, 22
sins of commission 32

Tor ohr

Redaktion: Jacqueline Tschiesche
Projektleitung und Graphik: Nadia Maestri
Computerlayout: Simona Corniola
Bildbeschaffung: Laura Lagomarsino

© 2006 Cideb

Erstausgabe: Mai 2006

Fotonachweis:
© Gilles Peress/Magnum: S. 26; © picture-alliance/dpa S. 56;
© InterCultura S. 86; © picture-alliance/dpa S. 87; © Troy
Wayrynen/Columbian/NewSport/Corbis: S. 89.

Wir würden uns freuen, von Ihnen zu erfahren, ob Ihnen
dieses Buch gefallen hat. Wenn Sie uns Ihre Eindrücke mittei-
len oder Verbesserungsvorschläge machen möchten, oder
wenn Sie Informationen über unsere Verlagsproduktion wün-
schen, schreiben Sie bitte an:
info@blackcat-cideb.com
blackcat-cideb.com

CISQ CISQ CERT
TEXTBOOKS AND
TEACHING MATERIALS
The quality of the publisher's
design, production and sales processes has
been certified to the standard of
UNI EN ISO 9001

ISBN 978-88-530-0592-2 Buch + CD

Gedruckt in Genua, Italien, bei Litoprint

Inhalt

ÜBUNGEN   12, 23, 33, 42, 51, 6...

INTERNETPROJEKT

ABSCHLUSSTEST

KLEINES FUSSBALLGLOSSAR

Die CD enthält den vollständigen Text.

 Das Symbol kennzeichnet den Anfang der ...

4

Auftakt

1 Schau dir diese zwei Bilder und das Wortmaterial an. Du brauchst es, um die Erzählung zu verstehen. Auch das Glossar auf S. 96 hilft dir.

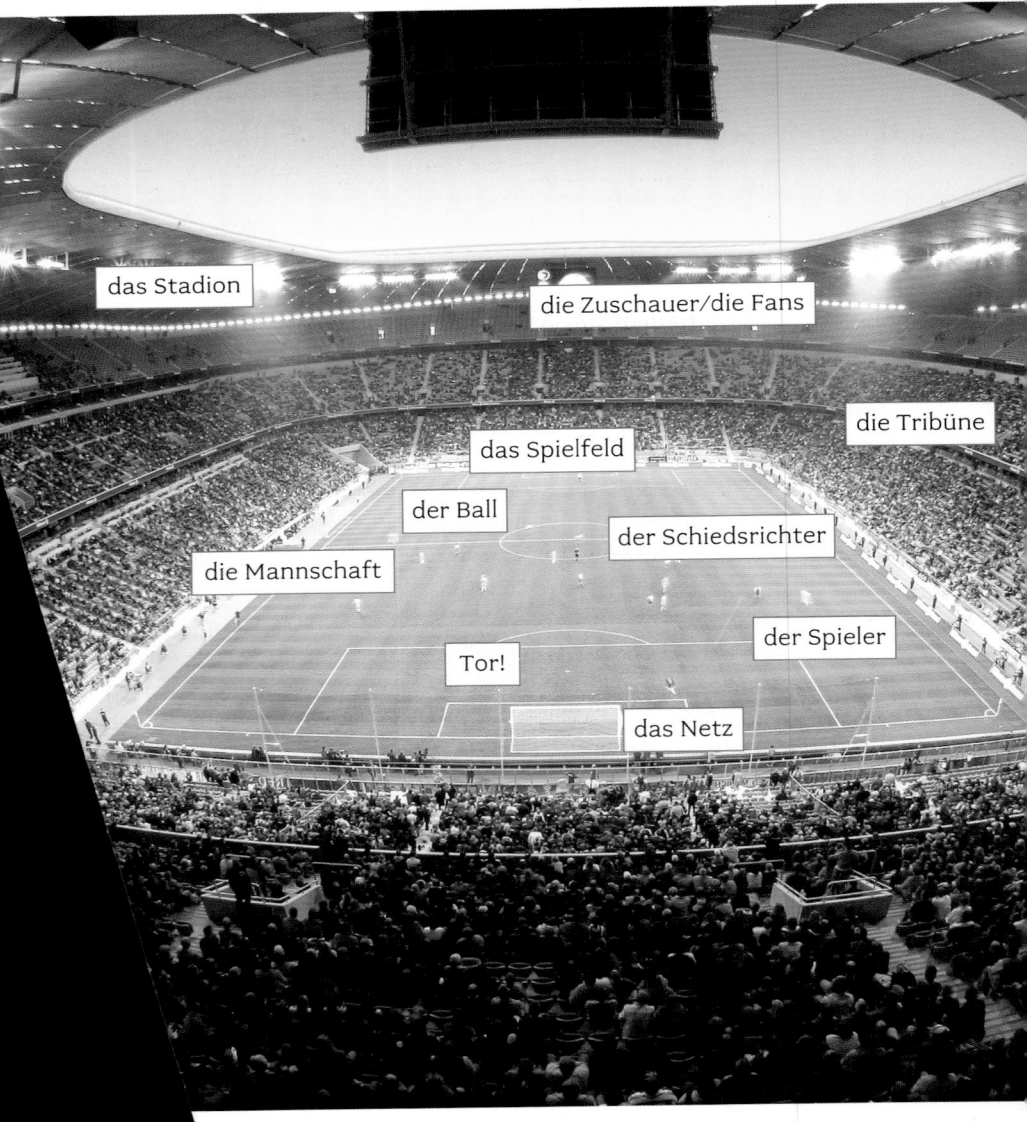

das Stadion

die Zuschauer/die Fans

die Tribüne

das Spielfeld

der Ball

der Schiedsrichter

die Mannschaft

der Spieler

Tor!

das Netz

2 Welche Wörter sind in deiner Sprache ähnlich?

3 Wie sagt man das in deiner Sprache?

    a die Mannschaft: ....

    b der Schiedsrichter: ....

    c das Stadion: ....

    d der Stürmer: ....

    e Tor!: ....

    f das Tor: ....

    g der Torwart: ....

4 Kennst du einige Namen von deutschsprachigen Fußballspielern?

Und hier die drei wichtigsten Spielfeldpositionen:

Angriff, Mittelfeld und Verteidigung

Lieber Juan

Hier wohne ich jetzt. Die Stadt heißt Gelsenkirchen und liegt im Westen von Deutschland, im Ruhrgebiet. Sie ist nicht groß, aber die Leute sind reich und alles ist sehr sauber. Viel reicher und sauberer als bei uns in Havanna. Alles ist ganz anders hier. Es ist August, aber es ist kalt. Es regnet heute, und auch gestern hat es geregnet. Die Sonne scheint nicht oft hier. In Kuba war es schöner, mit dir und mit unseren Freunden. Ich kenne noch niemanden. Morgen fängt die Schule an.
Ich schreibe dir bald wieder. Viele Grüße an alle.
Pedro

Pedro liest die E-Mail noch einmal durch und klickt auf ‚Senden'. Dann steht er auf und geht zur Kasse des Internetcafés. Ein Junge sitzt dort und langweilt sich.

„Nochmals vielen Dank", sagt Pedro. „Ohne deine Hilfe ..."

Pedro hat heute die erste E-Mail seines Lebens geschrieben. Der Junge hat ihm erklärt, wie es geht.

„Funktioniert doch", sagt der Junge. „Du hast es schnell gelernt. Die anderen Ausländer kapieren das nie."

Richtig, die Ausländer!

Tor ohne Grenzen

„Hier bin ich Ausländer", denkt Pedro. Das ist noch neu für ihn. Er spricht noch nicht gut Deutsch, hat einen starken spanischen Akzent. Er versteht nur schlecht, was die Leute sagen.

In Kuba hat sein Vater ihm immer wieder gesagt:

„Du musst Deutsch lernen. Du weißt doch, in Deutschland spricht niemand Spanisch."

Er hat es auch versucht. Aber es ist schwer. Ganz anders als Spanisch.

„Ich muss besser Deutsch sprechen", denkt Pedro.

Pedro geht nach Hause.

Es ist eine sehr lange Straße. Sie geht durchs Stadtzentrum und da dürfen fast keine Autos fahren. Fußgängerzone heißt das. Es gibt Geschäfte dort und Kaufhäuser, viele Geschäfte, eins neben dem anderen, und viele Kaufhäuser. Pedro sieht die Leute an den Imbissbuden[1] und in den Bäckereien stehen.

„Sie essen die ganze Zeit", denkt er. Hamburger, Currywurst mit Pommes, Döner Kebab, Pizza.

Pedro kriegt Hunger. Er hat drei Euro in der Tasche. Ein Brötchen oder ein Stück Pizza … ? Er kauft nichts.

„Zu Hause gibt es jetzt Abendessen", denkt er. „Und Mama wird böse, wenn ich nichts esse."

Er will sein Geld ja auch nicht zum Fenster hinauswerfen[2].

Sein Vater und seine Mutter arbeiten beide. Vater hat eine Arbeit in einer Fabrik gefunden und Mutter putzt morgens bei einer deutschen Familie. Sie verdienen nicht wenig, aber sie schicken Geld nach Kuba und Pedro hat auch noch zwei jüngere Geschwister.

---

1. **e Imbissbude (n)**: Wurst und Pommes Frites isst man da.
2. **s Geld zum Fenster hinauswerfen**: zu schnell zu viel Geld ausgeben.

Sie wohnen im neunten Stock eines zwölfstöckigen Hauses. Die Wohnung ist ok: ein Schlaf- und ein Kinderzimmer, ein kleines Wohnzimmer, Küche und Bad. Pedro gefällt es dort nicht, denn die Wohnung hat nicht einmal einen Balkon, nur kleine Fenster. In Kuba haben sie in einem kleinen Haus mit Garten gewohnt und die Kinder haben den ganzen Tag draußen gespielt.

Seiner Mutter hat er das gesagt. Da ist sie sehr böse geworden.

„Pedro! Unser Haus in Kuba war eine Hütte! Die Toilette war draußen im Garten und die Küche war klein und schmutzig! Sieh doch nur, wie schön unsere Wohnung jetzt ist!"

Die Familie sitzt schon beim Abendessen.

„Wo kommst du denn jetzt her?" fragt der Vater. „Wir haben auf dich gewartet!"

„'Tschuldigung", sagt Pedro „Ich war im Internetcafé und habe Juan eine E-Mail geschickt."

Pedros kleine Geschwister sitzen am Tisch und reden laut miteinander. Das tun sie immer.

„Morgen beginnt die Schule", sagt der Vater. „Freust du dich?"

„Weiß nicht."

„So lernst endlich andere Jungen kennen."

„Meinst du?"

„Am Anfang ist es für alle schwer, mit der Zeit ..."

„Vielleicht", antwortet Pedro.

Er will nicht mit seinem Vater sprechen.

Er will gar nicht sprechen.

Nach dem Essen steht er sofort auf und geht ins Wohnzimmer. Er macht den Fernseher an. Deutsch, Deutsch und immer wieder Deutsch. Er kann es nicht mehr hören.

Tor ohne Grenzen

„Was willst du denn?" sagt er zu sich selbst. „Wir sind hier in Deutschland. Wie sollen sie denn sonst sprechen? Portugiesisch?"

Es gibt einen Krimi. Das versteht er, aber er versteht nur wenig von dem, was die Leute sagen. Und jetzt kommen auch noch seine kleinen Geschwister ins Zimmer. Sie wollen schon wieder den Kinderkanal sehen. Sie verstehen zwar auch kaum etwas, aber das stört sie nicht.

Sie lachen die ganze Zeit.

Pedro steht auf und geht ans Fenster. Es ist acht Uhr. Es ist noch hell draußen und es regnet nicht mehr.

Vor dem Haus gibt es einen großen Parkplatz. Dahinter liegt ein Fußballplatz. Er ist nicht groß. Gerade richtig zum Trainieren.

Pedro sieht sich über den Platz laufen.

Da läuft er, unser Mittelstürmer [1] *Pedro Vaseros, sein Gegenspieler will ihn stoppen, aber Pedro läuft weiter, ein Schuss und ... Tooor!*

Pedro lächelt.

Wie gern möchte er jetzt mit seinen Freunden Fußball [2] spielen! Aber die sind weit weg.

Da hat er eine Idee. Er holt den Ball aus seinem Zimmer.

Die anderen sitzen immer noch vor dem Fernseher.

„Ich geh noch auf den Fußballplatz [3]!" ruft er ins Wohnzimmer.

Draußen ist es kühl.

Das ist ihm egal.

Er läuft über das Feld, das Tor vor sich.

1.-3. siehe S. 96.

10

Textverständnis

1 Pedro, der Protagonist. Was weißt du über ihn?

a   Er kommt aus ....

b   Er wohnt in ....

c   Er hat .... Geschwister.

d   Er spricht .... Deutsch.

e   Sein Vater arbeitet ....

f   Seine Mutter ....

g   Sein Freund in Kuba heißt ....

2 Was ist anders als zu Hause?

a ☐ das Wetter   b ☐ die Familie   c ☐ die Schule

d ☐ die Leute   e ☐ die Stadt   f ☐ die Sprache

g ☐ die Bücher

3 Wie ist Gelsenkirchen?

....

....

4 Wie ist Pedros Wohnung in Gelsenkirchen?

....

....

5 Was macht Pedro heute Abend?

a ☐ Er sieht den ganzen Abend fern.

b ☐ Er spielt Fußball mit seinen Freunden.

c ☐ Er spielt allein.

Wortschatz

1 Welches Wort passt nicht?

a ☐ Haus ☐ Hütte ☐ Villa ☐ Schule
b ☐ Deutsch ☐ Mathematik ☐ Spanisch ☐ Portugiesisch
c ☐ Wand ☐ Garten ☐ Feld ☐ Park
d ☐ E-Mail ☐ Computer ☐ Brief ☐ Telegramm
e ☐ Pizza ☐ Kebab ☐ Cola ☐ Brötchen

2 Kennst du die Namen der Länder und der Sprachen? Teste dich selbst.

a In Italien spricht man ....

b In Kuba sprechen die Leute ....

c Französisch spricht man in ....

d Wo spricht man Deutsch? In .... ,
in .... und in der ....

e In Großbritannien, in den USA und in vielen anderen Ländern
sprechen die Leute ....

Sprechen wir darüber?

1 Die deutsche Sprache.
Pedro findet Deutsch schwierig.
Und du? Findest du Deutsch auch
schwierig? Oder leicht?
Schwieriger oder leichter als
Englisch? Warum?

Schreiben

1 Pedro ist allein, denn er kommt aus einem fremden Land. Er möchte Freunde finden. Er liest die Anzeigen am Schwarzen Brett im Internetcafé und findet diese:

> Ich bin Karim und komme aus Ägypten. Ich wohne jetzt in der Nähe von Gelsenkirchen. Ich kann gut Englisch, aber Deutsch spreche ich noch schlecht. Ich spiele gern Fußball und sehe gern Krimis.
> Möchtest du mein Freund/meine Freundin werden?

Antworte auf diese Anzeige (zirka 50 Wörter). Vergiss die Anrede und die Grüße am Ende nicht.

Hallo ....,

_____

_____

_____

_____

_____

_____

_____

_____

_____

_____

_____

Tschüss

Das Ruhrgebiet

Wo ist das Ruhrgebiet?

Das Ruhrgebiet liegt im Westen von Deutschland. Auf der Landkarte sehen wir viele Städte, kleine und große: Bochum, Bottrop, Duisburg, Essen, Gelsenkirchen, Wanne-Eickel etc. Städte ohne große Tradition: sie haben keine Kriege geführt und keine Länder regiert. Sie liegen zwischen drei Flüssen: dem Rhein, der Ruhr und im Norden, der Lippe. Mehr als fünf Millionen Menschen leben dort. Was sie tun? Sie „malochen", oder auf gut Deutsch: sie arbeiten. Was noch wichtig ist: Fußball und Bier.

Früher ...

war das Ruhrgebiet kein Ferienparadies. Kohle und Stahl für ganz Europa kamen von dort. Mehr als hundert Jahre lang. Sauber war es auch nicht. Die Luft war schlecht, und im Rhein und in der Ruhr hat man jahrzehntelang keinen lebenden Fisch gesehen. Aber es gab Arbeit für alle, zu viel Arbeit. Fabriken und Bergwerke brauchten immer mehr Arbeiter. Erst holte man Männer aus Polen, dann aus Italien, aus Griechenland und aus der Türkei.

Heute ...

braucht Europa weniger Stahl und kaum noch Kohle. Die Industrie im Ruhrgebiet hat eine lange schwere Krise erlebt. Viele Männer und Frauen waren und sind arbeitslos. Moderne Industrie braucht Universitäten und wissenschaftliche Labors und eine ganz neue Art von Fabriken. Damit moderne Unternehmer kommen, sind zwei Dinge wichtig: Infrastrukturen und Lebensqualität.

Was machte man mit den alten Fabriken und Bergwerken? Man schafft Museen, Konzerthallen, Schwimmbäder ... und auch viele Grünflächen. Deshalb kommen heute viele Touristen ins Ruhrgebiet. Vor vierzig Jahren war das undenkbar. Was tun sie dort? Hier ein paar Beispiele:

Im **Bergbau-Museum** von **Bochum** können sie unter die Erde gehen und Bergbau und Maschinenlärm aus der Nähe erleben. Dann fahren sie mit dem Lift auf den Förderturm: frische Luft!

Der Förderturm des Bochumer Bergbau-Museums

In **Duisburg** gibt es den **Landschaftspark Duisburg-Nord**. Man kann da nicht nur joggen und schwimmen, sondern auch Freeclimbing an der Fabrikhalle ausprobieren oder im Ex-Gasometer unter Wasser gehen: da liegen auch ein paar Wracks von Schiffen.

Haben wir vielleicht das **Brauerei-Museum** vergessen? Das liegt in **Dortmund**. Dortmund gehört eigentlich schon zu Westfalen, aber ein bisschen auch noch zum Ruhrgebiet.

Noch etwas? Ja, das **Alpincenter** in **Bottrop** (Skifahren im Winter, Beachvolleyball im Sommer), der **Duisburger Zoo** und das **Bochumer Planetarium**.

1 Wähle die richtige Alternative.

Welche von diesen Städten gehören nicht zum Ruhrgebiet?

a ☐ Bottrop   b ☐ Köln   c ☐ München   d ☐ Berlin
e ☐ Duisburg   f ☐ Essen   g ☐ Stuttgart

2 Früher war das Ruhrgebiet

a ☐ ein reiches Land.
b ☐ ein großes Industriegebiet.
c ☐ ein wichtiges Touristenziel.

3 Heute kommen viele Touristen ins Ruhrgebiet, weil

a ☐ es dort viele alte Gebäude und Kirchen gibt.
b ☐ man sich dort gut entspannen kann.
c ☐ man „neue" und originelle Museen gebaut hat.

4 Antworte auf die folgenden Fragen.

a In den 1980er Jahren hatte der Sänger Herbert Grönemeyer großen Erfolg mit dem Lied *Bochum*. Das Lied beginnt mit den Versen: „Du bist keine Schönheit / vor Arbeit ganz grau". Warum?
b Ein anderer Vers lautet: „Du bist keine Weltstadt". Warum nicht?

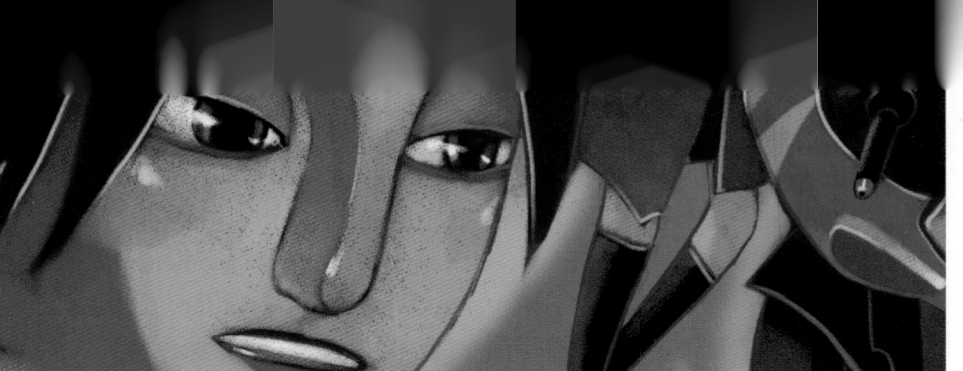

Ausländer

„Hast du den Neuen gesehen?" fragt Susanne Martha.

„Netter Typ, oder?"

„Ja, und der sieht auch gut aus. Die dunklen Augen und dann diese schwarzen Haare. Einfach süß. Und breite Schultern hat er auch."

„Na, hübsch ist er ja, aber irgendwie gefällt er mir nicht."

„Mir schon."

Pedro steht allein in einer Ecke in der neuen Klasse. Es ist Pause. Er ist etwas rot.

„Sehen die andern mich an? Sicher sprechen sie über mich."

Der Lehrer hat ihn vorgestellt: „Ihr habt ab heute einen neuen Mitschüler. Er heißt Pedro und kommt aus Kuba. Pedro, setz dich doch bitte dort neben Jochen hin. Der Platz ist frei."

Pedro setzt sich neben einen großen blonden Jungen.

„Hallo Pedro", sagt Jochen und gibt ihm die Hand.

„Hallo Jochen", antwortet Pedro. Soll er noch etwas sagen? Er spricht so schlecht Deutsch.

Pedro geht jeden Tag in die Schule. Zu Hause lernt er Deutsch. Er macht sich Listen mit Wörtern. Die hängt er an den Kühlschrank, an den Spiegel im Badezimmer. Er liest täglich

Zeitung und versucht, die Sendungen im Fernsehen zu verstehen. Es geht nur langsam, aber Pedros Deutsch wird besser.

„Es läuft nicht gut in der Schule", sagt er eines Tages zu seiner Mutter.

„Probleme in der Schule? Du warst doch immer der Klassenbeste!"

„Mama, ich verstehe nicht die Hälfte [1] von dem, was die Lehrer sagen."

„Ach Pedro, das wird sicher bald besser." Seine Mutter macht sich keine Gedanken.

Und Pedro lernt Deutsch. In der Schule versteht er jetzt immer mehr.

„Das geht doch schon viel besser", sagt auch der Klassenlehrer. „Nur beim Schreiben hast du noch ein paar Probleme. Aber mach nur so weiter. Du schaffst das schon."

Das denkt Pedro auch. Die deutsche Sprache ist nicht das Problem. Das Problem sind seine Mitschüler. Er hat noch keine Freunde in der Klasse.

„Es ist, weil du noch nicht so gut Deutsch kannst", erklärt ihm Susanne.

Susanne spricht oft mit ihm.

Wie sieht denn diese Susanne aus? fragt Juan in einer E-Mail.

Nicht schlecht, antwortet Pedro. Sie hat braune Haare und blaue Augen. Eine richtige Deutsche. Sie ist groß, aber nicht riesengroß wie andere Mädchen in der Klasse. Sie trägt die Haare kurz und zieht sich immer wie ein Junge an.

---

1. **e Hälfte (n)**: 50%.

Tor ohne Grenzen

Pedro sieht in Susanne nur eine Freundin. Nicht mehr. Ein anderes Mädchen in der Klasse gefällt ihm viel besser. Ihr Name ist Vanessa. Sie hat lange rote Haare, perlweiße Zähne und grüne Augen. Sie ist sechzehn wie die anderen, aber sie hat schon den Körper einer Frau. Die anderen Mädchen tragen Jeans. Sie ist immer sexy, mit engen Hosen und langen Stiefeln. Auch das gefällt Pedro sehr.

Susanne sieht, dass ihn Vanessa interessiert.

„Sie ist sehr hübsch, nicht wahr? Aber sie hat schon einen Freund. Es ist dein Banknachbar, Jochen Rheinald."

„Träumen darf man doch noch, oder?" erwidert Pedro und wird rot.

Nach dem Unterricht bleibt Pedro vor der Schule stehen. Er wartet auf Vanessa.

„Bis morgen, Vanessa", sagt er.

Sie antwortet nicht. Sie sieht ihn nicht einmal an.

Sie steigt zu Jochen aufs Motorrad.

„Armes Schwein! Der ist wohl in dich verliebt", sagt Jochen.

„Gut gesagt, mein Lieber. Ein armes Schwein, das ist er. Und wie du weißt, habe ich für arme Schweine nichts übrig [1]. Und für Ausländer auch nicht. Ich mag Siegertypen [2]. Männer wie dich."

Jochen hört es nicht gern, wenn Vanessa so spricht. Er kommt aus einer reichen Familie, hat ein schweres Motorrad und ist immer gut angezogen. Nur darum ist Vanessa mit ihm zusammen. Das weiß er gut.

Am Sonntag sind Pedro und seine Familie eingeladen. Es gibt ein großes Fest. Bei anderen Ausländern.

---

1. **nichts übrig haben für etwas/jdn**: etwas/jdn nicht gut oder interessant finden.
2. **r Siegertyp (en)**: Typ, der immer gewinnt.

Tor ohne Grenzen

„Ich möchte nicht so gern mitkommen. Kann ich nicht zu Hause bleiben?" bittet Pedro seinen Vater.

„Du willst nicht mitkommen?" fragt der Vater. „Unsere Freunde sind alle da. Wir essen zusammen, singen und tanzen, und du willst allein zu Hause sitzen?"

„Das sind eure Freunde, nicht meine. Für mich sind eure Feste ein bisschen ... langweilig."

„Pedro! Für eine halbe Stunde kommst du mit. Dann kannst du allein nach Hause gehen, wenn du willst."

Sie fahren in die Wohnung eines kubanischen Freundes. Viele Leute sind da. Männer, Frauen und viele Kinder. Die Musik ist laut, es gibt viel zu essen. Die Leute lachen und haben viel Spaß.

Pedro sitzt allein.

„Warum gehst du nicht zu den andern?" fragt ihn seine Mutter.

„Keine Lust."

Er isst etwas und geht dann.

Allein in der Stadt. Der Himmel ist grau und die Leute gehen schnell durch die stillen Straßen. Manchmal fährt ein Auto vorbei. Ein typisch deutscher Sonntag.

„Warum gehe ich nicht zurück?" fragt sich Pedro. „Zu dem Fest. Die lachen und haben Spaß. Da ist es wie bei mir zu Hause, in Kuba."

Er weiß die Antwort selbst: „Das ist nicht mehr mein Zuhause. Wer weiß, wann ich nach Kuba zurück kann. Und dann ... fühle ich mich sicher auch da wie ein Ausländer. Ausländer in Deutschland, Ausländer in Kuba, immer Ausländer."

Textverständnis

1 Was ist richtig (R), was ist falsch (F)

		R	F
a	Susanne mag Pedro.	☐	☐
b	Auch Martha mag Pedro.	☐	☐
c	In der Klasse gibt es zwanzig Schüler.	☐	☐
d	Pedro fühlt sich sofort wie zu Hause.	☐	☐
e	Pedro lernt sehr schnell Deutsch.	☐	☐
f	Pedro mag Vanessa sehr.	☐	☐
g	Auch Vanessa mag Pedro.	☐	☐
h	Jochen ist Vanessas Freund.	☐	☐
i	Pedros Eltern gehen zu einer Party.	☐	☐
j	Pedro möchte gern mitgehen.	☐	☐
k	Er hat auf der Party viel Spaß.	☐	☐
l	In Deutschland fühlt er sich als Ausländer.	☐	☐

2 Ergänze die folgende Tabelle. Wie sehen Pedro, Susanne und Vanessa aus?

	Haare	Augen	Sonstiges
Pedro	....	....	....
	....	....	....
Susanne	....	....	....
	....	....	....
Vanessa	....	....	....
	....	....	....

Grammatik

1 Benutze die folgenden Verben im Präsens.

> geben   finden   haben   leben   lieben
> schreiben   sein   sprechen   wollen

a Pedro .... schlecht Deutsch. Er .... Deutsch
sehr schwierig.

b Susanne .... die spanische Sprache, sie ....
mit Pedro nach Kuba fahren.

c Pedro .... an seinen Freund Juan. Er .... noch
in Kuba.

d Pedro .... in Vanessa verliebt, aber sie ....
schon einen Freund: Jochen.

e Am Sonntag .... es bei einem Freund von Pedros Familie
ein großes Fest.

2 Bilde die Imperativform wie im Beispiel.

Der Lehrer: Pedro, (sich setzen) neben Jochen.
→ *Setz dich neben Jochen!*

a Der Klassenlehrer:
„Pedro, (machen) weiter so.“

....

b Pedros Mutter:
„Pedro, (helfen) mir bei der Hausarbeit, bitte!“

....

c Pedros Vater:
„Pedro, (mitkommen) zur Party!“

....

d Susanne zu Pedro:
„(Sprechen) ein bisschen Spanisch mit mir!“

....

e Jochen zu Vanessa:
„(Steigen) aufs Motorrad!“

....

Lesen Plus

Den richtigen Partner finden

Viele sind auf der Suche nach ihrem idealen Partner. Aber wie muss er/sie sein?
Fülle den Fragebogen aus.

Aussehen
Er/sie ist

☐ klein ☐ mittelgroß ☐ groß ☐ sehr groß
☐ dünn ☐ schlank ☐ athletisch ☐ robust
☐ blond ☐ rothaarig ☐ braunhaarig ☐ schwarzhaarig

Er/sie hat

☐ helle ☐ graue ☐ dunkle ☐ braune ☐ blaue Augen

Persönlichkeit/ Charakter
Er/sie ist

☐ ruhig ☐ schüchtern ☐ süß ☐ sexy ☐ lebhaft ☐ energisch

Qualitäten
Welche drei Eigenschaften findest du am wichtigsten?

☐ Intelligenz ☐ Bildung ☐ gute Erziehung ☐ Reichtum
☐ Sympathie/ Nettsein ☐ Attraktivität ☐ Eleganz

Beruf
Was ist er/sie von Beruf? Kreuze an, was du nicht magst.

☐ Angestellte/r ☐ Lehrer/in ☐ Arbeiter/in ☐ Freiberufler/in
☐ Unternehmer/in ☐ Künstler/in (Schriftsteller/in, Maler/in) ☐ Automechaniker/in
☐ Polizist/in ☐ Tänzer/in ☐ Verkäufer/in

Hobbys
Treibt er/sie Sport?

☐ regelmäßig ☐ unregelmäßig ☐ gar nicht

Liest er/sie? (Bücher)

☐ viel ☐ wenig ☐ gar nicht

Er/sie geht gern ...

☐ ins Kino ☐ ins Theater ☐ ins Restaurant ☐ in die Kneipe

Er/sie macht gern Urlaub

☐ am Meer ☐ im Gebirge ☐ auf dem Land
☐ er besichtigt gern Städte ☐ er macht keinen Urlaub

Weitere Hobbys:

....

Migranten in D-A-CH

In Deutschland

Seit den 1960er Jahren kommen viele
Leute aus verschiedenen Ländern nach
Deutschland. Sie wollen dort arbeiten. In
den Sechzigern waren es Italiener, dann
Jugoslawen und Griechen, in den
Siebzigern Türken und nach dem Krieg in
Ex-Jugoslawien Serben, Montenegriner
und Kroaten. Es gibt ungefähr 7,4
Millionen Ausländer in Deutschland.
Nach einem Gesetz des Jahres 2000 ist
man „Deutscher", wenn man in
Deutschland als Kind von Eltern geboren
ist, von denen einer seit mindestens acht
Jahren in Deutschland lebt.

In Österreich

Von den drei deutschsprachigen Ländern
ist Österreich die Nation mit den
wenigsten Migranten. Sie kommen
hauptsächlich aus Serbien und
Montenegro und aus der Türkei.

In der Schweiz

Die Schweiz ist ein sehr „internationales" Land. 20% der Bevölkerung sind
Ausländer. Die meisten sind Italiener und Leute aus Ex-Jugoslawien.

DATEN

Deutschland	*Österreich*	*Schweiz*
Türken: 2,5%	Serben und Montenegriner: 1,6%	Ex-Jugoslawen: 4,8%
Italiener: 0,8%	Türken: 1,5%	Italiener: 4,5%
Serben und Montenegriner: 0,6%		Portugiesen: 2%
Kroaten: 0,2%		
Griechen: 0,3%		

1 **Was ist richtig?**

1 In Deutschland kommen die meisten Migranten aus

  a ☐ Italien.

  b ☐ den Ländern Ex-Jugoslawiens.

  c ☐ der Türkei.

2 Italienische Migranten kamen

  a ☐ gleich nach dem Zweiten Weltkrieg.

  b ☐ fünf Jahre nach dem Zweiten Weltkrieg.

  c ☐ fünfzehn Jahre nach dem Zweiten Weltkrieg
  nach Deutschland.

3 In der Schweiz bilden die Migranten

  a ☐ 10%

  b ☐ 20%

  c ☐ 30%

  der Bevölkerung.

4 Aus Serbien, Montenegro und Serbien kamen die Migranten
  hauptsächlich

  a ☐ nach dem Zweiten Weltkrieg.

  b ☐ nach dem Krieg in Ex-Jugoslawien.

  c ☐ in den Sechziger und Siebziger Jahren.

Sprechen wir darüber?

1 Findest du es gut, dass viele Migranten in einem Land leben?

2 Würdest gern in einem „internationalen" Land wie in der Schweiz leben?

3 Glaubst du, dass das deutsche Gesetz von 2000 richtig ist?

Fußball

Der Weg nach Hause ist weit. Mit dem Bus braucht Pedro eine halbe Stunde. Aber er will nicht mit dem Bus fahren. Er will lieber zu Fuß gehen. Er geht schnell. Sein Weg führt an seiner Schule vorbei.

Ein schönes, modernes Gebäude [1] mit einer großen Turnhalle [2]. Es gibt auch einen Fußballplatz.

Pedro bleibt stehen.

Die Mannschaft seiner Schule trainiert dort. Eine gute Mannschaft. Vielleicht wird sie dieses Jahr Landesmeister. Jochen, Pedros Banknachbar, ist der beste Spieler. Vielleicht wird er auch Profi-Spieler in der deutschen U-21 [3] Mannschaft.

Pedro hat noch nie auf diesem Platz gespielt. Er ist groß mit einer überdachten Tribüne. In Kuba gibt es nur wenige so schöne Plätze.

Der Eingang steht offen.

Pedro sieht sich um: kein Mensch zu sehen.

1. **s Gebäude (-)**: Haus.
2. **e Turnhalle (n)**: Gebäude, wo man Sport macht.
3. **U-21**: Nationalmannschaft mit Spielern unter 21 Jahren.

Da liegt noch ein Ball.

Pedro dribbelt ein bisschen. Dann schießt er den Ball ins Tor.

„Wen haben wir denn da?" Ein Mitschüler steht plötzlich hinter ihm. Hans. Am Rand des Spielfelds stehen auch die anderen. Pedro kennt sie alle. Frank, Jochen, Thomas, Vanessa und Susanne.

„Spiel doch weiter!" ruft Jochen. „Das war gar nicht schlecht." Pedro will nicht.

„Du kannst es wohl doch nicht, wie?" Vanessa lacht laut.

Das ist zu viel.

„Zu Hause war ich der beste", sagt er laut.

„Meine Damen und Herren: der beste Spieler von ganz Kuba!" ruft Vanessa.

Aber die anderen lachen nicht.

„Als was hast du denn gespielt?" fragt Jochen interessiert.

„Als Mittelstürmer", antwortet Pedro.

„Wie ich!" Jochen nimmt den Ball, legt ihn auf den Rasen [1] und schießt ihn ins Tor.

„Bravo!" ruft Vanessa.

Jochen holt den Ball und gibt ihn Pedro.

„Und jetzt du", sagt er.

Pedro geht langsam rückwärts. Erst dreißig Meter vom Tor entfernt bleibt er stehen.

„Das kann er nicht schaffen", sagt Jochen leise.

Ein Tritt [2]. Der Ball fliegt.

Tor!

„Super", ruft Susanne.

---

1. **r Rasen** (-): s Gras.   2. **r Tritt (e)**: gibt man mit dem Fuß.

Tor ohne Grenzen

„Wirklich gut", kommentiert Jochen.

Vanessa sagt nichts mehr.

„Willst du nicht in unserer Mannschaft mitspielen?" fragt Jochen Pedro.

„Du meinst, das geht?" fragt Pedro.

„Morgen spreche ich mit dem Trainer."

„Ja dann, bis morgen." Pedro geht.

Tor ohne Grenzen

Eine Hand legt sich auf seinen Arm. Es ist Susannes.

„Ich komme mit", sagt sie.

„Nein, ich komme mit. Hast du keine Angst?"

„Ach was", sagt Susanne. „Ich bin hier zu Hause. Angst! Wovor denn?"

„Es wird schon dunkel und du bist ein Mädchen und hier ist um diese Zeit kein Mensch mehr unterwegs.[1] Wo wohnst du denn?"

„Nur ein paar hundert Meter von hier."

„Dann bringe ich dich nach Hause."

Susanne lächelt.

„Ist der lieb", denkt sie, „ein richtiger Kavalier."

„Hoffentlich sehe ich dich bald spielen", sagt Susanne.

„Nun mal langsam, sie haben mir ja noch nicht einmal erlaubt bei ihnen mitzuspielen."

„Bestimmt fragen sie dich gleich morgen." Susanne ist sich da ganz sicher. „Und ... du sprichst jetzt wirklich gut Deutsch."

Vor Susannes Haustür umarmt er sie und gibt ihr einen Kuss auf die Wange[2].

„Bis morgen, Susanne", sagt er.

„Bis morgen."

Sie bleibt vor der Tür stehen und sieht ihm nach. Diese starken Beine, die breiten Schultern, die dunklen lockigen Haare.

„Susanne!" sagt sie zu sich: „Er ist in Vanessa verliebt. Und ich verliebe mich immer in den falschen. Oder ... ? "

Pedro geht in der Novemberkälte nach Hause. Aber ihm ist nicht kalt, und die Stadt ist ihm nicht mehr fremd. Zum ersten Mal ist er in Deutschland fast glücklich.

---

1. **unterwegs**: nicht zu Hause, auf Reisen.
2. **e Wange (n)**: rechts und links von der Nase.

Textverständnis

1 **Weißt du die Antwort?**

 a Wohin geht Pedro?

  ....

 b Wo bleibt er stehen?

  ....

 c Warum?

  ....

 d Wer kommt dann?

  ....

 e Wer schießt den Ball ins Tor?

  ....

 f Mit wem geht Pedro nach Hause?

  ....

 g Wer ist in Pedro verliebt?

  ....

 h Susanne findet Pedro sehr nett. Ein „Kavalier", sagt sie. Warum?

  ....

 i Glaubt Susanne, dass Pedro in sie verliebt ist?

  ....

2 **Wie sind Pedros Klassenkameraden?**

 1 Jochen: ....
 2 Susanne: ....
 3 Vanessa: ....

 a ☐ nett und freundlich
 b ☐ unsympathisch
 c ☐ sportlich

Wortschatz

1 Suche das passende Wort zu jeder Definition im Puzzle.

a   Der „Chef" der Fußballmannschaft.

b   Damit kannst du spielen.

c   Die von Pedro ist sehr modern.

d   Schnell zu Fuß.

e   Nach Oktober kommt ...

f   So heißt Pedros Freund.

g   Das Gegenteil von *weinen*.

h   Die Sprache von Pedro.

i   Pedro kommt von dort.

j   *Goal* auf Deutsch.

S	P	A	N	I	S	C	H
K	A	P	I	T	Ä	N	J
U	T	O	R	O	A	B	U
B	A	L	L	R	R	E	A
A	L	A	C	H	E	N	N
L	A	U	F	E	N	S	A
N	O	V	E	M	B	E	R
S	C	H	U	L	E	P	R

Wortschatz Plus

Fußballverben

anpfeifen/abpfeifen   angreifen   dribbeln

gegen den
Gegenspieler treten

ein Foul erleiden

zielen

schießen

den Ball verfehlen

klatschen

1 **Zu viele Verben? Schon vergessen? Versuchs noch einmal. Ergänze mit dem passenden Verb.**

a   Harald gibt den Ball nicht ab. Er .... den Ball an dem
Gegenspieler vorbei.

b   Er will nicht mehr in der Defensive spielen, er .... jetzt
....

c   Da, in der 44. Minute .... Diego noch ein Tor.

d   Jetzt ...... der Schiedsrichter .... Das Spiel ist zu Ende.

e   3:2 gewonnen. Die Fans ....

Grammatik

1 **Wie kommen diese Leute zur Schule? Ergänze mit den richtigen Präpositionen und Artikeln (wo nötig).**

a   Pedro fährt .... Bus.

b   Vanessas Vater fährt sie .... Auto.

c   Susanne geht .... Fuß.

d   Jochen fährt .... Motorrad.

e   Der Klassenlehrer fährt .... Zug.

2 **Welche Präposition wählst du?**

1   Pedro spielt .... Stadion.

   a ☐ im   b ☐ ins   c ☐ auf dem

2   Pedro schießt den Ball .... Tor.

   a ☐ in den   b ☐ ins   c ☐ im

3   Ein Mitschüler steht .... ihm.

   a ☐ hinter   b ☐ zu   c ☐ in

4   Pedro bleibt dreißig Meter .... dem Tor stehen

   a ☐ vor   b ☐ an   c ☐ in

5   Pedro geht .... Hause.

   a ☐ im   b ☐ zu   c ☐ nach

6   Susanne sagt:

   Hier bin ich ......Hause

   a ☐ zu   b ☐ nach   c ☐ auf

7   Er umarmt Susanne .....Tür.

   a ☐ vor   b ☐ unter   c ☐ auf

8   Pedro ist ..... Vanessa verliebt.

   a ☐ in   b ☐ auf   c ☐ für

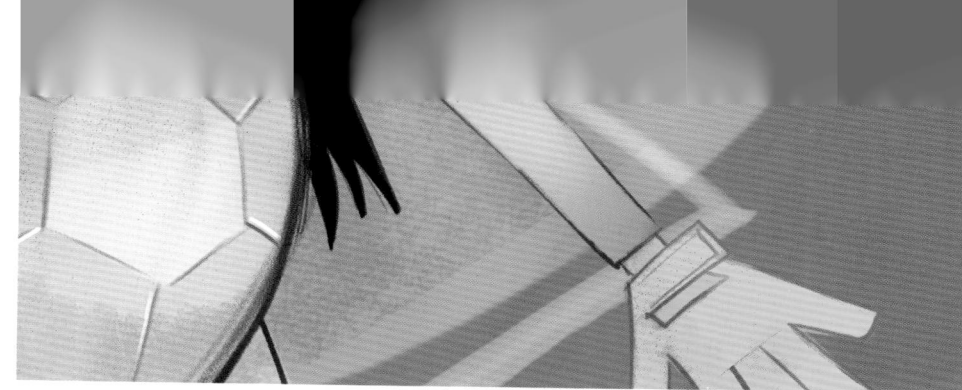

Das Spiel

Am nächsten Morgen gibt es einen Mathetest. Pedro hat viel dafür gelernt. Denn Mathematik ist in Deutschland anders als in Kuba und es ist nicht leicht für ihn!

„Du bist hier Ausländer und musst besser sein als die anderen", sagt sein Vater immer wieder.

In der Pause sieht er Jochen mit dem Sportlehrer sprechen.

„Vielleicht sprechen sie über mich", denkt Pedro. Soll er Jochen fragen? Nein. Pedro wartet.

„Wenn nicht, dann nicht. Sollen sie doch ohne mich spielen."

Samstag Nachmittag spielt die Schülermannschaft Gelsenkirchen gegen Wanne-Eickel.

„Spielst du auch mit?" fragt Susanne.

„Nein. Jochen hat mit mir nicht mehr über die Mannschaft gesprochen."

„Das kann doch nicht sein. Hast du ihn denn nicht mehr gefragt?"

„Nein."

„Vielleicht hat er das vergessen", sagt Susanne, aber sie glaubt das selbst nicht.

Tor ohne Grenzen

Sie sieht ihn an.

„Aber du kommst doch zum Spiel? Wir können zusammen hingehen. Hast du keine Lust?" fragt sie.

Pedro antwortet nicht. Er hat keine Lust, andere Leute spielen zu sehen, wenn er selbst nicht spielen kann ...

„Pedro! Ein Fußballspiel! Unsere Mannschaft spielt gut. Komm doch mit!"

„Na gut."

Viele Leute kommen das Spiel sehen. Das Stadion ist voll. Die meisten Schüler sind da, auch Lehrer und Eltern sind gekommen, und viele, die nichts mit der Schule zu tun haben.

„Siehst du", sagt Susanne. „Siehst du, wie viele Leute da sind? Die kommen, weil es hier guten Fußball zu sehen gibt."

Sie setzen sich zu den anderen aus ihrer Klasse.

Das Spiel beginnt.

Mal hat die eine Mannschaft den Ball, dann die andere. So geht es eine Zeit lang hin und her [1]. Da nimmt Jochen einem Gegenspieler den Ball ab, er schießt ihn nach vorne, läuft hinterher. Zwei Spieler der anderen Mannschaft wollen ihn aufhalten. Aber er ist schneller. Er schafft es bis ganz nah ans Tor. Eine Zehntelsekunde [2] Pause. Konzentration. Schuss. Der Ball fliegt über den Rasen. Tor!

„Tor!" Jochen umarmt seine Mitspieler.

Das Spiel geht weiter. Wieder ist Jochen am Ball. Wieder läuft er auf das Tor zu. Doch ein Gegenspieler [3] tritt ihn gegen das Bein. Foul! Jochen liegt auf dem Rasen und hält sich das Bein. Er will aufstehen. Es geht nicht. Die anderen Spieler helfen ihm und

1. **hin und her**: vor und zurück.
2. **e Zehntelsekunde (n)**: 1/10 Sekunde.
3. siehe S. 96.

bringen ihn vom Feld. Er spricht mit dem Trainer. Sie schauen auf die Tribüne. Sehen sie Pedro an? Dann kommt auch der Trainer zu Pedro auf die Tribüne.

„Du heißt Pedro, stimmt's?" fragt der Trainer.

„Ja."

„Pedro, ich habe niemanden, den ich aufs Feld schicken kann. Heute sind alle krank. Du weißt schon, diese dumme Grippe. Willst du es nicht versuchen? Ich gebe dir zehn Minuten. Wenn es nicht gut läuft, bist du draußen."

„Typisch Deutsch", denkt Pedro.

„Alles klar", sagt Pedro.

Zweite Halbzeit[1]. Ein Tor für die andere Mannschaft. Es steht eins zu eins.

Pedro steht auf dem Feld.

Seit wann war er nicht mehr bei einem richtigen Spiel dabei? Seit vier oder fünf Monaten? Oder ist es noch länger her? Aber jetzt fühlt er sich wie zu Hause. Das Stadion ist sein Zuhause.

Er läuft. Da ist der Ball. Pedro nimmt ihn dem Gegenspieler ab. Übers Mittelfeld[2]. Er dribbelt den Ball an zwei Gegnern vorbei. Schafft er es bis ans Tor? Ein dritter Spieler steht vor ihm. Pedro sieht nur den Ball. Er tanzt um den Gegner herum. Der Ball ist frei.

Vor ihm das Tor.

Pedro schießt.

„Tor!" Das Publikum brüllt[3].

Auf der Tribüne fragt man jetzt: „Wer ist denn das? Wie heißt er?"

1.-2. siehe S. 96.
3. **brüllen**: sehr sehr laut rufen.

Tor ohne Grenzen

„Pedro, er heißt Pedro."

Nur den Namen. Mehr brauchen sie nicht. Immer wieder rufen sie seinen Namen.

„Pedro! Pedro! Pedro!"

Das Spiel geht weiter. Ein Tor für die Mannschaft aus Wanne-Eickel.

„Die Verteidigung[1] ist zu schwach", kommentiert Jochen auf der Reservebank. „Die Verteidigung ...“

Noch fünf Minuten.

Wieder ist Pedro am Ball.

Zwischen ihm und dem Tor stehen zwei Gegenspieler. Links von ihm steht ein anderer Gelsenkirchener, Jens. Pedro gibt den Ball ab. Jens läuft nach vorne, will schießen — da kommt ein Gegenspieler und tritt ihn von hinten ans Bein. Jens fällt zu Boden. Noch ein Foul.

Der Schiedsrichter pfeift. Elfmeter[2].

Pedro soll den Elfmeter schießen.

Pedro steht elf Meter vor dem Tor.

Pedro konzentriert sich. Den Kopf zwischen den Schultern, läuft er ein Stück und tritt gegen den Ball.

Der Ball fliegt über dem Kopf des Torwarts ins Tor.

„Tor!" brüllen die Leute, und „Pedro, Pedro, Pedro."

Drei zu zwei.

1.-2. siehe S. 96.

Textverständnis

1 **Was passiert? Wähle die richtige Alternative.**

1 Wann ist das Fußballspiel?

    a ☐ Am Samstag   b ☐ Am Sonntag   c ☐ Am Freitag

2 Wer spielt gegen wen?

    a ☐ Die Schülermannschaft gegen die Lehrermannschaft Gelsenkirchen.

    b ☐ Die kubanische Mannschaft gegen die deutsche Mannschaft.

    c ☐ Die Schülermannschaft Gelsenkirchen gegen die Mannschaft Wanne-Eickel.

3 Im Stadion gibt es

    a ☐ sehr wenige Leute b ☐ nicht viele Leute c ☐ viele Leute

4 Mit wem geht Pedro ins Stadion?

    a ☐ Mit Vanessa   b ☐ Mit Susanne   c ☐ Allein

5 Wer hat während des Fußballspieles einen kleinen Unfall?

    a ☐ Jochen   b ☐ Hans   c ☐ Pedro

6 Wer spricht mit Pedro während des Spiels?

    a ☐ Jochen   b ☐ der Trainer   c ☐ der Kapitän

7 Viele Spieler sind nicht da. Warum?

    a ☐ Sie sind krank.

    b ☐ Sie sind in Urlaub.

    c ☐ Sie sind in der Schule.

8 Pedro spielt

    a ☐ sehr gut b ☐ ziemlich gut c ☐ nicht so gut

2 **Wie steht es am Ende des Spiels? Wer hat wie viele Tore geschossen?**

....

....

....

Wortschatz und Grammatik

1 Verbinde die Fragen mit den richtigen Antworten.

1 ☐ Wie viele Leute sind da?   **a** Ja!
2 ☐ Wie heißt er?   **b** Doch.
3 ☐ Seit wann spielt er nicht?   **c** Mindestens Zweitausend.
4 ☐ Hast du keine Lust?   **d** Pedro.
5 ☐ Willst du es versuchen?   **e** Seit fünf Monaten.

2 Lückentest. Ergänze den Text mit den richtigen Wörtern.

Pedro findet Mathematik schwer. Es ist hier anders (**1**) ....
in Kuba und gar nicht leicht (**2**) .... ihn.

Die Schülermannschaft spielt (**3**) .... eine andere Mannschaft.

Pedro will nicht (**4**) .... Spiel gehen; er hat (**5**) .... Lust,
die anderen spielen zu sehen.

Pedro und Susanne setzen (**6**) .... zu den anderen aus
(**7**) .... Klasse.

Jochen (**8**) .... auf dem Rasen, dann spricht er (**9**) ....
dem Trainer.

Jetzt spielt Pedro und (**10**) .... ein Tor. Die Zuschauer brüllen
(**11**) ....Namen.

1 **a** ☐ als   **b** ☐ wie   **c** ☐ von
2 **a** ☐ von   **b** ☐ für   **c** ☐ als
3 **a** ☐ für   **b** ☐ mit   **c** ☐ gegen
4 **a** ☐ zu   **b** ☐ zum   **c** ☐ zur
5 **a** ☐ keine   **b** ☐ kein   **c** ☐ nicht
6 **a** ☐ sie   **b** ☐ sich   **c** ☐ dich
7 **a** ☐ seinen   **b** ☐ ihrer   **c** ☐ ihrem
8 **a** ☐ legt   **b** ☐ liegt   **c** ☐ stellt
9 **a** ☐ mit   **b** ☐ an   **c** ☐ für
10 **a** ☐ schießt   **b** ☐ tut   **c** ☐ kommt
11 **a** ☐ seinen   **b** ☐ seine   **c** ☐ ihren

Hören

6 Fußball und Geld. Wie viel haben die Vereine für ihre Fußballspieler bezahlt?

1 Ergänze die folgende Liste.

	Zinédine Zidane	Luis Figo	Hernàn Crespo
Summe			
von Verein 1			
zu Verein 2			
Jahr			

2 Jetzt höre den zweiten Teil und schreibe die Nationalität jedes Fußballspielers auf.

Fußballspieler   Nationalität

Zinédine Zidane   ....

Luis Figo   ....

Hernàn Crespo   ....

Sprechen wir darüber?

1 Für die Positionen innerhalb der Mannschaft muss jeder Spieler gewisse Eigenschaften haben. Welche?

> aggressiv   aufmerksam   diszipliniert
> kreativ   intelligent   schnell   vorsichtig
> wach   zuverlässig

a Der Mittelfeldspieler: ....
....

b Der Stürmer: ....
....

c Der Torwart: ....
....

d Der Verteidiger: ....
....

2 Und welche Qualitäten muss man für diese Sportarten haben?

> Aggressivität   Ausdauer   Disziplin
> Kraft   Kreativität   Schnelligkeit

a Basketball: ....
....

b Gewichtheben: ....
....

c Rugby: ....
....

d Triathlon: ....

e Wrestling: ....
....

45

Pedro, der Goldjunge

  Pedro ist immer noch derselbe, aber sein Leben hat sich sehr verändert.

Pedro ist jetzt der Star der Fußballmannschaft. Alle kennen ihn. Man nennt ihn den Goldjungen, *el pibe de oro*, wie sie vor vielen Jahren Diego Maradona genannt haben.

Diego Maradona ist klein und sieht ein wenig plump [1] aus. Pedro ist groß und dünn. Maradona kommt aus Argentinien und er ist aus Kuba. Aber das ist nicht so wichtig. Beide sprechen Spanisch und beide werden auf dem Spielfeld zu Zauberern [2].

Sofort nach dem Spiel kam der Trainer zu Pedro.

„Willst du bei uns mitspielen?" hat er gefragt.

„Na klar", hat Pedro geantwortet. „Als was denn?"

„Als Mittelstürmer, natürlich. Neben Jochen."

Pedros Tage sind jetzt sehr stressig. Morgens geht er in die

---

1. **plump**: nicht fein, nicht elegant.
2. **r Zauberer (-)**: Magier.

Schule, nachmittags lernt er und dann geht er zum Training. Dreimal pro Woche. Am Wochenende muss er spielen.

Seine Mutter macht sich Gedanken.

„Pedro, ist das nicht alles zu anstrengend [1] für dich?" fragt sie ihn. „Du hast ja keine freie Minute mehr. Und du schläfst zu wenig. Um Mitternacht gehst du ins Bett und um sechs Uhr bist du schon wieder auf den Beinen."

„Da hast du Recht. Aber morgens muss ich mir noch einmal ansehen, was ich gelernt habe. Auf Deutsch ist alles so schwierig ..."

„Wenigstens abends brauchst du doch ein bisschen Ruhe. Das Training dauert immer so lange."

„Das Training! Das macht mir doch Spaß!"

Pedro führt jetzt ein anstrengendes Lebe, das ist richtig. Aber das gefällt ihm so.

Wenn er über das Spielfeld läuft, dem Ball hinterher, wenn er am Gegner vorbei dribbelt, und natürlich, wenn der Ball ins Tor geht und das Publikum brüllt „Tor! Tooor!" Das alles macht ihn glücklich.

Er schreibt es auch Juan:

> Ich habe Freunde gefunden. Ausländer oder Deutscher – das ist den anderen jetzt egal. Ich bin ein guter Fußballspieler. Und nicht nur das. Ich bin Pedro, ihr Freund.

Das ist richtig. Pedro ist jetzt nicht mehr allein. Oft geht er mit seinen neuen Freunden aus, mit denen von der Mannschaft und auch mit Mädchen.

Auch heute, am Donnerstag. Nach dem Training fahren sie alle zusammen ins Stadtzentrum. Sie gehen eine Pizza essen. Die Jungen aus der Mannschaft: Hans und Jens, die Verteidiger, und

---

1. **anstrengend**: was Energie kostet und müde macht.

Thomas, der Torwart. Vanessa und Susanne, Franziska und Jessica kommen auch mit.

Pedro sitzt neben Jochen.

Sie sind jetzt Freunde. Mit Jochen kann Pedro über alles sprechen.

„Gehst du nicht mehr mit Vanessa? Man sieht euch gar nicht mehr zusammen."

„Nein, das ist vorbei", antwortet Jochen. „Aber ..."

„Ja?"

„Pedro, ich weiß, dass dir Vanessa gefällt. Vergiss sie. Die ist nichts für dich."

„Warum denn nicht?" Wenn Pedro sich etwas in den Kopf setzt[1]... .

„Was ist eigentlich mit Susanne? Die mag dich. Das sieht man. Hübsch ist sie auch, und gar nicht blöd. Nicht so wie Vanessa."

Susanne? Eine Freundin, nicht mehr.

Hinten am Tisch sitzt Vanessa neben Jens, Jens Petersen aus der Klasse über ihnen.

„Der Typ da", sagt Jens zu Vanessa, „der geht mir total auf die Nerven. Der muss weg."

Er meint Pedro, den Mittelstürmer. Jens spielt jetzt in der Verteidigung. Das gefällt ihm nicht.

„Da kommt dieser Ausländer und nimmt mir einfach meinen Platz weg. Dat is nich richtig!"

Vanessa findet das auch.

Nach dem Essen gehen Pedro und Susanne zusammen nach Hause. Wie immer, sprechen sie viel, über Gott und die Welt. Pedro hört ihr gern zu. Mit Susanne ist es nie langweilig.

---

1. **sich etwas in den Kopf setzen:** etwas wollen.

Tor ohne Grenzen

„Gehen wir morgen Abend zusammen ins Kino?" fragt er.

„Es läuft *Das Wunder von Bern* und ..."

Er spricht nicht zu Ende.

„Oh ja, super", antwortet Susanne.

Zum ersten Mal lädt Pedro sie ein.

An der Tür umarmt er sie, fester [1] als sonst. Susanne geht langsam nach oben in ihre Wohnung.

„Morgen ... morgen ... vielleicht denkt er nicht mehr an Vanessa. Vielleicht ..."

Sie ist glücklich. Sie möchte singen und tanzen.

1. **fest**: stabil, *hier*: mit Kraft (Energie).

Textverständnis

1 **Weißt du die Antwort?**

a Die anderen Jungen nennen Pedro den „Goldjungen", auf Spanisch
„el pibe de oro". So heißt auch ein berühmter Fußballspieler.
Kennst du ihn?

....

b Was haben Pedro und dieser Fußballspieler gemeinsam?

....

....

c Wer ist nicht glücklich?

   a ☐ Susanne **b** ☐ Pedro **c** ☐ Vanessa **d** ☐ Jochen

Warum?

2 **Was steht im Text, was nicht?**

a ☐ Pedros Mutter macht sich Gedanken um ihren Sohn.

b ☐ Pedro trainiert sehr gern.

c ☐ Pedro mag sein Leben nicht, denn es ist zu anstrengend.

d ☐ Jetzt hat Pedro Freunde.

e ☐ Pedro ist in Susanne verliebt.

f ☐ Er hat Vanessa vergessen.

g ☐ Pedro und Susanne sprechen viel.

h ☐ Vanessa ist noch Jochens Freundin.

i ☐ Pedro lädt Susanne ins Kino ein.

j ☐ Susanne mag Pedro nicht mehr.

k ☐ Jens mag Pedro nicht.

l ☐ Susanne und Pedro tanzen zusammen

Wortschatz

1 Fußball ist ein schöner Sport und der populärste in Europa. Aber es gibt auch andere Sportarten. Wie heißen sie auf Deutsch?

1 Basketball	2 Eishockey	3 Schwimmen
4 Radfahren	5 Leichtathletik	6 Marathonlauf
7 Tennis	8 Skilaufen	9 Formel 1

2 Setze die Namen der passenden Sportarten ein.

> Basketball   Eishockey   Formel 1
> Leichtathletik   Marathonlauf   Radfahren
> Schwimmen   Skilaufen   Tennis

a   Noch ist Jan Ullrich der erste. Aber da stoppt er. Hat er vielleicht Probleme mit einem Rad?

Sportart: ....

b   Tergat und Selassie laufen vorne. Zirka hundert Meter hinter ihnen laufen die nächsten.

Sportart: ....

c   An diesem Grand Prix wird auch ein deutscher Rennfahrer teilnehmen: Michael Schumacher.

Sportart: ....

d   Jetzt muss die deutsche Spielerin Anna-Lena Grönefeld schlagen.

Wenn sie dieses Match gewinnt, spielt sie gegen die russische Spielerin Anna Kournikova.

Sportart: ....

Hören

1 Junge Leuten sprechen über Sport. Wer treibt welche Sportart?

a   Martha: ....

b   Selina: ....

c   Jochen: ....

d   Johann: ....

2 Höre dir den Text noch einmal an. Was ist richtig (R), was ist falsch (F)?

			R	F
1	a	Martha fährt gern Fahrrad, aber auch Auto.	☐	☐
	b	Martha trainiert viel.	☐	☐
	c	Martha gehört zu einer Schülergruppe.	☐	☐
2	a	Selina spielt jeden Tag Fußball.	☐	☐
	b	Sie möchte aber Lehrerin werden.	☐	☐
	c	Frauenfußball wird in Deutschland immer wichtiger.	☐	☐
3	a	Jochen hat immer in der Stadt gelebt.	☐	☐
	b	Jochen findet es natürlicher, Ski zu fahren als zu Fuß zu gehen.	☐	☐
	c	Viele Leute sagen, dass Jochen nicht sehr gut ist, aber er denkt, er kann trotzdem ein großer Skifahrer werden.	☐	☐
4	a	Johann macht alle Spezialitäten der Leichtathletik.	☐	☐
	b	Johann läuft jetzt kurze Distanzen.	☐	☐
	c	Johann läuft auch Marathon.	☐	☐

WM Deutschland 2006

Wann?

Vom 9. Juni bis 9. Juli 2006 findet in Deutschland die Fußballweltmeisterschaft statt.

Wo?

In den Stadien von zwölf Städten in ganz Deutschland.

Das Stadion von Berlin, das Olympiastadion, ist das größte. Es hat Platz für mehr als 70000 Zuschauer.

Wer?

Aus Afrika, Europa und Südamerika kommen je fünf Mannschaften. Aus Asien, Nord- und Zentralamerika und der Karibik je vier Mannschaften, Australien schickt eine Mannschaft.

Von den vier deutschsprachigen Ländern nehmen Deutschland und die Schweiz an der WM teil. Österreich und Liechtenstein haben sich nicht qualifiziert.
Zum ersten Mal dabei: Angola, Elfenbeinküste, Ghana, Tobago, Togo, Trinidad, Ukraine. Serbien und Montenegro nehmen nicht zum ersten Mal an der Fußballweltmeisterschaft teil, denn früher haben sie in der jugoslawischen Mannschaft mitgespielt.

Die deutsche Nationalmannschaft 2006

Länder von Fußballweltmeisterschaften:

1930 Uruguay	1962 Chile	1986 Mexiko
1934 Italien	1966 England	1990 Italien
1938 Frankreich	1970 Mexiko	1994 USA
1950 Brasilien	1974 Deutschland	1998 Frankreich
1954 Schweiz	1978 Argentinien	2002 Japan
1958 Schweden	1982 Spanien	2006 Deutschland

1 **Bist du fit für die Fußballweltmeisterschaft? Teste dich selbst.**

1 Die Fußballweltmeisterschaft 2006 findet in

   a ☐ fünf   **b** ☐ acht

   c ☐ zwölf   **d** ☐ achtzehn

   deutschen Städten statt.

2 Das größte Stadion in Deutschland ist in

   a ☐ Frankfurt   **b** ☐ Berlin   **c** ☐ München.

3 Einige Mannschaften haben noch nie an den Fußballweltmeisterschaften teilgenommen. Sie kommen hauptsächlich aus

   a ☐ Europa   **b** ☐ Asien   **c** ☐ Afrika

   d ☐ Amerika   **e** ☐ Australien.

4 In welchen Ländern haben die Fußballweltmeisterschaften in den letzten Jahren zweimal stattgefunden?

   a ☐ Italien   **b** ☐ Deutschland   **c** ☐ Frankreich

   d ☐ England   **e** ☐ Argentinien   **f** ☐ Mexiko

   g ☐ Brasilien   **h** ☐ USA.

Zauberpillen

9 Samstag gibt es ein wichtiges Spiel. Pedros Mannschaft steht auf dem zweiten Platz der Tabelle und spielt heute gegen den Tabellenersten [1].

Pedro ist schon früh auf dem Spielfeld.

Er will sich vor dem Spiel warmlaufen und Stretching machen.

Es ist kalt draußen und für seine Muskeln ist das immer noch ein Problem.

Am Eingang zum Stadion steht Vanessa.

„Hallo, Pedro!" Sie lächelt ihn an.

„Ist sie schön!" denkt Pedro.

Vanessa trägt einen engen Jeansrock und schwarze Stiefel.

„Gehen wir etwas trinken?" fragt sie ihn.

Was ist das? Ein Traum?

„Trinken? Vor dem Spiel? Ich möchte ja gern, Vanessa, aber es geht nicht."

„Eine Cola ..."

„Ein Glas Mineralwasser vielleicht."

---

1.   **r/e Tabellenerste**: wer in der Tabelle auf dem ersten Platz steht.

Tor ohne Grenzen

„Ach, diese Sportler!" sagt sie und lächelt wieder.

Zusammen gehen sie ins Café am Stadion. Es ist noch leer. Zwei Stunden vor dem Spiel.

Vanessa spricht mit ihm und lächelt.

„Was ist denn nur los?" fragt er sich. „Warum ist sie so nett zu mir? Hat ihr jemand einen Zaubertrank[1] gegeben."

In der Klasse haben sie gestern die Geschichte von Tristan und Isolde gelesen. Die trinken da so etwas und verlieben sich.

„Gibt's das?" fragt sich Pedro. „Na ja, man weiß ja nie."

Er braucht keinen Zaubertrank. Er ist sowieso schon bis über beide Ohren verliebt[2].

Sie setzen sich an einen Tisch.

Pedro holt eine Tasse Kakao für Vanessa und ein Glas Wasser für sich selbst.

Sie sprechen über die Schule und über Fußball.

Sie nimmt seine Hand und sieht ihm tief in die Augen.

„Du wirst sicher einmal ein großer Fußballspieler."

Dann stehen sie auf. Pedro muss gehen. Sie umarmt ihn und gibt ihm einen Kuss auf die Wange. So glücklich ist Pedro noch nie gewesen. Nicht einmal, wenn er ein Tor schießt.

Er geht in den Umkleideraum[3]. Drei seiner Freunde sind schon da.

„Na, wie geht's?" fragt er Jochen.

„Nicht schlecht, und bei dir?"

„Wunderbar. Weißt du, dass …"

Pedro kann nicht zu Ende sprechen.

---

1. **r Zaubertrank**: magisches Getränk.
2. **bis über beide Ohre verliebt sein**: sehr verliebt sein.
3. **r Umkleideraum ("e)**: wo man sich umzieht.

Der Trainer kommt herein. Er sieht böse aus.

„Was gibt's?" fragt Jochen.

„Ich muss ... Kontrolle! Macht eure Taschen auf, Jungs! Pedro ... deine Tasche."

„Ja, aber ... meine Tasche? Warum ... ?"

Der Trainer nimmt Pedros Tasche und nimmt die Schuhe heraus, dann das T-Shirt, die Shorts, ein Handtuch [1] und ... ein kleines Päckchen.

„Was ist das?"

Pedro antwortet nicht.

„Pedro, ich warte!"

„Ich ... ich weiß es nicht. Das ist nicht meins! Nie gesehen."

Der Trainer macht das Päckchen auf.

„Nun?"

Vier kleine Schachteln [2] sind im Päckchen. Schachteln mit Tabletten. Der Trainer liest, was auf den Schachteln steht.

„Tabletten", sagt er.

Pedro versteht nicht.

„Was für Tabletten?" fragt er.

„Zauberpillen. Was der Spieler so braucht. Damit läuft er schneller, reagiert schneller und wird nicht müde."

Pedro versteht noch immer nicht.

„Was heißt das?"

„Mensch, Doping!" brüllt der Trainer. „Pedro! Das ist Doping!"

Keiner sagt mehr etwas.

„Das sind nicht meine ... davon wusste ich nichts ..."

Pedro weiß nicht, was er sagen soll.

---

1. **r Handtuch ("er)**: zum Abtrocknen.
2. **e Schachtel (n)**: kleiner Behälter.

Tor ohne Grenzen

„Ok, Pedro. Das war's dann. Du kannst nach Hause gehen. Du spielst nicht mehr mit. Nie wieder."

„Aber ... ich habe ..."

„Nimm deine Tasche und geh!" brüllt der Trainer. „Und komm mir nicht wieder unter die Augen!"

Vorbei. Pedro versteht die Welt nicht mehr.

„Und die hier ... die nehme ich mit."

Der Trainer geht, das Päckchen mit den Tabletten in der Hand.

Die anderen Jungen sagen nichts. Auch Jochen nicht.

Pedro nimmt seine Tasche und geht zu ihm.

„Ich habe nichts mit diesen Tabletten zu tun", sagt er. „Aber du glaubst mir ja wohl auch nicht, oder?"

Jochen sieht Pedro nicht an.

„Wir spielen fair. Doping gibt's bei uns nicht", sagt er.

Pedro geht. Es hat keinen Sinn[1] mehr. Da kann er tausendmal sagen: „Ich nehme diese Zauberpillen nicht!"

Niemand glaubt ihm. Das Päckchen hat in seiner Tasche gelegen.

Wer hat es in die Tasche gelegt? Wann und wie?

---

1. **Es hat keinen Sinn**: es geht nicht, hat keine Resultate.

Textverständnis

1 Was ist richtig?

1 Pedro ist früh am Fußballplatz, weil er
- **a** ☐ Vanessa treffen möchte.
- **b** ☐ mit seinen Kameraden ein bisschen spielt.
- **c** ☐ sich vor dem Spiel warmlaufen will.

2 Vanessa ist
- **a** ☐ unfreundlich
- **b** ☐ freundlich
- **c** ☐ sehr nett

zu ihm.

3 Pedro ist jetzt sehr glücklich, weil
- **a** ☐ Vanessa ihn küsst.
- **b** ☐ Susanne ihn küsst.
- **c** ☐ er Fußball spielt.

4 Der Trainer will
- **a** ☐ alle Taschen
- **b** ☐ Pedros Tasche
- **c** ☐ Jochens Tasche

kontrollieren.

5 In Pedros Tasche findet er
- **a** ☐ Pillen.
- **b** ☐ Pulver.
- **c** ☐ Aspirin.

6 Der Trainer sagt zu Pedro, dass er
- **a** ☐ nie wieder spielen darf.
- **b** ☐ jetzt nicht spielen darf.
- **c** ☐ zur Polizei gehen soll.

7 Alle denken jetzt, dass
- **a** ☐ Pedro gedopt ist.
- **b** ☐ Pedro ein Krimineller ist.
- **c** ☐ Pedro ein schlechter Fußballspieler ist.

2 Und du, was glaubst du? Ist Pedro gedopt oder nicht? Warum waren Pillen in seiner Tasche?

Wortschatz

1 Was gibt es in der Tasche eines Sportlers? Schreibe unter jedes Bild den richtigen Namen.

Duschgel	Energieriegel	Handtuch
Handy	Sportschuhe	T-Shirt

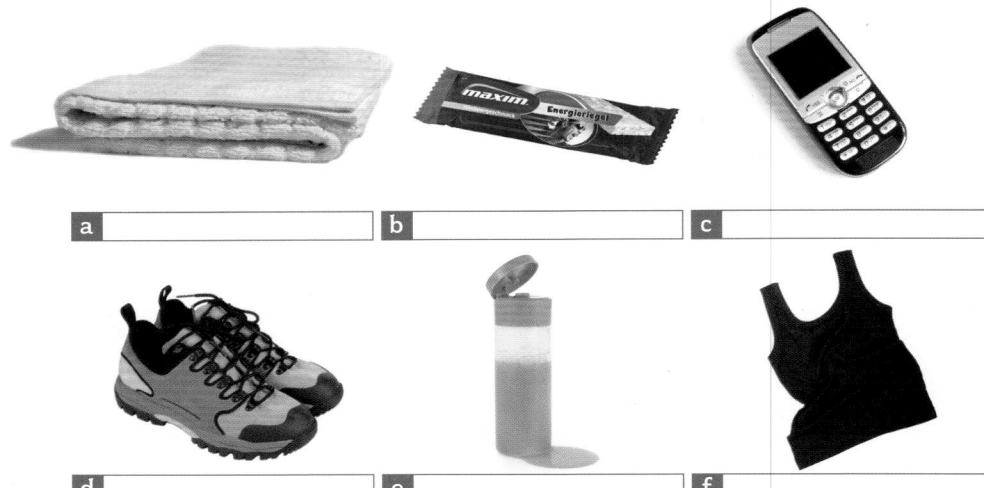

a _____ b _____ c _____

d _____ e _____ f _____

Grammatik

1 Adjektive. Setze die richtigen Endungen ein (wo nötig).

a Heute gibt es in der groß (**1**) ……… Stadt ein wichtig (**2**) ……… Spiel. Der best (**3**) ……… Spieler einer Mannschaft ist aber nicht da: er ist krank (**4**) ……… . Es ist kalt (**5**) ……… , trotzdem sind viele Leute aus dem ganz (**6**) ……… Land gekommen. Einige möchten auch das neu (**7**) ……… und modern (**8**) ……… Stadion sehen.

b Das Spiel ist vorbei. Das Ergebnis war 0:0. „Das war ein uninteressant (**1**) ……… Match", sagen die Zuschauer. „Es war wirklich langweilig (**2**) ……… . Sie haben schlecht (**3**) ……… gespielt." Viele gehen ins Stadioncafé und trinken ein warm (**4**) ………

Getränk. Viele nehmen das Auto oder den Bus und fahren weg.
Es gibt überall stark (**5**) .... Verkehr.

c   Ich habe auch das Fußballspiel gesehen, aber im Fernsehen. Ich
    habe in meinem bequem (**1**) .... Sessel gegessen und habe ein
    lecker (**2**) .... Sandwich gegessen und Cola getrunken. Dann sind
    meine klein (**3**) .... Geschwister gekommen. Das Spiel war
    langweilig (**4**) .... Deshalb habe ich den Fernseher ausgemacht
    und habe ihnen eine Geschichte aus ihrem neu (**5**) .... Buch
    vorgelesen. Das war eine schön (**6**) .... und lang (**7**) ....
    Geschichte.

Lesen und Hören

1 **Als Pedro mit Vanessa im Café ist, denkt er,
       dass sie vielleicht einen Zaubertrank
       getrunken hat. Kennst du die Geschichte
       von Tristan und Isolde? Nein? Hier ist eine
       kurze Zusammenfassung. Einige Wörter
       fehlen. Höre dir die Geschichte auf der CD an
       und ergänze.**

Tristan und Isolde

Tristan fährt nach (**1**) .... und dort
holt (**2**) .... die schöne Isolde. Sie
muss mit ihm nach England fahren und den (**3**) .... von
Tristan, (**4**) ...., heiraten. Auf der (**5**) .... aber
trinken Tristan und Isolde aus Versehen einen (**6**) .... Den
hatte Isoldes (**7**) .... für ihre Tochter und Marke zubereitet,
damit sie glücklich werden konnten. Doch nun sind Tristan und Isolde
ineinander verliebt. Sie lieben sich sehr, aber sie dürfen nicht heiraten.
Marke soll Isoldes Mann (**8**) ....
Auch nach der (**9**) .... treffen sich Tristan und Isolde
heimlich immer wieder. Marke entdeckt das und sie müssen weg vom
Hof. Sie leben im Wald und sind (**10**) .... , aber Marke will
Isolde zurück. Tristan muss weg aus dem Königreich, Isolde bleibt bei
Marke, aber (**11**) .... Tristan trotzdem.

Pedro sucht Hilfe

Pedro will noch nicht nach Hause gehen. Er ist zu traurig. Mehr als traurig: er weiß nicht, wie es weitergehen soll. Jetzt darf er nicht mehr mitspielen, die Freunde wollen nichts mehr von ihm wissen, alle ... Niemand glaubt, was er sagt.

Doch! Es gibt jemanden, der ihm glaubt. Susanne.

„Ich muss mit Susanne sprechen", denkt er.

Aber Susanne ist nicht zu Hause. Sie ist im Stadion bei den anderen.

„Soll ich hingehen? Das geht nicht. Dann fragen mich alle ... oder sie wissen es schon".

Ich muss sie anrufen. Das Handy! Susanne hat ihm sein altes geschenkt. Sie hat ein neues Modell.

Susanne antwortet sofort.

„Pedro! Warum bist du nicht ... ?"

„Ich spiele heute nicht mit."

„Warum denn nicht? Geht es dir nicht gut?"

„Nein ... doch. Es ist etwas passiert."

„Was denn?"

„Das kann ich dir am Telefon nicht sagen. Können wir uns treffen? Im Café hinter dem Stadion?"

„Ok, ich komme."

„Willst du nicht erst das Fußballspiel sehen?"

„Ohne dich? Nein."

Fünf Minuten später treffen sie sich im Café.

Hier ist Pedro heute schon einmal gewesen. Das war vor etwas mehr als einer Stunde. Da war die Welt noch in Ordnung. Und jetzt ...

„Wie siehst du denn aus?" fragt Susanne. „Sag schon! Was ist passiert?"

Pedro erzählt ihr alles.

Susanne kann es nicht fassen [1].

„Wie können die Tabletten in deine Tasche gekommen sein?"

Pedro sieht sie an.

„Also glaubst du mir?"

„Natürlich. Ich kenne dich doch. Sind wir Freunde oder nicht?"

„Danke."

„Aber es muss doch eine Erklärung geben. Wie sind die Pillen ... oder besser: wer hat die Pillen in die Tasche getan? Und warum? Wir brauchen das Motiv."

„Was willst du damit sagen?"

„Hast du vor dem Spiel jemanden getroffen?"

„Ja, Vanessa, und sie ..."

„Vanessa?"

"Wir sind zusammen hier ins Café gegangen. Ich habe natürlich nur ein Glas Wasser getrunken. Sie war ... sie war so nett zu mir."

„Vanessa? Zu dir? Moment mal: du hast die Getränke geholt, oder?"

„Natürlich."

„Und deine Tasche hast du hier am Tisch stehen lassen."

„Was denn sonst?"

---

1. **etwas nicht fassen**: etwas nicht glauben können.

„Dann hat sie das Päckchen in deine Tasche getan."

„Vanessa? Aber nein, wie kannst du …"

„Also, mein lieber Pedro. Erstens: Vanessa mag keine Ausländer. Zweitens: Vanessa hasst dich, denn du spielst besser als ihr Jens. Du bist der beste Spieler der Mannschaft."

„Ich war der beste."

„Lass mich nur machen."

Die Mannschaft verliert das Spiel. Ohne Pedro hatte sie keine Chance.

Alle wissen, was passiert ist. Alle reden darüber.

Auch abends, nach dem Spiel, in der Pizzeria. Alle haben schlechte Laune[1]. Vor allem Jochen.

„Pedro gedopt. Es ist wirklich nicht zu glauben. Ich kann es nicht glauben …"

„Du hast dat[2] doch gesehen. Die Tabletten waren in seiner Tasche", sagt Jens.

„Ich habe es mir schon gedacht", sagt Vanessa. „Wie der gelaufen ist …"

„Ach was!" Jochen lässt sie nicht ausreden. „Pedro ist ein großartiger Spieler."

„Großartig?" fragt Jens ironisch. „Mit einem Kilo Tabletten im Bauch spielt auch mein Großvater ganz großartig."

Niemand lacht.

„Selten ist das ja nicht", weiß Hans. „Es sind doch alle gedopt. Alle großen Sportler. Fahrradfahrer, Marathonläufer, Fußballspieler. Und in der DDR hat das der Staat selbst organisiert …"

Jochen hört ihm nicht zu.

Er denkt an Pedro, der nicht mehr mitspielt.

1. **schlechte Laune haben**: nicht lustig sein, sondern böse und/oder traurig.
2. **dat**: *das* im Dialekt des Ruhrgebietes.

Textverständnis

1 Was ist richtig (R), was ist falsch (F)?

		R	F
a	Pedro weiß, dass Susanne ihm glaubt.	☐	☐
b	Er will sofort ins Stadion gehen.	☐	☐
c	Er ruft Susanne an.	☐	☐
d	Susanne ist jetzt zu Hause.	☐	☐
e	Pedro und Susanne treffen sich im Café.	☐	☐
f	Pedro erzählt ihr, was passiert ist.	☐	☐
g	Susanne glaubt, dass Vanessa die Pillen in Pedros Tasche getan hat.	☐	☐
h	Ohne Pedro hat die Mannschaft das Spiel verloren.	☐	☐
i	Die Spieler der Mannschaft gehen nach dem Spiel in eine Pizzeria.	☐	☐
j	Sie sprechen über Pedro.	☐	☐

2 Susanne sagt, dass Vanessa Pedro nicht mag. Welche Gründe hat sie dafür?

a ....
....

b ....
....

3 Vanessa ist nicht die einzige, die Pedro nicht mag. Wer mag ihn auch nicht?

....

Wortschatz

1 Wie heißt das Gegenteil?

1	☐ hassen		a	vor
2	☐ traurig		b	mit
3	☐ ohne		c	alle
4	☐ niemand		d	lieben
5	☐ spät		e	glücklich
6	☐ nach		f	früh

2 Welche von diesen Sätze haben dieselbe Bedeutung?

1 Was ist passiert?
 a ☐ Wie geht's? b ☐ Was ist los? c ☐ Was machst du?
2 Sie hat keine Chance.
 a ☐ Sie muss nicht. b ☐ Sie darf nicht. c ☐ Sie schafft es nicht.
3 Es ist nicht zu glauben.
 a ☐ Ich kann es nicht glauben. b ☐ Ich glaube es.
 c ☐ Ich muss es glauben.

Grammatik

1 Setze die Sätze ins Perfekt.

*Pedro **isst** ein Brötchen.* → *Pedro **hat** ein Brötchen **gegessen**.*

a Die Schule organisiert das Spiel. ....
b Er denkt an Pedro. ....
c Pedro spielt nicht. ....
d Ich weiß es. ....
e Wir gehen ins Café und trinken etwas zusammen. ....
 ....
f Sie glaubt ihm. ....
g Sie hat einen Plan. ....
h Was passiert? ....

Lesen Plus

**Doping im Sport. Lies den Text aus einer
Jugendzeitschrift und beantworte die Fragen.**

Journalist: Man spricht immer wieder von Doping im Sport. Leider nehmen viele Topsportler Substanzen, um bessere Leistungen zu erbringen. Was sind diese Substanzen?

Arzt: Es gibt viele Substanzen: von anregenden Mitteln bis zu Hormonen, von Anabolika bis zu diuretischen Präparaten.

Journalist: In den letzten Jahren hat man viel von EPO gesprochen. Was ist EPO?

Arzt: EPO ist ein Mittel, mit dem mehr rote Blutkörperchen gebildet werden. Es ist verboten, denn das Risiko ist groß.

Journalist: Ist Doping ein heutiges Phänomen?

Arzt: Nein, eigentlich nicht. Auch in der Vergangenheit waren viele Sportler gedopt. Berühmte Beispiele sind die Athleten der Ex-DDR. Da bekamen viele Athleten verbotene Substanzen von Ärzten und Sportfunktionären.

Journalist: Aber diese Substanzen schaden dem Körper. Sie können auch zum Tod führen. Wissen die Athleten das nicht?

Arzt: Doch natürlich wissen sie das, aber viele denken, dass das wichtigste ist, der beste zu sein. Oft wissen die Athleten aber gar nichts. In der Ex-DDR hat man ihnen gesagt, sie bekommen Vitamine.

Journalist: Und das haben sie geglaubt?

Arzt: Dem Trainer glaubt ein Sportler normalerweise.

Journalist: Ist Doping auch im Fußballspiel verbreitet?

Arzt: Ja, viele Skandale zeigen das. Zum Beispiel der von der italienischen Mannschaft Juventus. Leider.

Journalist: Was halten Sie von Doping?

Arzt: Ich spreche als Sportler und Fußballfan. Ich finde Doping schlecht, nicht nur, weil es schädlich ist, sondern auch weil Doping bedeutet, zu betrügen, schmutzig zu spielen.

1 Weißt du die Antwort?

a Wer macht Doping?

....

b Ist EPO eine Droge oder ein Blutmittel?

....

c Die Athleten der Ex-DDR bekamen schädliche Substanzen. Wer gab sie ihnen?

....

d Welches Beispiel für Doping im Fußball nennt der Arzt?

....

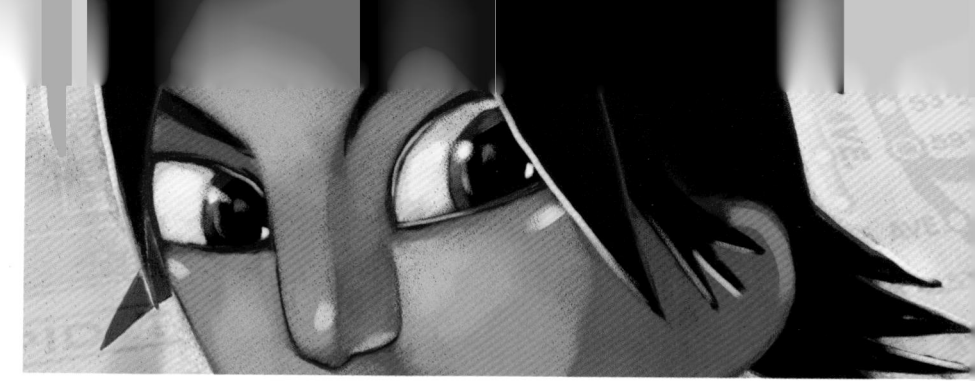

Die Falle

 Montag sind sie alle in der Schule. Ein Tag wie jeder andere? Nicht für Pedro.

Er kommt um acht. Keine Minute zu früh. Es ist still in der Klasse. Alle sehen ihn an. Wie am ersten Tag. Aber diesmal sind die anderen nicht neugierig. Sie sind böse.

Pedro nimmt seine Tasche und setzt sich neben Susanne. Sie lächelt ihn an.

„Die wissen es alle schon, stimmt's?" fragt er sie.

„Ich glaube schon, aber mach dir keine Gedanken. Das wird schon wieder."

In der Pause geht Pedro mit Susanne nach draußen. Jens, Franz und Hans warten auf ihn.

„Pedro, du siehst nicht gut aus heute. Hast du keine Tabletten mehr? Findet ihr nicht? Der ist blass heute, unser Pedro!" sagt Jens.

Alle lachen. Pedro antwortet nicht.

„Komm, lass die doch!" sagt Susanne.

Aber Jens steht schon neben ihm.

Tor ohne Grenzen

„Ganz klein heute, unser großer Mittelstürmer, wat [1]? Na, ohne seine Tabletten läuft natürlich nix!"

Das ist zu viel. Pedro brüllt: „Ich nehme keine Tabletten und habe nie welche genommen, du … du …"

Susanne nimmt ihn am Arm: „Komm schon, keine Dummheiten, Pedro!"

In der vierten Stunde haben sie Sport. Alle gehen in die Turnhalle.

Susanne geht zur Lehrerin.

„Vanessa geht es heute nicht so gut. Ich bleibe bei ihr" sagt sie.

„Vanessa? Was hat sie denn?"

„Bauchschmerzen. Ich dachte, ich gehe mit ihr einen heißen Tee trinken. Vielleicht wird es dann besser."

„Na gut. Dann geht mal euren Tee trinken."

Aber die beiden gehen nicht Tee trinken. Sie gehen in den Aufenthaltsraum [2].

„Nun sag schon! Was gibt's denn?" Vanessa versteht nicht, warum Susanne sie hierher gebracht hat.

„Ich wollte mit dir über Jochen sprechen", erklärt ihr Susanne.

„Über Jochen? Mit dem … das hat doch Zeit bis nach der Schule."

„Nein." Susanne sieht jetzt sehr ernst [3] aus.

„Nein?"

„Jochen hat mir gesagt, er will zum Trainer gehen und ihm von dir erzählen."

„Von mir?" Vanessa wird langsam unruhig.

---

1. **wat**: *was* im Dialekt des Ruhrgebietes.
2. **r Aufenthaltsraum ("e)**: Saal für freie Stunden.
3. **ernst**: lächelt nicht.

„Ja. Diese Geschichte mit den Tabletten in Pedros Tasche geht ihm nicht aus dem Kopf. Und da gibt es etwas, was er dem Trainer...“

„Was denn?“ Vanessa ist jetzt sehr blass.

„Heute morgen vor dem Spiel hat Jochen dich mit Pedro ins Café gehen sehen. Das hat ihn natürlich neugierig gemacht.“

„Ich kann doch wohl ins Café gehen, mit wem ich will!“

„Jochen hat euch durch das Fenster gesehen. Pedro ist aufgestanden und hat die Getränke geholt und du ...“

„Ich? Was?“ fragt Vanessa böse.

„...du hast das Päckchen in Pedros Tasche gelegt.“

„Das glaubst du doch selber nicht. Ich? Ich soll dem Kubaner da ...?“

„Jochen hat es gesehen. Frag ihn selbst. Aber vielleicht hat er es ja schon dem Trainer gesagt.“

„So etwas tut Jochen nicht!“

„Was du getan hast, war auch nicht sehr schön.“

„Das ist nicht wahr, ich habe nichts getan.“

„Pedro hat nichts getan, Vanessa. Alle haben ihn gern und ...“

„Jetzt mag ihn niemand mehr!“ sagt Vanessa triumphierend.

Das ist der richtige Moment. Susanne fragt:

„Was hast du denn gegen Pedro? Warum hasst du ihn so?“

„Den? Hassen? Das glaubst du doch selbst nicht!“

„Ja, und jetzt weiß ich auch warum“, sagt Susanne. „Er spielt besser als Jochen, viel besser als Jens und als alle anderen. Ein Ausländer! Nicht wahr? Das darf nicht sein?“

Vanessa sagt nichts. Susanne spricht weiter.

„Pedro ist der beste, nicht nur beim Fußball, auch in der Schule ...“

Vanessa lacht.

„Leider spricht er Deutsch wie ein Baby."

„Aber er lernt schnell. Und Deutsch ist nicht seine Muttersprache. Bei ihm zu Hause ..."

„In Kuba! Warum ist er nicht in Kuba geblieben? Bei seinen Kamelen! Die kommen hier zu uns und glauben, sie machen alles besser! Alles nehmen sie sich!"

„Alles was?"

„Alles! Er ist jetzt unser Mittelstürmer. Pedro der Star! Hast du nicht gehört, wie die Leute ihm applaudiert haben. Wie sie brüllen: Pedro! Pedro! Pedro!" Vanessa lacht leise.

„Und darum hast du ihm das Päckchen in die Tasche gelegt!"

Vanessa sieht sich um. Der Aufenthaltsraum ist leer.

„Ja. Ich habe ihm das Päckchen in die Tasche gelegt. Jens hat es mir gegeben. Es war nicht schwierig, und es hat gut funktioniert, oder? Pedro! Pedro! Das ist jetzt vorbei!"

„Danke, Vanessa. Das wollte ich nur hören.

Vanessa sieht sich um.

„Aber Susanne. Was soll denn das? Das glaubt dir niemand. Du bist Pedros Freundin und niemand wird ..."

Susannes Tasche ist offen. Sie zieht ihr Handy heraus und sagt laut: „Ok."

Die Tür zum Aufenthaltsraum geht auf.

Jochen und Hans stehen da, jeder sein Handy in der Hand. Sie lächeln.

„Alles klar?" fragt Susanne.

„Glasklar", sagen die beiden.

Textverständnis

1 **Weißt du die Antwort?**

a Pedro kommt in die Klasse. Wie reagieren seine Schulkameraden?
....

b In der vierten Stunde ist Sport. Wohin gehen die Schüler?
....

c Wohin geht Susanne mit Vanessa?
....

d Was sagt sie der Lehrerin?
....

e Susanne sagt, dass sie mit Vanessa über etwas reden will. Worüber?
....

f Was will Susanne von Vanessa hören?
....

g Wer hört auch, was Vanessa sagt?
....

2 **Vanessa sagt: „Warum ist er nicht in Kuba geblieben? Bei seinen Kamelen?" Aber sie macht einen großen (geografischen) Fehler. In Kuba gibt es keine Kamele. Warum denkt sie an Kamele?**

Wortschatz

1 **Welches Wort passt nicht?**

a ☐ brüllen   ☐ sagen   ☐ laut sprechen   ☐ gehen
b ☐ spielen   ☐ applaudieren   ☐ bravo sagen   ☐ klatschen
c ☐ Hotel   ☐ Café   ☐ Kneipe   ☐ Bar
d ☐ gern haben   ☐ mögen   ☐ hassen   ☐ lieben
e ☐ erster   ☐ vierter   ☐ später   ☐ zweiter

2 Was bedeuten diese Sätze?

1 Deutsch ist nicht seine Muttersprache.

a ☐ Seine Mutter ist keine Deutsche.

b ☐ Er hat als Kind nicht Deutsch gesprochen.

c ☐ Nur sein Vater spricht Deutsch.

2 Das ist jetzt vorbei.

a ☐ Das ist jetzt aktuell.

b ☐ Das war einmal, heute ist es anders.

c ☐ Das ist schnell gegangen.

3 Glasklar ist

a ☐ gar nicht klar.

b ☐ sehr klar.

c ☐ ziemlich klar.

Grammatik

1 Welches Verb passt?

| legen | liegen | stehen | stellen |

a Er .... das Handy auf den Tisch.

b Vanessa .... das Päckchen in Pedros Tasche.

c Der Ball .... auf dem Feld.

d Pedro .... am Netz.

e Hans .... auf dem Boden. Er kann nicht stehen.

f Susanne .... das Buch in das Bücherregal.

g .... das Glas auf den Tisch, bitte!

Sprechen wir darüber?

1 Vorurteile. Was man so sagt. Die Ausländer...

a ☐ nehmen unsere Arbeit weg. b ☐ verkaufen Drogen.
c ☐ benehmen sich wie Kinder. d ☐ haben kriminelle Tendenzen.
e ☐ sind weniger intelligent. f ☐ sind schmutzig.

2 Vanessa ist in einer multikulturellen Gesellschaft keine Ausnahme. Es gibt viele Vorurteile gegen Ausländer. Was sagt man in deinem Land? Diskutiere darüber.

Hören

1 Einige dieser Filme hast du sicher gesehen! Hör dir die Filmreklame an. Welcher Text passt zu welchem Film?

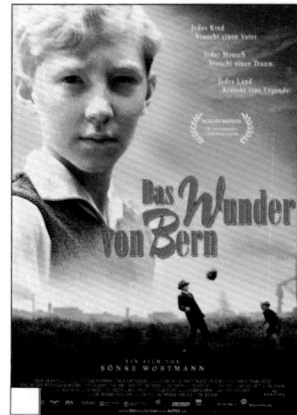

Happy End

 Es ist Samstag. Ein Frühlingssamstag. Die Sonne scheint über Gelsenkirchen.

Die Mannschaft steht schon auf dem Feld. Elf junge Männer. Jochen, Hans, Harry, Andreas, Thomas, Michael, Lars, Markus, Kevin, Rainer und ... Pedro. Das Publikum ruft seinen Namen. Er ist wieder da.

Er ist der beste, der beliebteste Spieler von allen. Mit ihm werden sie die Meisterschaft gewinnen.

Auf der Tribüne sitzt Susanne, seine Freundin.

„Wenn ich heute ein Tor schieße, ist es für dich!"

Er sieht sie an und wirft ihr einen Kuss zu.

Vor dem Spiel geht Jochen zu ihm und legt ihm eine Hand auf den Arm.

„Pedro, heute müssen wir gewinnen."

Pedro lächelt.

„Wir tun, was wir können, oder?"

„Mehr! Besser!"

Pedro und Jochen sind jetzt Freunde.

Er war der erste, der sich bei Pedro entschuldigt hat.

„Tut mir Leid. Wirklich. Warum habe ich dir nicht geglaubt? Wir sind doch Freunde."

Tor ohne Grenzen

Pedro hat ihm die Hand gegeben und gelächelt.

Heute sind alle ins Stadion gekommen. Nur Vanessa und Jens sind nicht da. Seit ein paar Tagen kommen sie auch nicht mehr in die Schule. Man sagt, sie wollen die Schule wechseln.

Am Montag wird in Pedros Klasse gefeiert. Pedro steht im Mittelpunkt. In der linken Hand hält er den Pokal, mit der rechten umarmt er Susanne. Eine Mitschülerin bittet ihn um ein Autogramm. Alle lachen.

„Lacht nur", sagt sie, „es dauert nicht mehr lange, dann sehen wir Pedro nur noch im Fernsehen."

Hat sie Recht? Pedro bleibt nicht bei seiner Schulmannschaft. Die Zeitung schreibt über ihn. Ein Trainer der Jugendmannschaft von Schalke 04 will den Goldjungen aus Kuba haben. Auch Borussia Mönchengladbach ist interessiert. Doch Mönchengladbach, sagt Pedro, ist zu weit weg. Er will für Gelsenkirchen spielen. Dort ist er zu Hause. Dort wohnt Susanne.

Und Kuba? Das hat er natürlich nicht vergessen. Er schreibt immer noch an seinen Freund Juan:

Lieber Juan,
jetzt geht es mir gut, sehr gut hier. Ich habe viele Freunde. Ich bin mit Susanne zusammen – weißt du noch? Sie war von Anfang an nett zu mir.
Auch die Stadt gefällt mir gut. Ich soll jetzt in der Jugendmannschaft von Schalke 04 spielen. Aber ich denke oft an Kuba und an euch alle. Ich hoffe, ich kann euch bald besuchen.
Bis bald
Pedro

Textverständnis

1 **Die folgenden Sätze fassen das letzte Kapitel zusammen. Ergänze.**

1   Es ist ....

2   Pedro spielt wieder in der ....

3   Er ist der .... Spieler von allen.

4   Pedro und Jochen sind jetzt ....

5   Heute sind alle ....

6   Nur Vanessa und Jens ....

7   Was schreibt Pedro an seinen Freund Juan?

    a   Es geht ihm ....

    b   Er ist jetzt ....

    c   Er hofft, ...

2 **Gefällt dir das Ende?**

a   ☐ ja   b   ☐ nein

Warum (nicht)?

....

....

3 **Wen magst du am meisten?**

a   ☐ Pedro   b   ☐ Susanne   c   ☐ Jochen

Warum?

....

....

4 **Wie findest du die Geschichte?**

a   ☐ realistisch   b   ☐ unrealistisch

c   ☐ interessant   d   ☐ uninteressant

e   ☐ romantisch   f   ☐ zu „sportlich".

Fußballwelt D-A-CH
und ... *Frauenfußball*

Die deutsche Bundesliga

Die deutsche Meisterschaft heißt Fußball-Bundesliga. Das ist die höchste Spielklasse im deutschen Fußball und eine der wichtigsten Meisterschaften Europas.

Seit Beginn der 1990er Jahre ist die Bundesliga wieder populärer geworden, denn sie hat mehr Erfolg: dritter Weltmeisterschaftstitel 1990 und dritter Europäischer Meisterschaftstitel 1996.

In der Saison 2004/5 gab es einen Zuschauerrekord: fast 12 Millionen Zuschauer besuchten die 306 Spiele (also fast 37781 Zuschauer pro Spiel). Das Interesse an der Bundesliga war im Jahr vor der Weltmeisterschaft 2006 in Deutschland enorm hoch, auch weil die neuen Stadien die modernsten der Welt sind, darunter die Veltins-Arena (Gelsenkirchen) oder die Allianz-Arena (München).

Die besten Mannschaften

Der FC Bayern München ist mit über 100000 Mitgliedern nach dem FC Barcelona der Verein mit den meisten Mitgliedern der Welt.

Er ist auch der erfolgreichste deutsche Fußballverein (u.a. 19 Meistertitel).

Zwei Vereine aus dem Ruhrgebiet, der Gelsenkirchener FC Schalke 04 und Borussia Dortmund sind sehr beliebte deutsche Fußballclubs. Bekannt sind auch Borussia

Ein typischer Schalke 04-Fan

Mönchengladbach, der Hamburger Sport-Verein (HSV) und der VfB Stuttgart. Der VfB ist mit über 30000 Mitgliedern der drittgrößte Verein Deutschlands und der größte Baden-Württembergs.

Borussia Dortmund komplett

Oliver Kahn in Aktion

Die besten Fußballspieler

Oliver Kahn wurde 1969 in Karlsruhe geboren, man nennt ihn „Titan" und er ist Tormann. Er spielt beim FC Bayern München (seit 1994), wo er viele Titel gewonnen hat. Er wurde 1994, 1997 und 1998 als bester Bundesliga-Torhüter prämiert.

Michael Ballack, geboren 1976 in Görlitz, spielt seit 2002 beim FC Bayern München. Er gehört zu den besten Mittelfeld-Spielern der Welt.

Miroslav Klose wurde 1978 im polnischen Oppeln geboren. Seit dem Sommer 2004 spielt er beim SV Werder Bremen. Er hatte große Erfolge bei der WM 2002.

Die österreichische Bundesliga

Die österreichische Fußball-Bundesliga ist die höchste Spielklasse im österreichischen Fußball. Es gibt sie seit der Saison 1974/75. Die österreichische Mannschaft hat sich nicht für die Weltmeisterschaft 2006 qualifiziert.

Die besten Mannschaften

Der SK Rapid Wien, österreichischer Rekordmeister mit 31 Meistertiteln und der FK Austria Wien.

Die besten Fußballspieler

Ivica Vastic wurde 1969 in Split geboren, seit 2005 spielt er bei Lask Linz; er spielte auch in Deutschland (Duisburg) und für Austria Wien und in der Nationalmannschaft. Er ist einer der besten österreichischen Spieler der Neunziger Jahre. Es gibt in Österreich keinen Spieler, der im Abschuss zwischen 15 und 20 Metern vor dem Tor besser ist als Ivo.

Die schweizerische Super League

Schweizerischer Fußballverband (SFV), so heißt die Organisation der Schweizer Fußballvereine. Die höchste Spielklasse in der nationalen Liga ist die Super League, wo zehn Mannschaften um den Meistertitel und um Europacup-Plätze kämpfen. Für die WM 2006 in hat sich die Schweiz qualifiziert.

Die besten Mannschaften

Der Grasshopper-Club Zürich ist die erfolgreichste Mannschaft der Super League, aber bei den europäischen Pokalspielen hat sie nie viel Glück gehabt. Sehr populär ist auch der FC Basel.

Die besten Fussballspieler

Alexander Frei wurde 1979 in Basel geboren. Seit 2003 spielt er bei der Mannschaft Rennes. Für die Schweizer Fußballnationalmannschaft ist Frei ein sehr wichtiger Mann. In 42 Länderspielen schoss er 23 Tore.

Johann Vogel wurde 1977 in Genf geboren. Er ist Mittelfeldspieler und Kapitän der Schweizer Nationalmannschaft, wo er bislang 77 Länderspiele absolvierte. 2005 verließ er die Schweiz und spielt jetzt bei der italienischen Mannschaft AC Milan.

Frauenfußball

Heute ist der Frauenfußball in vielen Ländern bei jungen Mädchen und Frauen die beliebteste Sportart.

1991 wurde die Frauen-Bundesliga

Worldcup 2003: Birgit Prinz (Nr.9) gegen die Amerikanerin Joy Fawcett

eingeführt. Doch spielen hier in erster Linie Amateure, die neben dem „normalen" Beruf dem Training nachgehen. Frauen verdienen im Fußball sehr viel weniger als die Männer.

Die deutsche Frauen-Fußball-Bundesliga ist neben der schwedischen die führende Fußball-Liga in Europa.

Nach dem Gewinn der Weltmeisterschaft 2003 ist der Frauenfußball in Deutschland sehr populär geworden. Trotzdem kommen nur relativ wenige Zuschauer/innen zu Spielen der Frauen-Bundesliga.

1 **Weißt du die Antwort?**

1 Fußball ist in Deutschland in den Neunziger Jahren noch populärer geworden. Warum?

....

2 Wie heißen zwei der neuen deutschen Stadien?

a ....

b ....

3 Und zwei der größten Fußballvereine in Deutschland?

a ....

b ....

4 Welcher deutsche Fußballspieler ist in Polen geboren?

....

2 **Ergänze jetzt diese Sätze über österreichischen und Schweizer Fußball.**

a Die österreichische Bundesliga entstand ....

b Die österreichische Mannschaft ist nicht mehr so stark wie in den Achtziger Jahren, deshalb ....

c   Die zwei besten Mannschaften sind beide aus der Stadt
....

d   Der beste österreichische Fußballspieler heißt
....

e   Die Schweizer Bundesliga heißt ....

f   Die Schweizer Mannschaft hat sich für die Weltmeisterschaft
2006 ....

g   Die zwei besten Mannschaften in der Schweiz heißen
.... und .... Die zwei
berühmtesten Spieler sind .... und
....

3 Frauenfußball

1   Frauenfußball ist in den letzten Jahren
   a ☐ populärer geworden, aber immer noch weniger populär
   als Männerfußball.
   b ☐ so populär wie Männerfußball.
   c ☐ gar nicht populär geworden.

2   Die deutsche Mannschaft ist 2003
   a ☐ Europameister
   b ☐ Weltmeister
   c ☐ Olympiasieger
   geworden.

3   Jetzt hat Frauenfußball
   a ☐ viele Zuschauer.
   b ☐ noch nicht so viele Zuschauer wie Männerfußball.
   c ☐ relativ wenige Zuschauer.

INTERNETPROJEKT

Möchtest du eine offizielle deutsche Fußball-Webseite besuchen?

Gib das Wort *Deutscher Fußballverband* in die Suchmaschine ein.
Da ist eine sehr große Seite mit vielen Daten.

1 Klicke auf: *Nationalmannschaft*. Du siehst eine Liste.
   Suche in der Liste Informationen, um diese zwei Fragen zu beantworten:

   a Wer sind die Trainer der Nationalmannschaft?
   ....
   ....

   b Woraus besteht das Team? (nur 4 Namen)
   ....
   ....

2 Klicke jetzt auf *Frauennationalmannschaft* und suche den Namen des Trainers/der Trainerin:
   ....

3 Die Seiten über die *Fußballweltmeisterschaften* sind besonders interessant.
   Wie oft hat Deutschland die Weltmeisterschaften gewonnen?
   ....
   ....

4 In der Liste siehst du auch *Bundesliga*. Du weißt, was die Bundesliga ist *(Seite 85)*. Sieh dir den Kalender an. Wann beginnt die Fußballsaison in Deutschland?
   ....

5 Ist es derselbe Zeitpunkt wie in deinem Land?
   ....
   ....

1 Hier hast du eine Zusammenfassung des ersten Teils der Geschichte. Setze die fehlenden Wörter ein.

a Pedro kommt aus (1) .... und wohnt in einer deutschen Stadt, die (2) .... heißt. Pedro ist aber nicht glücklich. Er kann wenig (3) .... , er hat keine
(4) ...., er fühlt sich (5) ....
Er geht in die Schule; in der Klasse (6) .... Susanne ihn sehr attraktiv. Er aber (7) .... ein anderes Mädchen, Vanessa.

b Eines Abends (1) .... Pedro allein auf dem Spielfeld der Schule. Hier sehen ihn seine (2) ....
Er (3) .... ihnen, dass er sehr gut Fußball spielt. Am Tag des Fußballturniers spielt Pedro mit der (4) ....
der Schule. Er schießt zwei Tore. Von jetzt ab ist Pedro Mitglied der Mannschaft. Er spielt als (5) ....

2 Jetzt ergänze die folgenden Sätze über den zweiten Teil der Geschichte.

a Pedro ist mit Susanne befreundet, aber er mag Vanessa, weil sie
....

b Die Leute nennen Pedro *El pibe d'oro*, das heißt ....

c Pedro hat viel zu tun, denn ....

d Eines Tages kommt der Kapitän in den Umkleideraum der Jungen und ....

3 Pedro ist sehr traurig, nur Susanne glaubt ihm. Sie hat aber eine Idee. Was macht Susanne? Um das vorletzte Kapitel zu rekonstruieren, brauchst du nur auf diese Fragen zu antworten.

a Wo und wann stellen die anderen Vanessa die Falle?

b Was macht Susanne?

c Was sagt sie Vanessa?

d Was sagt Vanessa?

Quiz – Fußball auf Deutsch

1 **Kennst du dich auf Deutsch im Fußball wirklich gut aus?**

1 Wie viele Spieler sind pro Mannschaft auf dem Feld?

    a ☐ 10   **b** ☐ 11   **c** ☐ 15

2 Wie heißt der Spieler am Netz?

    a ☐ Torwart   **b** ☐ Fan   **c** ☐ Spieler

3 Wer ist der Mann in schwarz?

    a ☐ der Schiedsrichter

    b ☐ der Trainer

    c ☐ der Zuschauer

4 Was passiert bei einer roten Karte?

    a ☐ Der Spieler muss etwas bezahlen.

    b ☐ Der Spieler muss zehn Minuten auf der Bank sitzen bleiben.

    c ☐ Der Spieler darf nicht weiterspielen.

5 Wie heißt es, wenn ein Spieler den Ball ins Netz schießt?

    a ☐ Tor   **b** ☐ Netz   **c** ☐ Spiel

6 Wo ist das größte Stadion in Deutschland? In

    a ☐ München   **b** ☐ Frankfurt

    c ☐ Berlin   **d** ☐ Gelsenkirchen

7 Welcher von diesen Spielern spielt nicht mit der Mannschaft?

    a ☐ der Kapitän   **b** ☐ der Trainer   **c** ☐ der Verteidiger

8 Hast du ein gutes Gedächtnis? Schreib die Namen der bekanntesten deutschen (auch schweizerischen und österreichischen) Mannschaften und ihrer wichtigsten Fußballspieler auf.

Mannschaft:

D: ....

A: ....

CH: ....

Fußballspieler:

D: ....

A: ....

CH: ....

Lösungen

1 a   1 Kuba 2 Gelsenkirchen 3 Deutsch 4 Freunde 5 allein 6 findet 7 mag

b   1 spielt 2 Klassenkameraden/Mitschüler 3 zeigt 4 Mannschaft 5 Mittelstürmer

2 a sehr sexy ist b Goldjunge c er lernt und trainiert viel d kontrolliert Pedros Tasche

3 a In der Schule in der Sportstunde/während des Sportunterrichts. b Susanne geht mit Vanessa in den Aufenthaltsraum. c Sie sagt, Vanessa habe die Pillen in Pedros Tasche gelegt und Jochen habe sie gesehen. d Am Ende sagt sie, es ist wahr.

Quiz – Fußball auf Deutsch

1 b 2 a 3 a 4 c 5 a 6 c 7 b

8 Mannschaften:

D: FC Bayern München, Schalke 04 A: SK Rapid Wien, FK Austria Wien
CH: Grasshopper Zürich, FC Basel

Fußballer:

D: Oliver Kahn, Michael Ballack A: Ivica Vastic CH: Alexander Frei, Johann Vogel

Kleines Fußballglossar

Deutsch	English	Français	Italiano	Español

r Elfmeter (-)	penalty kick	le penalty	il rigore	el penalti
r Fan (s)	fan	le supporter	il tifoso	el aficionado
s Foul (s)	foul	la faute	il fallo	la falta
r Fußball ("e)	football (GB) soccer (USA)	le football	il (gioco del) calcio	el fútbol
r Fußballplatz ("e)	football pitch	le terrain de football	il campo da gioco	el campo de fútbol
r Gegenspieler (-)	opposing player	l´adversaire direct	l'avversario	el contrincante
e Halbzeit (en)	half-time	la période	il (primo/secondo) tempo	la mitad del partido
e Mannschaft (en)	team	l'équipe	la squadra	el equipo
s Mittelfeld (er)	midfield	le milieu de terrain	centrocampo	el centro del campo
r Mittelstürmer (-)	center forward	avant-centre	centravanti	defensa central
s Netz (e)	net	le filet	la rete	el red
e Niederlage (n)	defeat	la défaite	la sconfitta	la derrota
r Pokal (e)	cup	la coupe	la coppa	la copa
r Schiedsrichter (-)	ref	l´arbitre	l´arbitro	el árbitro
r Sieg (e)	victory	la victoire	la vittoria	la victoria
s Spiel (e)	game	le match	il gioco, la gara	el juego
r Spieler (-)	player	le/la joueur(-euse)	il/la giocatore (-trice)	el/la jugador(a)
s Spielfeld (er)	pitch	le terrain	il campo da gioco	el campo de juego
s Stadion (en)	stadium	le stade	lo stadio	el estadio
r Stürmer (-)	striker	attaquant	attaccante	el atacante
s Tor(e)	goal	le but	il goal	el gol
r Torwart ("er)	goalkeeper	le gardien de but	il portiere	el portero
r Trainer (-)	coach, team manager	l'entraineur	l'allenatore	el entrenador
e Tribüne (n)	stand	la tribune	la tribuna	la tribuna
e Verteidigung (en)	defence	la defense	la difesa	la defensa
e Weltmeisterschaft (en)	the World Cup	la coupe du monde, le mondial	la coppa del mondo, i mondiali	el mundial